Academic Work and Careers in Europe: Trends, Challenges, Perspectives

The Changing Academy – The Changing Academic Profession in International Comparative Perspective 12

Scope of the series

As the landscape of higher education has in recent years undergone significant changes, so correspondingly have the backgrounds, specializations, expectations and work roles of academic staff. The Academy is expected to be more professional in teaching, more productive in research and more entrepreneurial in everything. Some of the changes involved have raised questions about the attractiveness of an academic career for today's graduates. At the same time, knowledge has come to be identified as the most vital resource of contemporary societies.

The Changing Academy series examines the nature and extent of the changes experienced by the academic profession in recent years. It explores both the reasons for and the consequences of these changes. It considers the implications of the changes for the attractiveness of the academic profession as a career and for the ability of the academic community to contribute to the further development of knowledge societies and the attainment of national goals. It makes comparisons on these matters between different national higher education systems, institutional types, disciplines and generations of academics, drawing initially on available data-sets and qualitative research studies with special emphasis on the recent twenty nation survey of the Changing Academic Profession. Among the themes featured will be:

1. Relevance of the Academy's Work
2. Internationalization of the Academy
3. Current Governance and Management, particularly as perceived by the Academy
4. Commitment of the Academy

The audience includes researchers in higher education, sociology of education and political science studies; university managers and administrators; national and institutional policymakers; officials and staff at governments and organizations, e.g. the World Bank.

More information about this series at
http://www.springer.com/series/8668

Tatiana Fumasoli • Gaële Goastellec •
Barbara M. Kehm

Editors

Academic Work and Careers in Europe: Trends, Challenges, Perspectives

 Springer

Editors
Tatiana Fumasoli
ARENA Centre for European Studies
University of Oslo
Oslo
Norway

Gaële Goastellec
Observatory Science, Politics and Society
University of Lausanne
Lausanne
Switzerland

Barbara M. Kehm
Robert Owen Centre for
    Educational Change
University of Glasgow
Glasgow
UK

ISBN 978-3-319-10719-6   ISBN 978-3-319-10720-2 (eBook)
DOI 10.1007/978-3-319-10720-2
Springer Cham Heidelberg New York Dordrecht London

Library of Congress Control Number: 2014954242

Printed on acid-free paper

Springer is part of Springer Science+Business Media (www.springer.com)

Contents

Chapter 1
Introduction: Understanding Change in the Academic Profession Through the Perceptions of Academics and Institutional Leadership

Tatiana Fumasoli, Gaële Goastellec, and Barbara M. Kehm

1.1 The EuroAC Project: The Impact of Social Change on the Academic Profession in Europe

The major transformations encountered by the higher education systems during the last half-century have changed the face of the academic profession. Mass higher education, financial restrictions and a shifting relationship with the state are just a few changes that have affected higher education and have questioned its role in society. In Europe the growing diversification of higher education has led to an increasing public debate, not only within nations and societies, but also at the level of the European Union. Hence the Lisbon Agenda as well as Strategy 2020 have featured universities as catalysers of the emerging knowledge society, driving innovation and promoting technology transfer. In a similar vein, the development of a European charter for researchers and code of conduct for the recruitment of researchers illustrates this renewed interest for higher education and the political will to develop an "attractive, open and sustainable European labour market for researchers" (European Commission 2005, p. 4).

T. Fumasoli (✉)
ARENA Centre for European Studies, University of Oslo, Blindern, P.O Box 1143, Oslo 0318, Norway
e-mail: Tatiana.Fumasoli@arena.uio.no

G. Goastellec
Observatory Science, Politics and Society, University of Lausanne, Quartier UNIL-Mouline, Bâtiment Géopolis, Lausanne 1015, Switzerland
e-mail: Gaele.Goastellec@unil.ch

B.M. Kehm
Robert Owen Centre for Educational Change, University of Glasgow, St. Andrew's Building, 11 Eldon Street, Glasgow G3 6 NH, UK
e-mail: Barbara.Kehm@glasgow.ac.uk

© Springer International Publishing Switzerland 2015   1
T. Fumasoli et al. (eds.), *Academic Work and Careers in Europe: Trends, Challenges, Perspectives*, The Changing Academy – The Changing Academic Profession in International Comparative Perspective 12, DOI 10.1007/978-3-319-10720-2_1

In this context, the European Science Foundation decided, in 2008, to support, along with various national European research promotion agencies, four comparative European research projects in the thematic area of "Higher Education and Social Change in Europe". Amongst those, a collaborative research project entitled "The Academic Profession in Europe: Responses to Societal Challenges" (EuroAC), coordinated by Ulrich Teichler and Barbara M. Kehm, University of Kassel, (Germany) was devoted to studying the academic profession. EuroAC has involved eight European countries – Austria, Croatia, Germany, Finland, Ireland, Poland, Romania and Switzerland – that have been funded by their national research councils.

This project has its roots in previous international research such as the Carnegie study on the academic profession from the early 1990s, which investigated US academic profession in comparison to that of 14 other countries (cf. Boyer et al. 1994). Particularly however, EuroAC is built on the findings of "The changing Academic Profession" (CAP) project, a major comparative survey of the academic profession focusing on 18 countries from 5 continents, of which 7 were European, conducted predominantly in the years 2007–2008 (Teichler et al. 2013). The EuroAC project has two strong connections with the CAP project: first and overall, the quantitative dimension of the research borrowed the questionnaire used in the CAP survey and adapted it to the specificities of the higher education systems under scrutiny (cf. Teichler and Höhle 2013). Second, two countries involved in the EuroAC research were previously part in the CAP survey: Germany and Finland.

Enriched by this affiliation, the EuroAC project has developed a broader perspective on the academic profession: in so doing it questions the processes through which the academic profession is being shaped by changes in the socio-economic environment as well as in the institutional and organisational fabric of higher education systems and institutions.

Three stages characterised the research. A first step was devoted to an extensive and explorative literature review that led to a state of the art of the knowledge on the academic profession. In a first book (Kehm and Teichler 2013) eight dimensions were identified as structuring the academic profession and in need for further scrutiny.

– First, the blurring boundaries of professional identities in the university;
– second, the decommissioning of the academic profession since the 1990s;
– third, the tensions between academic values and managerial values in a context of changing governance of higher education systems;
– fourth, the emergence of a new group of hybrid professionals in higher education (so-called HEPROs) as a result of the overlap of certain academic and administrative tasks and functions;
– fifth, the challenges faced by the traditional structure of academic career paths in the emerging European labour market;
– sixth, linked to the previous dimension, the internationalisation of academic markets and careers has become a constraint and a resource for both individuals and institutions;

– seventh, the emergence of new challenges in terms of quality, societal relevance and research excellence calls for new forms of organisation of academic work;
– eighth and last, the growing importance of the third mission in European universities is stretching academics' activities.

These dimensions underscore a growing complexity and an expansion of the academic profession on the one hand, and they highlight important facets to be researched further on the other hand.

The second book (Teichler and Höhle 2013), compares the situation of individual academics (i.e. employed at least 50 %) and of the organization of their working time in higher education institutions in 12 European countries. It is based on the EuroAC quantitative survey conducted in 2010, whereby data from Romania could not be used for methodological reasons, as well as on the data provided for the Netherlands, Italy, Norway and the UK between 2007 and 2010 in the framework of the CAP project.

This book sheds light on these under-explored issues relating to the academic profession by highlighting the diversity of academic career paths, the intertwinement of academic work, working conditions and job satisfaction, gender differences and inequalities in the academic profession, the combination of teaching, research and service functions, the academics' perceptions of the shift from self-governance and collegiality to executive university management and leadership. Last but not least the perceptions on evaluation of research and teaching, of the internationalisation of academic markets, of changing careers and profession are also explored. This book is thus the third and last volume of a series of three. It proposes a qualitative approach to answer the question: how does the academic profession in various European countries perceive, interpret and interact with changes in the socio-economic environment and in the organisational fabric of higher education systems and institutions?

This third volume is based on interviews with academic staff and representatives of institutional leadership probing into their perceptions about the changes in academic careers and academic work experienced in recent years. Emphasis is put on academic career paths, impacts of new forms of quality management, changes in employment and working conditions as well as academics' perceptions of their professional contexts, interactions between academic staff and higher education professionals, and finally the public engagement of academic staff in the context of universities third mission. This volume is organized in a thematic manner, i.e. each contribution consists of an analysis of the interviews carried out in all eight countries involved in the EuroAC project with regard to the respective thematic focus, except for chapter 7 on community engagement, which compares three countries of the sample. Altogether the eight European countries involved in EuroAC have been examined: Austria, Croatia, Finland, Germany, Ireland, Poland, Romania, and Switzerland.

1.2   Methodological Challenges in Qualitative Comparative Analysis of Higher Education

Comparison has long been thought as the principal tool of science: "Thinking without comparison is unthinkable. And, in the absence of comparison, so is all scientific thought and scientific research" (Swanson 1971, p. 145). "It is through comparison, and of comparables, that whatever heart we can actually get to is to be reached." (Geertz 1983, p. 233).[1] The higher education field does not make an exception: since the 1970s, international comparisons of higher education systems have become an important research tool. This reflects a change in the object of analysis, that is of higher education itself (Teichler 1996). The globalization process has opened up the research possibilities, leading scholars to think further about the pertinent level of analysis. The macro level of analysis has been identified as an important resource to study not only national differences but also transnational and global dynamics, and, since the 1990s, the macro level has gained interest, questioning the transformations of institutions' social functions as well as the changing interdependency dynamics at play.

Gold mine of research, international comparison is thus acknowledged as a heuristic tool to challenge the conceptual frames and enrich the debates regarding innovation in higher education. Still, as Kogan recalled (1996, 395), "comparative studies are always being attacked for, or are self-defensive about their inadequacies." The EuroAC qualitative research, characterized by the building up of a common methodological and conceptual frame, can hope to escape most of the basic critiques faced by comparative research: it is not a sole juxtaposition of cases, nor a benchmarking (Barbier 2005), nor a political command. Still, international comparative qualitative research faces a certain number of difficulties and limits, of which the researchers involved in EuroAC are well aware. The difficulties in building up a common interview grid, to be used in diverse national and higher education contexts, as well as the language issue, should not be underestimated. These difficulties have been worked on, first by attempting to build up a common research culture within the group of researchers, by regular meetings aimed at the joint designing of every step of the qualitative research, including firstly long hours of work on conceptual definitions. This stage was absolutely central to overcome disciplinary, culture, and language heterogeneity and build a common understanding and a shared vocabulary regarding research questions and methods. Once this was done and the fieldwork carried out, the thematic analysis was achieved by going back and forth between all the national teams and the responsible teams of each thematic analysis. In this regard the thematic strength of each team as well as the contextual in-depth knowledge of all teams was efficiently articulated.

At a more pragmatic level, the sample of the respondents has been selected so as to be as similar as possible to the CAP sample. This implies that target groups,

---

[1] For a comprehensive approach of comparison in higher education, see for example Goedegebuure and Van Vught 1996; Välimaa 2008 or Rothblatt and Wittrock 1993.

Table 1.1 Qualitative interview schedule

Time for interview	Interview-part		
20 %	A common core		
20 %	B 1	B 2	4B 3
	Subtheme:	Subtheme:	Subtheme:
	Governance	Professionalization	Academic careers
60 %	C special thematic area within a subtheme		
60 interviews per country (based on CRP framework proposal)	20 interviews	20 interviews	20 interviews

disciplines, gender, institutional types have been taken into consideration in all eight European countries.

At the beginning of each interview basic information was gathered with respect to the interviewee. Date, duration, name, academic position (e.g. full professor, assistant professor) and function (e.g. dean) as well as disciplinary field, institutional and sub-unit affiliation were reported at the top of each interview report.

The content of individual interviews was standardized according to the main research topic on the one hand, in order to produce findings that could be compared across countries, institutional types, disciplines, positions and functions. Table 1.1 summarizes how the different national teams in the EuroAC project have proceeded in data collection.

The most important objective of this methodology was to ask the same questions on basic core issues in order to provide a common framework for comparative analysis. Different national teams were responsible for one of the three subthemes, governance, professionalization, and academic careers.

Questions in the common core of the interviews addressed institutional status, recruitment (e.g. Where are you in the "map" of the profession/status?); identity (e.g. Who do you feel belongs to the university, only colleague next door or e.g. president?); international status (e.g. Are you integrated in international networks?); perception of societal expectations (e.g. What does the institutional and societal context expect from you?/e.g. Civic mission); perception of being researcher or teacher (or both); perception of having control over one's own work vs. being driven by others (e.g. What do you believe you can do in your academic life?; What the personal chances are, what the professors etc. let you do?); perceptions of the institution's expectations (e.g. How do you (try to) represent your institution/make your institution look good?).

Coming to the subthemes, governance was operationalized as follows: structure of institutional/internal governance (micro level), structure of external governance (macro level), quality management, perceptions of change. In the latter case senior staff were privileged as informants on the overall situation and on the historical perspective of the last years. The governance subtheme was articulated around three levels of analysis: first, at system level higher education steering has been observed through legislation and funding. The main research question in this regard is

"How have the changes that have taken place at national level affected your professional role as an academic?" Second, at institutional level, information about management and decision making within the university was gathered in order to understand how the increasing power of academic leaders and managers has affected an academic's professional role. Finally, at individual level, the impact of management in terms of decision-making powers and new practices has been scrutinized in order to compare the different value systems at work, that is the managerial and the academic ones. In this respect university members' identity and ownership of the academic professions has been tackled. Each national team has written a descriptive paper concerning the national governance framework of its own country according to system governance, steering by financial regulation and by information as quality assurance. This background paper has provided a basis to all national teams to support their thematic analysis across countries. Moreover it has focused on academic careers by describing the process of access to the current position of the interviewees, the criteria for recruitment and promotion.

When it comes to academic careers, the following issues were addressed: perceptions of the logic underpinning career paths, suggestions for improvement, recruitment processes and actors, mobility (inter-institutional, occupational, international); relevance of international experiences for progression, hierarchy in terms of social distance among status groups, with a particular focus on senior-junior relationships. To be noticed that the term "career progression" has been used in order to include more career phenomena than the traditional path of "up or out".

Questions about professionalization have been posed particularly to new groups of professionals within the university. The different dimensions of professionalization have affected academics' qualifications: traditional ones such as being a good researcher and teacher, but also emerging ones, like for instance being able to manage research projects and apply for external funding. At the same time the increasing professionalization of academic leadership, institutional management and administration as well as the professionalization of the academics themselves has been examined. Against this backdrop the implications for academic work, for the new higher education professionals (HEPROs), for the balance between teaching and research, between external and internal pressures have been highlighted. Respondents were also explicitly required to speak about their level of job satisfaction, about service to society functions beyond transfer of knowledge and applied research.

Professionalization has required different questions and perspectives in order to explore and shape an understanding with respect to HEPROs. The main research questions were: How did you get your job? Who has defined your role? How have your interactions and experiences with academics evolved? How have interactions with the institutional management, in particular bridging functions, developed? If the respondents were academics, the main questions and perspectives on academics were: how do you describe your experiences with HEPROs? How do you perceive an impact of the HEPROs on core tasks of academics?

Related to the evolving academic profession, the university's third mission has been also investigated. The concept of third mission is connected to the expectation towards universities to be relevant to society: in this perspective the knowledge produced in higher education institutions should also be applied and exploited to the benefit of the social, cultural and economic development. This can be translated in technology transfer and, more broadly, to socio-economic development and external stakeholder relations. Respondents were asked how they perceive their role in community and society; whether it is a voluntary work; whether they are pushed into third mission activities or any other distinctive activities in special areas; finally how much autonomy academics have in their research and teaching activities.

Each national team has conducted around 60 interviews. All interviews addressed the core part (A), 20 interviews have focused on part B1 (Governance, with at least 1/3 of respondents being managers), 20 interviews have tackled questions on part B2 (Academic Careers), 20 interviews posed questions on part B3 (Professionalization, with at least 1/3 of respondents being HEPROs). As of the C part (sub-themes Governance, Academic Careers, Professionalization) every team asked questions according to its specific C-part.

Drawing on the rationale of qualitative comparative research, it is more relevant to consider the typical common characteristics than giving prominence to exceptional cases and features. However the research design has to "guarantee" the difference of each country's situation. The choice of contextual variables reflects the survey conducted in 2010. Along this line important comparative aspects of the sample are countries, teaching/research institutions (types of institutions), career stages of the interviewees (senior, junior), disciplinary fields and gender.

In sum, more than 500 structured interviews have been conducted in the eight relevant countries. They all have taken place either face-to-face (most of them) or by phone and skype. The average duration was 35 minutes, however the longest lasted 2 hours. All interviews have been transcribed or summarized in detailed reports in each team's national language. A standardized report has been produced for each interview in English, coding interviewees' personal characteristics and providing as many quotations as possible. These standardized reports have been shared among the national EuroAC teams and every team could ask all other teams for further details. In fact in order to check the accuracy of information, the content of the empirical chapters has been controlled by all the other teams regarding each country's characteristics.

1.3 Emerging Issues in the European Academic Profession

In Chap. 2 the Austrian team explores European variations of career paths in academia by focusing on personal perspectives and experiences of academics. According to Brechelmacher, Park, Ates and Campbell, embarking on an academic career appears to be a risky undertaking. Across all eight countries many interviewees claim that what is needed is perseverance and persistence, not giving up (you need an "absolute will to do it"), steadfastness, ambition, obstinacy, flexibility and a willingness to take risks. Young academics must face periods of uncertainty, in the words of one interviewee it is vital "not to have a need for security". Uncertain employment prospects, in many cases adverse financial circumstances, quite often slightly above the 'at-risk-of-poverty' level go hand in hand with self-exploitation and long working hours at the expense of a private life. Also, mobility and willingness to go abroad and cultivate international experiences are increasingly required for an academic career. This chapter tries to identify and analyze different phases of an academic career from the early stages as a PhD candidate via the selective postdoctoral phase towards reaching permanent employment, preferably but not necessarily as a tenured university professor. Academic career paths and perspectives are currently in a state of transformation and recent national attempts to give new structure and perspective to academic careers (e.g. tenure-track) are discussed along with alternative career models (externally funded positions, cross employment).

In Chap. 3 "The changing paths in academic careers in European Universities: minor steps and major milestones" Kwiek and Antonowicz focus on how competition affects progress in academic careers. The Polish team argues that the academic career model in Europe used to be much more unstructured and much less competitive than today. There are significant variations across the European countries studied regarding the level of competition, often different according to the different positions occupied in the academic hierarchy. Nonetheless increasing competition has pervaded the academic profession and seems to be bound to stay: it takes the shape of rivalry for part-time and full-time academic positions, for research grants and research funding, and for tokens of academic prestige (e.g. publications). The academic progression today has to be made systematically, in increasingly clearly defined timeframes, and the academic career seems to be sliced into comparable time periods across European systems. Usually, the timeframes are doctoral studies, employment in postdoctoral and junior positions, employment in lower-level senior positions and, finally, in higher-level senior positions (such as traditional chair holders and/or full professorships), and all career steps have to be reached within a certain time period. The competition in academic settings means most often measurable research outputs expected from academics for particular time periods or for particular stages of the academic career. Expectations from academics in the same stages of their careers are becoming largely similar throughout Europe. Under such conditions often marginal differences in performance make the winners secure a position in the academic system, and make their marginally lower-performing competitors lose the battle for entering the higher education system.

In Chap. 4 the Swiss team investigates recruitment processes in academia focusing on their formal and informal organization, the configuration of actors at play, the variety implied in national settings, institutional types and disciplines as well as the constraints and opportunities experienced by academics in coping with their own career progress. In this framework Fumasoli and Goastellec discuss how recruitment represents a key dimension of academic labour markets. Not only such processes organise academic influxes – specifying the scientific and human composition of the academic workforce – they also testify of the configuration at play in each higher education sector (configuration they contribute to shape), and of the embedding of academic labour markets in the general economy of the country. Particularly, the interaction of diverse models (disciplinary, institutional, national, global) is observed in order to understand how distinctive logics coexist, generating similar and different practices. This contribution explores and analyzes academic recruitment processes as a structuring dimension of both academic careers and organisations. Embedded in career structures, higher education institutions' organisation, and disciplinary identities, recruitment processes can be described as two-sided. On the one hand, a formal framework features the scientific qualifications required for each status, as well as the steps through which an application can be made, at the level of the institution and/or at national level. On the other hand, local practices are often specific, influenced by the disciplinary academic community, by the available different types of resources and by the position of the faculty in the national and international market, as well as by the attractiveness of the private sector.

The changing employment and working conditions are analyzed in Chap. 5 by Aarrevaara, Dobson and Wikström. The chapter by the Finnish team considers the academic working environment reporting particularly on academics' impressions of the changes undergone in recent years. A focus is provided on the extent to which the content of academic work in these countries is similar or different; on the nature of academics' working conditions and on how they have changed; and finally on how academics' affiliations are articulated. The analysis also considers differences according to seniority. This contribution offers an analysis of how changes in working conditions, in employment and in modes of operation have affected scholarly work and related activities, as well as how academic freedom is being affected.

The perception academics have of their professional contexts is investigated by the Irish team in Chap. 6. Clarke, Drennan, Hyde and Politis build on the notion of academic profession as a variegated combination of functions and profiles. The authors argue that the role of the academic profession is recognized internationally as comprising teaching, research and administration, however the concept of an academic profession is relatively new and includes a mixture of profiles. This is due to the move to mass higher education, the development of international markets for students, the establishment of quality assurance systems, increased competition between universities, and other organizations in the knowledge economy. The diversity within the academic profession suggests that it cannot be viewed as one where traditional divisions within the roles are clear-cut. The findings from the eight country EuroAC study are interpreted within Bourdieu's sociology of academia (1988), which highlights the tensions academics experience in their professional roles: teaching, researching, managing, writing and networking. The authors point out how academics experience significant challenges between the scientific capital (or prestige) routes and the academic capital routes. This is so both within their roles and within the demands made by the institutions where they work.

Relating to the stretching of the notion of academic profession, the Croatian team examines academics' community engagement in selected European countries. The aim of Ćulum, Turk and Ledic in Chap. 7 is to contribute to the ongoing discussion on community engagement by focusing on the nature, on the extent and on the evaluation of academics' community engagement in three European countries – Croatia, Germany and Ireland – and their different social, cultural, political and economic contexts. Differences in such contexts can be reflected in differences in the involvement of the university with the university wider community. The main topics addressed in this chapter are twofold: on one side the nature and extent of academics'/participants' public engagement in the community/society with non-economic stakeholders, on the other side the status of their community engagement in the frame of institutional commitment to value that kind of activities and academics' public engagement. Different dynamics emerge in how widely or narrowly academics interpret and enact community engagement, whom they target for knowledge transfer, how they build partnerships and networks, what activities they find themselves engaged with, and which incentives enhance their involvement. This variegated picture accounts for distinctive country specific models, as well as for specific institutional strategies in communicating the importance of academics' community engagement.

In Chap. 8 Moraru, Praisler, Marin and Bentea scrutinize the implementation of quality assurance systems (QAS) according to academic staff perceptions. The study of the Romanian team identifies and examines numerous challenges posed by standardization and a global approach of quality assurance, and their implications for educational restructuring. Moreover special attention is paid to new forms of quality assurance systems covering the relationship between teaching and research, students' feedback vs. students' involvement, and cross-institutional assessments. The main themes are direct statements extracted from the interviewees' responses that were considered to be the most meaningful to the central areas of inquiry. They are: QAS significance; satisfaction with QAS; QAS implementation issues; QAS organizational benefits; quality vs. quantity; research vs. teaching in terms of QA; standardization/general model vs. flexible approach; structural changes; and cross-institutional assessment tools.

In Chap. 9 Kehm contends that the more new forms of managerial governance emerge in higher education institutions the higher becomes the number of a particular group of people that we call the 'new higher education professionals' (HEPROs). By looking at the relationship between HEPROs and the academic profession, the German team points out how HEPROs act as change agents at various levels of the institutions (departmental, faculty, central levels) and help prepare management decisions or support their implementation. They are experts providing innovative or extended types of services within higher education institutions. In particular three dimensions of HEPRO work are emphasized: as experts, as facilitators, and as service providers. It turns out that HEPRO work is highly appreciated by academic staff as long as it unburdens the academic staff from administrative duties, however conflicts are emerging if HEPROs demand additional work from academic staff. Most importantly however, the HEPRO phenomenon changes the configuration of power within the higher education institutions and creates an as yet precarious new balance between the "academic oligarchy", a strengthened central management, and the HEPROs themselves.

The final chapter (chap. 10) pulls together the main findings presented in the book and discusses their implications for academic work conditions and academic careers in Europe. It puts a particular emphasis on European changes in academic careers and the new requirements emerging for progress and potential tenure. The EuroAC qualitative study has been built to permit a systematic comparison of the academic profession in highly diverse national contexts. The focus on Europe allows questioning the emergence of a regional structure of the academic profession in the higher education context, following the work of international relations sociologists such as Badie (1995) and Laïdi (1994), who hypothesize a trend toward the emergence of neo-regionalism. Still, the systematic work of comparison shows the remaining importance of national frames, as underlined in other research fields by Petiteville (1997), and underline that the European reference does not constitute yet a semantic space (Laïdi 1994). Against this backdrop, the final chapter underlines the common trend towards the formalization and professionalization of the academic profession in Europe but also the remaining influence of the specific historical roots of higher education systems that lead, as already pointed out by Ramirez and Christensen (2013) in other contexts, to the building up of different answers to the same pressure.

References

Badie, B. (1995). *La fin des territoires*. Paris: Fayard.

Barbier, J.-C. (2005). When words matter. Dealing anew with cross-national comparison. In J.-C. Barbier & M. T. Letablier (Eds.), *Cross-national comparisons: Epistemological and methodological issues* (pp. 45–70). Brussels: Peter Lang.

Boyer, E. L., Altbach, P. G., & Whitelaw, M. J. (1994). *The academic profession: An international perspective*. Princeton: Carnegie Foundation.

European Commission. (2005). *The European charter for researchers. The code of conduct for the recruitment of researchers*. Brussels: European Commission.

Geertz, C. (1983). *Local knowledge. Further essays in interpretative anthropology*. New York: Basic Book.

Goedegebuure, L., & Van Vught, F. (1996). *Comparative higher education studies: The perspective from the policy science*. Higher Education, *32* (4), 371–394.

Kehm, B. M., & Teichler, U. (Eds.). (2013). *The academic profession in Europe: New tasks and new challenges*. Dordrecht: Springer.

Kogan, M. (1996). Comparing higher education systems. *Higher Education, 32*, 395–402.

Laïdi, Z. (1994). *Un monde privé de sens*. Paris: Fayard.

Petiteville, F. (1997). Les processus d'intégration régionale, vecteurs de structuration du système international? *Etudes Internationales, 28* (3), 511–533.

Ramirez, F. O., & Christensen, T. (2013). The formalization of the university: Rules, roots and routes. *Higher Education, 65*, 695–708.

Rothblatt, S., & Wittrock, B. (1993). Introduction: Universities and higher education. In S. Rothblatt & B. Wittrock (Eds.), *The European and American university since 1800* (pp. 1–16). Cambridge: Cambridge University Press.

Swanson, G. (1971). Frameworks for comparative research: Structural anthropology and the theory of action. In K. Vallier (Ed.), *Comparative methods in sociology: Essays on trends and applications* (pp. 141–202). Berkeley: University of California Press.

Teichler, U. (1996). The state of comparative research in higher education. *Higher Education, 32* (4), 431–465.

Teichler, U., Arimoto, A., & Cummings, W. K. (2013). *The changing academic profession: Major findings of a comparative survey.* Dordrecht: Springer.

Teichler, U., & Höhle, E. (Eds.). (2013). *The work situation of the academic profession in Europe: Findings of a survey in twelve countries.* Dordrecht: Springer.

Välimaa, J. (2008). On comparative research in higher education. In A. Amaral, I. Bleiklie, & C. Musselin (Eds.), *From governance to identity – A Festschrift for Mary Henkel* (Higher education dynamics 24, pp. 141–155). Dordrecht: Springer.

Chapter 2
The Rocky Road to Tenure – Career Paths in Academia

Angelika Brechelmacher, Elke Park, Gülay Ates, and David F.J. Campbell

2.1   Introduction

Embarking on an academic career apparently is a risky undertaking. Across all eight countries many interviewees claim that what is needed is perseverance and persistence, not giving up (you need an "absolute will to do it"), steadfastness, ambition, obstinacy, flexibility and a willingness to take risks. Young academics must face periods of uncertainty, in the words of one interviewee it is vital "not to have a need for security". Uncertain employment prospects, in many cases adverse financial circumstances, quite often slightly above the 'at-risk-of-poverty' level (Ates and Brechelmacher 2013), go hand in hand with self-exploitation and long working hours at the expense of a private life. Also, mobility and a willingness to go abroad international experiences are increasingly requirements for an academic career. Coincidence also play a role as several interviewees claim that it was ultimately luck that got them where they are ("being in the right place at the right time"), however, as one interviewee points out: "Women say their academic careers are based on luck, men claim it was their competence".

This chapter tries to identify and analyse different stages of an academic career from the early stages as a PhD candidate via the selective postdoctoral phase towards reaching permanent employment, preferably but not necessarily as a tenured university professor. As academic career paths and perspectives are currently in a state of transformation recent national attempts to give new structure and perspective to academic careers (tenure-track) will be discussed as well as alternative career models that are possibly emerging (externally funded positions, cross employment). Focusing on the personal perspectives and experiences of academics

A. Brechelmacher (✉) • E. Park • G. Ates • D.F.J. Campbell
IFF Institute for Science Communication and Higher Education Research, Universität Klagenfurt-Graz-Wien, Schottenfeldgasse 29, Vienna 1070, Austria
e-mail: Angelika.Brechelmacher@uni-klu.ac.at

© Springer International Publishing Switzerland 2015   13
T. Fumasoli et al. (eds.), *Academic Work and Careers in Europe: Trends, Challenges, Perspectives*, The Changing Academy – The Changing Academic Profession in International Comparative Perspective 12, DOI 10.1007/978-3-319-10720-2_2

the situation and problems they currently find themselves confronted with will be reflected.

2.2 The PhD Phase: Entering an Academic Career

In the following a brief insight into the early stages of an academic career, before completion of the doctoral degree will be given. The analysis centers on the following questions: Is a doctorate required for an academic career? What tasks are expected of early career researchers? How do PhD-candidates perceive their situation? How satisfied are they with their working conditions?

In Austria a doctoral degree is still the first requirement for an academic career. Short-term positions as tutors, student assistants, assistants on research projects or as pre-doctoral assistants, are seen as important first steps towards entering an academic trajectory. One interviewee stated that her career started with the first employment in a pre-doc position, which was an "entry ticket to the institution". (AT46) According to many interviewees – especially university managers and professors – the ideal start into an academic career is to secure a place in one of the newly established structured doctoral programmes. Entering these highly selective programmes is reserved for only a few successful candidates. "It is impossible to finance everyone, and not everyone is able to do a doctorate." (AT34) Both juniors and seniors at Austrian universities see involvement in research projects, integration into the department, building up networks, active participation at conferences and journal publications as important elements for career advancement in academia. Some of the interviewed seniors recommend that being mobile is also important during this early career stage. Regarding the profile and status of pre-doctoral junior academics, changes are observed:

> Today's pre-docs are equal to former university assistants, but have to remain in the role of students, they are employed through projects and lab-jobs, whereas former university assistants were firmly integrated into the team/institute. (AT47)

In Switzerland an academic career starts right after a master thesis by being employed as an assistant and doing a PhD. Interestingly, many junior respondents mention getting their post was easy and without any competition.

Swiss funding and the recruitment procedures are dynamic, which makes it very attractive to do a PhD in Switzerland. However, it is also mentioned that structured doctoral schools tend to overburden young scientists. Junior respondents from Swiss universities list teaching, correcting exams of undergraduates or supervision of master thesis, doing laboratory jobs, and publication of articles as important tasks. One of the respondents observes that teaching has been devalued and there is too much focus on research:

> Everybody at [my institution] always says that teaching is important and so on, but in the end I want to get my PhD, and for my PhD [my institution] doesn't care how much teaching I did but how many results I have. [...] So it's always if I spend more time on teaching, I

spend less on research, I have less results and in the long term I have some smiling faces of the students but it's not helpful for me at all. (CH34)

The interviewee thinks that the tension between teaching and research comes partly because of a lack of rules regulating the time devoted to teaching and research.

An influx of highly educated German PhDs in Switzerland could contribute to an increasingly competitive environment for Swiss PhDs: "Doing a PhD in Switzerland could become less attractive." (CH24) Not least because of this, being mobile before or after obtaining a PhD seems to be highly common at Swiss universities.

Also at Polish universities, doctoral degrees are required for an academic career. However, interviewees repeatedly point to an insufficient funding level for pre-docs. The salaries of junior position holders seem to be low and additional remuneration is required. One of them underlines:

If a young researcher has no decent place to live, faces problems in providing sufficient income for the family, then research career development is wishful-thinking. And the lack of academic leaders and research teams makes it difficult to absorb external funding. (PL6)

Furthermore, both senior and junior interviewees criticise still predominantly feudal senior-junior relationships.

Taking advantage of younger academics unfortunately seems to be an integral part of higher education in Poland. Fortunately, the new generation of senior academics who are more internationally oriented know that feudalism in science is already a thing of the past. (PL50)

At Finnish universities too, doing a PhD is a requirement for an academic career. As in Austria and Switzerland, structured doctoral programmes have recently been established. The standard time to complete a degree has been decreased to 4 years. Research merits, social skills and networking have until recently belonged to the post-doctoral phase. The norms for these abilities, skills and competences are subject to change. These and are now to be developed in the doctoral phase. However, compared to before, the supervisors now support the doctoral candidates more fully and are responsible until completion of the doctoral thesis.

Because of the required competence profile for doctoral candidates it seems that Finish junior researchers have to postpone the time of being abroad to the postdoctoral phase. Job opportunities for PhDs are rare inside of academic institutions:

When I started as a doctoral student most graduates stayed in the academia. Now we have quite a few doctoral graduates who work outside academia. (FIJW71)

In Germany the PhD is still seen as an extended training phase. Currently established structured doctoral programmes and excellence initiatives of German universities are considered as a good start into an academic career. However, many juniors feel pressurized into finishing their degree in 4 years as required by the new doctoral programmes. Doctoral candidates at German universities list as their core duties: being involved in teaching and research activities, supervising Bachelor- and Master students, supporting the professor, administrative tasks, publishing, being mobile and finally, writing a PhD. In addition, doctoral candidates in structured programmes mention a specific amount of courses as further required activities. Respondents in junior positions find it difficult to go abroad under these circumstances. One of them underlines that one needs a high frustration tolerance (0310SS). The situation during the doctoral phase is described as follows:

> I definitely think that there is very big competition among the doctoral candidates and the team work suffers. Those who compete for the next position are known. The dissertation's quality suffers, because one is left alone. In addition, the readiness to work more than eight hours a day, is required. It is important to commit oneself completely to this career, which is actually no career. This includes working late, at weekends and travelling a lot. (. . .) I would be happy with my job, if I knew that the work would pay off. (0120SH)

Despite the high performance pressure, low income and 60 hours per week workload, some of the junior researchers are highly motivated and satisfied with their situation. "I have fun in scientific work and teaching. My work is creative." (0120 MB)

Working at Croatian universities requires a PhD too. The allocated time for a doctoral degree has been reduced to 6 years. Also in Croatia there is a trend to faster completion of the doctorate. Junior researchers mention that their scientific performance should include research and teaching activities, publishing as many articles as possible, gaining international experience and the active participation in conferences. Many criticise the high teaching workload, which prevents them from completing their PhD.

> My teaching workload is a major problem. Although my contract says I should spend 25 percent of my time in teaching and 75 percent in research work, in reality it is the other way around. (HR48)

Junior interviewees also complain about a lack of participatory rights and collegial support. However, one interviewee points out the freedom and autonomy to "define my own field of research and the opportunity to suggest and implement changes relating to the teaching process and my work with students" (HR6).

Obtaining a PhD is a requirement for an academic career also in Romania. There have been recent changes and adaptions in line with the European doctoral programmes. Often a lack of funding and/or low salaries for young academics are deplored. It is expected of doctoral candidates to participate at conferences and postgraduate programmes, besides doing research to attend professional training programmes for teachers, to publish articles in prestigious journals and to access grants and scholarships. One interviewee stresses the importance of belonging to a research team:

> This is the only way to achieve performance in research. [. . .] To be a member of a sound research team favours publication and has a positive effect on the academic prestige of scientists. (RO19)

One of the senior respondents from a Romanian university talks about the important fruitful interrelation of senior and junior scientists. He highlights the relevance of communicating with junior researchers and motivating them to take part actively at competitions and conferences (RO39MAN).

In conclusion, in most of the countries analysed the completion of a PhD is a requirement for an academic career. However, Ireland stands apart from the previously examined countries. Here bachelor graduates already have the opportunity to enter academia. Nevertheless, the increasing importance of doctoral degrees is noted as an upcoming trend. While in Croatia and Romania the doctorate is the final degree of the training phase, at Swiss, Finnish, Polish, German and Austrian universities, the doctorate is merely an intermediate degree before a habilitation or an equivalent post-doctoral degree.

Regarding competition, Swiss, Romanian and Polish respondents, find the application procedures for positions to obtain a doctoral degree not competitive. On the contrary, pre-doc position and structured programme applications procedures in Austria, Germany and Finland are highly competitive and selective. In nearly all countries, junior positions are fixed-term, precarious and have low incomes.

The expected tasks and core elements of the early career stages in nearly all countries are the advancement of teaching and research skills, participation in conferences, building up networks and publishing articles. With the exception of Finland, mobility requirements during the doctoral phase are strongly increasing in all countries.

Regarding the job satisfactions of junior academics, there is mixed evidence. However, a common impression is an increasing time pressure to finish the degree, and a heavy teaching workload which further impedes the completion of the thesis. Finally, regarding the senior-junior relationship, a hierarchical structure can be observed in nearly all countries.

2.3   The Critical Post-doctoral Phase: A Double Bottleneck?

The phase after completion of the doctorate and thus after the last steps of training or education as an academic, is considered by many as the hardest and most difficult phase during an academic career. The training phase to becoming an academic is over and young postdoctoral researchers enter the academic labour market. They need to find their first university position, even if only on a fixed-term basis, and then manage to progress on to permanent, tenured employment. Interviewees portray the postdoc phase as a double bottleneck at the stage of entering it after the PhD (trying to obtain a postdoctoral position) and at the stage of leaving it by securing permanent, tenured employment. The postdoc phase emerges as a highly risky and uncertain period at the end of which you either "make it to the safe side" (DE0318PF) or you have to leave the university. Many interviewees described this phase as most "critical", "problematic" or "difficult". Obtaining postdoc-positions after finishing your education is also becoming "increasingly harder". (AT01, AT19MAN) Interviewees claim that post-doctoral positions are rare and there is fierce and increasing competition for the few available posts. There are simply "not as many positions as applicants". (CH22) Several Finnish interviewees attribute this lack of open postdoc positions to the fact that the number of PhDs has increased in recent years, while the number of postdoctoral and professorial positions remained the same. One Finnish interviewee claims that "there are lots of PhDs [. . .] but after that it gets more complicated. Academic posts have not increased although more PhDs are trained." (FILP12) Another Finnish colleague (junior) notices the same change: "Previously there were less researchers, and it was possible that some day you get a professorship. Nowadays there are so many researchers, that there are no positions for everyone." (FILP17) There simply is "not enough work in the academy for doctoral graduates nowadays". (FIJW80) One Austrian postdoctoral researcher even considers his career atypical, because of the fact that he managed to obtain a postdoctoral position at all. (AT01)

How arduous and difficult it is today to obtain university employment as a postdoctoral researcher is stressed in many interviews. There is also wide agreement among interviewees that the postdoctoral phase is the most competitive phase in an academic career. A Finnish junior summarises what many others said:

> The post-doctoral phase is very exhausting, there is harsh competition going on and you usually have to work under fixed-term contracts for a very long time until you get a permanent position; if you ever get one. (FILP7)

The risky nature of an academic career and the uncertainty during the postdoctoral phase is also highlighted in other interviews: "One has to deal with a lot of insecurity" (FILP18) as "the path is unclear" (AT05).

Further, there is no guarantee that after competing on the tough academic job market a permanent position will open up at the end. Many will be forced to leave the university, having to end their academic career at a relatively late age (AT20MAN "at the age of forty academic corpses turn up – people who are too good for industry"). Ultimately, the postdoctoral phase is characterised by the race towards (permanent, tenured) university employment or dropping out of the race and having to leave academe (FILP18, AT19MAN).

The unpredictability of an academic career during this stage is also reflected in the interviews. Many claim that it was mere "coincidence" or "luck" that got them where they are (among others AT58, AT48, CH52, FILP4, FILP5, FILP8, FILP12).

There is also a growing pressure for mobility as in some countries academics are required or expected to leave their university after completion of the PhD. These mobility requirements present a further problem to postdoctoral academics as they collide with family and life-planning which usually takes place between the age of 30 and 40 (see also Sect. 2.3.4 on mobility). One Austrian interviewee states that "the decision to have a family, does not depend on your age, but on your employment contract" (AT48).

There is consensus, among university managers and academics alike that it is vital to structure the postdoc career phase more clearly and to provide perspectives for young academics during this phase. As a reaction to the high uncertainty and lack of concrete perspectives which makes the planning of an academic career difficult if not impossible, there have been recent attempts to structure the somewhat chaotic, highly risky postdoctoral phase, most notably through the introduction of new career models such as the tenure-track, a career track that is intended to lead postdocs to permanent employment on the condition that certain, previously outlined qualification requirements are fulfilled (see Sect. 2.3.3).

2.3.1   Fixed-Term Employment and Precarious Working Conditions

The prevalence of fixed-term contracts is one of the central problems associated with the postdoctoral phase. Most postdoctoral employment contracts are fixed-term as universities often consider this phase to be the last selective phase for professorial, tenured positions and it is thus in this phase – between the age of 30 and 45 depending on the country and structure of the HE system – that precarious employment situations occur most frequently: One fixed-term employment contracts follow after the other with no guarantee of a positive outcome. A Swiss interviewee claims that as a "postdoc people become eternal temporary workers". [...] "Getting a chair is an ambition but not a possibility" (CH4).

Many interviewees in several countries are under the impression that there have been changes in employment contracts at universities in recent years. They notice a rise and increase of fixed-term positions in academe and a trend towards less secure working conditions. (for example, AT24HE, DE01227BK, DE0201MH, DE0113DT). The "turnover" at universities is high (DE0215JR) and "contrary to former times staff today needs to be more flexible" (DE0301NA, DE0616AB). Due to contract limitations, performance pressure and competition increase (DE0120SG).

Several interviewees claim that formerly it was easier to obtain permanent employment at universities. "In the past" tenure was granted more or less automatically at the end of a contract (CH38), you simply had to "wait in line or queue" for a professorship after completing your PhD and habilitation (DE0215JR). According to the interviewees there used to be clearly outlined paths and employment prospects which no longer exist:

> An academic career was previously very clear, now it is very uncertain. I do not imagine that I will get a permanent position from the university, but probably some temporary posts. There are discussions in my department about strengthening career paths, but I am very sceptical about this. (FILP15)

This clear notion of an increase in fixed-term employment is linked to and explained by the need for flexibility and budgetary constraints universities are facing, both by academics and university managers. In the opinion of an Austrian junior researcher "university Human Resources planning is getting more strategic: departments tactically try to avoid being 'blocked' [with permanent positions] and aim at preserving flexibility in hiring." Many academics, especially in Austria, a country that only recently underwent drastic university reforms in the direction of New Public Management, are under the impression that university leadership is opting mostly for fixed-term junior positions and is reluctant to create permanent positions in order to maintain flexibility (AT25) "aims to keep the numbers of core [i.e. permanent] staff low for budgetary reasons" (AT09, also AT31HE).

Generally, university management underlined the need for a certain degree of flexibility in HR management in the interviews. An Austrian university manager explained the increase in fixed-term positions "as a reaction to relatively relaxed hiring policies before, which gave even less well qualified staff access to permanent [civil servant] positions." (AT12MAN). Another Austrian university manager argued in defense of an increase in non-permanent positions that he "also experienced phases of 100 % permanent employees, where positions were simply 'sat out'" (AT19MAN).

Not surprisingly, academics on fixed-term positions experience their personal employment situation mostly negatively and voiced their dissatisfaction in the interviews (with few exceptions, one interviewee claimed the fixed-term nature of his job was a "motivation and a chance", DE0523KS). However, there is support from senior academics who found the strongest words, when considering their younger colleagues' situation. An Austrian senior found the situation "absolutely horrific" (AT34), another called it "scandalous. [...] Fixed-term employment contracts force talented people to leave. This is not conducive to scientific work. In the social sciences people develop hopes, are actively involved and are then left with nothing" (AT38). Another professor found it "a catastrophe [...] We are burning an entire generation." At her department, [postdoctoral] university assistants are employed for 4 years, after this time the assistant "automatically" has to leave the department. This happens at a time in the academic's career "where other universities are more than happy to have him or her [...], it is a brain drain without comparison" (AT34). The resulting brain drain due to a lack of permanent academic positions is also mentioned in a German interview (DE0317NN). Higher Education systems with a high rate of fixed-term positions are considered increasingly "internationally unattractive" (AT34). France and the UK on the other hand are mentioned repeatedly as systems with better career prospects (AT01, AT01, AT48). Besides the inherent financial and personal uncertainty of fixed-term positions also the lack of institutional affiliation and participation in university governance (DE0118BK, AT50 "Loyalty cannot be developed this way") is seen as a reason why fixed-term employment is problematic and possibly detrimental. It was also mentioned that the quality of research suffers from time-pressure and temporal delimitations.

Most interviewees on fixed-term positions expressed their hopes for permanent employment after a long and exhausting phase of having taken "constant steps into financial uncertainty" (AT15). A Swiss postdoctoral researcher summarises: "Of course there is the anguish of having a position which you like but which is fixed in time. I have 5 years ahead then I hope I will finally get something permanent." (CH24)

Permanent employment, but not necessarily a professorial position: one interviewee's states that she does not aim for a "career" or a professorship, she only wants a "permanent position on which to do research" (AT15). Another interviewee from Austria claims that "his aim is a professorship or another permanent university position, such as the senior lecturer in the UK (AT02). However, according to the interviewee, such positions do currently not exist in his country [and] tenure-track positions are currently not available in his field". A male Austrian interviewee who is currently cross-employed as a consultant and works on a project basis at the university claims that as he started having a family "future fantasies of a permanent position" emerged. Apparently a permanent position to him is nothing but a fantasy, an unrealistic dream to him, which he claims he has now given up (AT58).

Another postdoctoral researcher from Austria recounts his career and looks back on over 25 years of precarious, fixed-term employment. This interviewee only recently obtained a position as university assistant (also fixed-term), "for which he is actually too old" and claims that "for the first time in 25 years I knows what to live on for the next 4 years." It is "strange not to have to permanently worry about finances." The interviewee financed his life through projects and worked on research that interested him on the side, often unpaid (AT29).

2.3.2   The – Changing? – Role of University Assistants

The position as "university assistant" represents the traditional continental European model for postdoctoral employment (especially prevalent in the German speaking area or countries with a chair-system, this applies to Switzerland, Austria, Germany, Finland, Croatia, in the EuroAC survey). University assistants (both pre-doc and postdoc) are assigned to a professor, they belong to the "infrastructure" of a professorial chair and are in many ways tied and strongly dependent on the chair-holder. These positions are mostly fixed-term. After the postdoctoral assistant's position expires, the only other option besides leaving the university was the application or appointment ("call") to a full professorship (usually after the completion of the habilitation around 45 years of age). This model is currently subject to change due to the introduction of tenure-track structures and attempts to foster earlier academic independence. An Austrian senior/manager summarises:

> The trend is away from traditional assistant positions that depend on professors towards early academic independence. [In] the old model young academics remained on assistant positions for a relatively long period of time, today comparative evaluations and reviews take place at a much earlier point in a career. (AT28MAN)

The traditional role of university assistants as an 'asset' of the professor was outlined in many interviews. Professors "have" or even "share" and "bring" their "own" assistants (CH28, CH17, CH48, AT10) "Some professors still keep assistants like in the old school." (AT39) All pre- and post-doc positions are "tied to professors, they are only assigned to close collaborators of professors." (AT48) An Austrian interviewee speaks of a "'feudal system' in the German speaking area" (AT57).

For professors, these human 'resources' are valuable, however: A Croatian senior sees a positive change in having assistants, because

[it] allows me to do those tasks I really love – writing books and working on my own improvement. Assistants do those less attractive tasks, such as evaluating students' progress, monitoring their work during the year, evaluating their seminar papers etc. (HR15)

University assistants traditionally got chosen by the professors they are assigned to (CH37, CH23) and they tend to depend strongly upon the chair-holder under and for whom they are working, in turn they (can) receive support from their mentor. This was the traditional model of academic career advancement but this model seems to be changing as an Austrian senior (AT41) notes that "formerly it was common that the assistant wrote the scientific paper and the professor put his name under it. In return the professor mentored and supported his assistant. Today, assistant positions are fixed-term, the assistants no longer work for the professors and do not take on administrative tasks any more, instead they have to closely watch and work on their own scientific performance."

However, others claim that the old model is still present: "At other institutes research assistants have to make copies for the professor" (AT32). Regarding the division of labour between professors and assistants, a Swiss professor mentions that "he doesn't go into the lab anymore. It is the PhDs and the post-docs who do the experiments. There is a pyramidal division of labor. [. . .] His job is mainly to "have new ideas of research", to find money to finance it, drive the research projects and write or rewrite the papers of his PhDs before sending it to journals" (CH54). That junior staff (both predoc and postdoc) does most of the academic "groundwork" is also recounted in other interviews in Austria and Switzerland: "Question: Whenever there is a publication it is co-signed by the head? Answer: Yes. Question: Always? Answer: Yes, no publication without the name of the professor and it is often written by himself" (CH29).

Several interviewees mention the high workload (especially in teaching and student supervision) assigned to assistants which impedes the completion of larger research projects such as the habilitation (AT48). An Austrian interviewee notices "that assistants have to carry the load of the high number of students, they are the ones standing in the lecture halls, they have to correct exams and they are blocked in their own academic careers." (AT17). In addition, university assistants are faced with a pressure to publish during this phase: High research performance is expected of them as a position as university assistant is still considered a qualification position in the academic career.

Still, institutions rely on the work and contributions of university assistants. While an Austrian senior academic is generally in favour of "raising the number of professorial positions", he states that "we cannot play America and pretend there are only professors", his university needs assistant positions to be able to fulfil the large teaching obligations and administrative tasks (AT12MAN).

2.3.3   New Career Tracks: The Tenure-Track as a Solution?

In many Higher Education systems there have been attempts to restructure the often unregulated and chaotic academic career paths during the critical postdoctoral phase. New career tracks were introduced to provide a clearer perspective and to create an outlined track or pathway towards permanent, tenured employment for highly qualified young academics in recent years. In some countries, such as Austria, Switzerland and Finland a tenure-track system more or less loosely based on the US American tenure-track has recently been established. The tenure-track intends to bridge the gap between fixed-term university assistant positions and professorial appointments by introducing a trial period from assistant to associate and full professor based on the fulfillment of certain previously outlined qualification requirements. While in Switzerland and Finland the tenure-track leads up to the position of full professor, in Austria promotion on the tenure-track ends with an associate professorship. The position of full professor can still only be reached via a "call" or professorial appointment procedure.

In Germany, the so-called "junior professorship" has been established, an intermediary position and a – previously missing – link between fixed-term university assistant positions and the full professorship. Also in Ireland which already foresees a clear path toward permanent employment, changes in the career-paths of academics were implemented aiming at more simplified structures. In Poland the "road towards tenure" is generally not considered a problem, a clear tenure-track from associate to full professor was and is in place and most postdoctoral academics follow this path. In Poland the problematic aspect of postdoctoral academic careers (as assistant or associate professors) is not so much obtaining a permanent position as the low salary level these positions offer.

Interviewees in the countries which recently implemented the tenure-track model expressed hopes that the tenure-track will provide perspectives to academics and give more clarity and predictability to the academic career path. Generally, the introduction and underlying idea behind the tenure-track is regarded overwhelmingly positively by junior and senior academics alike. They welcome "the existence of a foreseeable career path with predefined procedures" (AT44). The tenure track "offers permanence and continuity" (AT08), "clear requirements and perspectives" (AT06) and overall "attractive conditions" (AT54), some even describe it as "ideal" (AT35).

"A tenure track system for young promising postdocs might create new options for strategic long term recruitment" (FIJW73), an Austrian academic even claims that "tenure-track positions are 'the only adequate possibility' to make academic careers more secure, in order not to fall out of the system right before the habilitation: 'Long-term perspectives are very, very important'" (AT37).

However, while the concept is considered good, many interviewees also state that the number of these newly created positions is very limited, that there are "too few positions" (AT01, AT08), "assistant professorships are rare" (AT05), "available only for a limited number of people" (FILP4), their numbers are "not sufficient" (AT27HE). Another interviewee claims that "the financial situation of universities allows only for a limited number of tenure-track positions". (AT08) The insufficiency of funds to create an adequate number of tenure-track positions is also noticed by other interviewees: "Actually now my HEI says that we have a tenure track, but unfortunately we do not have enough funding for it" (FIJW75, also AT20MAN). "For the first time in a long time a career model exists, however, there are only few available tenure-track positions, because these positions cost money" (AT42). "Not all docents proceed to the higher levels, because there are not professorships enough. They do not have funding to establish new professorships to all who would be qualified for it" (FILP13).

The view that the number of available tenure-track positions has to be increased is shared by several interviewees. Tenure-track positions are highly sought after and attractive to young postdoctoral academics (AT15, AT48, AT35) and reaching a tenure-track position is the declared goal and aim of many junior academics we interviewed. However, one Austrian junior claims that obtaining a tenure-track position remains "an illusion" (AT55).

Due to the limited amount of available tenure-track positions the competition for the few available posts is fierce. "Tenure-track positions are only foreseen for a small group: it is a competition-oriented system. They offer concrete perspectives and predictability for those who get in" (AT29). Only few achieve an academic career this way: all others are "temporalised staff. This leads to an intensification of competition" (AT08).

The strongly competitive nature and highly selective recruitment procedure for tenure-track positions is underlined and pointed out by several interviewees. Young academics seem pinned against each other (FILP17, CH59, AT27HE). And there will inevitably are also be losers in this race as "many who would be good enough, will not make it. The system thus loses excellent people, many of them women" (AT52, also FIJW73).

However, competition for tenure-track positions in the new career model takes place at an earlier stage in the academic career, not around the age of 40 or 45 (applying for full professorship after the habilitation) which is mostly regarded positively. One senior academic notes: "The tenure-track system enables young academics to start an academic career early on and to prove themselves on the international market. Comparative evaluations and reviews take place at a much earlier point in a career [...] not during professorial appointments" (AT28MAN). Especially in the German interviews the lowering of the age structure was mentioned several times in regard to the "junior professorship": The newly appointed colleagues are "younger than they were in the past" (DE0203VS, also DE0208HPG). Junior professorships can begin at the age of 27, which is seen as a "decisive change in academic careers" (DE0208JR) compared to formerly, when there were 'waiting loops' before you could hold a chair at the age of 40–50 years. Due to the introduction of the junior professorship, the decision for or against an academic career will take place earlier in life (DE0124RL). Generally, "faster careers are registered, the times for study, promotion and habilitation decreased. Often a call is issued at the age of 35–41" (DE0308TH).

However, this trend towards earlier tenure is also criticised: "Especially in the humanities or education, where personal maturity is very important, I do not want to imagine a 30-year old professor teaching 20-year old students" (DE0525CLN). Another German interviewee notices an increasing number of young professors and claims that "the duties are often over their head, because of a lack at maturity, experience and practice. They purport to be someone who they couldn't be, because of their age. Overambitious and inexperienced people will acquire junior professorships" (DE0601KP).

There is also a recurring notion among interviewees that tenure-track positions do not favor the life-planning of women (AT22, AT51, AT11HE). "In critical phases women decide against their career, for example by refusing to go abroad for private reasons" (AT50).

While qualification requirements during the trial period on the tenure-track are generally considered high, regarding the tasks and the institutional role of tenure-track staff, several Swiss interviewees mention that staff on the tenure-track is often spared time-consuming teaching and administrative duties as they have to focus on research and publications in order to fulfill their qualification requirements (CH35, CH36). In contrast to this view, an Austrian junior claims that the involvement in institutional self-governance as well as the higher teaching load for tenure-track staff than for assistants or other postdoc researchers represents a disadvantage for staff on the tenure-track (AT15).

2.3.4   Mobility and the Requirement of International Experience

Internationalisation in higher education addresses a wide range of research topics in literature (Kehm and Teichler 2007). Considered from the historical point of view, an increasing importance of scholars' mobility and a "re-internationalisation" of the higher education sector are noticed (Teichler 2004). This also includes the increasing mobility of non-professorial academic staff. Musselin (2004) states that in the relevant literature, generally, every kind of mobility is presented as a positive career step and as "associated with all kinds of benefits". She sees these arguments as largely "diffused and taken for granted in many higher education and research public policies. Specific measures and devices are developed by many countries in order to promote academic mobility" (Musselin 2004, p. 56). Especially in the postdoc phase, international (or at least institutional) mobility is expected by higher education management and the established scientific community. Interviewees' responses confirm a shift from only punctual international contacts (e.g., attending conferences) to a vital requirement for longer-term stays abroad. In Switzerland in particular, long-term mobility seems to be an obligatory phase during the postdoctoral stage and a condition for academic career progress. Experiences abroad are more and more expected (CH21). "In the last three to five years, there have been two changes: a lot of people willing to have an academic career [. . .] and a lot of mobility required. In order to do an academic career, you have to be very flexible" (CH22). As a common career path at high-ranked institutions, a Swiss interviewee describes the following steps:

> I did my diploma and my PhD at this institution. Then I went to the US to do a post-doc. After two years in the US, I came back and prepared my habilitation in this institution before going to another European country to become a full professor. Finally, four years later, I was asked to come back to Switzerland to become a full professor. (CH48)

Also in the Finnish higher education system, research mobility in the post-doctoral phase is highly common. A Finnish manager stresses the strategic point of view at his institution:

> Researchers in the post-doctoral phase should be encouraged to work abroad for some time. After completing a PhD the university is not responsible anymore for the PhDs. They should qualify themselves abroad, and if they are successful, they might be able to get a position at their home university or some other institution in Finland. (FILP9)

The post-doctoral phase in Austria is also increasingly defined by longer-term research experiences abroad (AT03). One of the interviewed professors stresses that, especially in the phase after the PhD, young academics are strongly advised to leave the university and to go abroad, since "there should not be continuous careers at one university only" (AT34). The later international mobility is planned, the more difficult it is to undertake it for personal reasons, as will become apparent below.

In Croatian interviews, international mobility is mentioned more often for the pre-doctoral phase than the phase after the doctorate (HR17, HR55). In some cases, it facilitates the entry to postgraduate doctoral study (HR6).

In the German and Polish interviews, research mobility was not systematically addressed but some of the interviewees brought up the topic themselves. There are no statements on international mobility in the Irish or Romanian interviews.

In accordance with Musselin, we note that in most cases post-doctoral mobility is part of a personal strategy to advance an academic career in the home country. "Most 'mobile' academics generally favour careers in their native country and use mobility as a 'plus'" (Musselin 2004, p. 66). Not least, the lack of post-doctoral positions and the strong competition for tenured positions force young academics to flesh out their profile by international experience. To better understand what research mobility is about, both positive and negative arguments will be discussed, even while the predominant tenor stresses the importance and the advantages of international mobility.

The benefits interviewees frequently ascribe to international mobility are the following:

(A) Networking and accumulating social capital: Unquestionably, the benefit that was mentioned most often for the individual academic and his or her institution was participation in international scientific networks (FILP15, FILP16). During an international fellowship, the reputation of the host university is not of

negligible importance: "That provides respect and also helps to build social capital and networks all around the world" (PL25; similarly HR6). In this context, Swiss universities seem to be highly attractive as host institutions with regard to both scientific reputation and working conditions.

(B) *Independence and self-assertion*: To assert oneself in a foreign academic environment is seen as an opportunity to increase young academics' self-confidence, to be one's "own master". The time abroad is considered "the most important for my academic career progression" (AT07). Dauntlessness and her "strongly international orientation" contributed to her success, claims a young Austrian professor (AT34). Independence of the supervising professor can be a decisive step into scientific self-fulfilment, particularly in a disharmonic senior-junior-relationship. "The early opportunity through scholarships to go abroad has become important, so you don't need to be a slave and do henchman jobs for your professor while you are writing for your habilitation", mentions a German junior academic (0607RSK).

In Musselin's words, "post-docs mostly see this international period as a risky but unavoidable phase to improve their situation in their home country" (Musselin 2004, p. 69). Nevertheless, some interviewees mention negative effects and experiences.

(A) *Missing estimation when coming home*: Negative experiences can be related to the process of transferring the knowledge academics gained abroad to the department upon their return. The interest from colleagues or professors in what the postdoc scholar has learnt can be weak (Melin 2005, p. 235). Similar experiences are framed in answers of several interviewees. "We have all gone abroad, the problem is that nobody is waiting for you when you come back. Seniors are under pressure and do not want competition from the lower levels" (CH28). Despite positive experiences during post-doc fellowships abroad, some interviewees were disappointed about the faint response at the home institution (HR41). "This was priceless research experience. [. . .] Unfortunately, it does not seem to be important for my formal career path development" (PL40).

(B) *Neglecting time and job opportunities in the home country*: The existence of strong time limitations of a maximum of 5 years to work for the habilitation is a problematic factor, mentions an interviewee in Germany. The required stay abroad during the post-doctoral phase implies an additional abbreviation of the period allowed (0113SH). A decreasing tendency in international mobility due to national competition for available positions has been observed by Finnish interviewees: "People stay more in Finland after PhD, [. . .] they keep active their contacts in Finland and are ready to apply for posts when they become available" (FILP7).

(C) *Work-life-balance*: One of the most discussed critical aspects of research mobility is its irreconcilability with family needs, especially for women. "Going abroad is becoming more and more important, and for women with a family, it is very difficult" (CH25, female). Particularly in Austrian interviews, that issue is often taken up. Academics' post-doctoral mobility – on average in their early or mid-30s – coincides with the phase of family formation (AT24HE, female). "Some women accomplish a career with children or in difficult family situations. However, women need more strength and endurance. Mobility requirements in the post-doc phase are harder to fulfil for women" (AT28MAN, male). But men also take up the topic as a crucial test of their academic career. "International experience and stays abroad are gaining in importance". This is difficult for one interviewee "as my life-partner would also have to be willing to go abroad [which is not the case]" (AT41, male). Expected mobility is compared to "the sword of Damocles. The decision to move to another city means to be torn out of your family and your social networks" (AT10, male). As a general problem, work-life-balance in the scientific community is summarized by a Romanian professor: "We have to identify ourselves more with our profession, thereby reducing the time devoted to extraprofessional activities" (RO42, female) – a requirement, which obviously is not backed by a number of interviewees.

2.4 Alternative Career Models: Externally Funded Positions and Cross-Employment

2.4.1 An Alternative Career-Track or a Dead-End Road: Externally Funded Project Work

External funding of research projects has been on the rise in recent years and it has taken on a significant role in the formation of academic careers. While – even fixed-term – university positions are rare and hard to come by, working on an externally funded position can be an alternative to a regular university post. While externally funded positions and working on research projects certainly present an opportunity for young pre-doc researchers to enter academe (one interviewee expressly mentioned that "the main purpose of external funding is to create positions for young academics", AT28MAN), externally funded academic positions become more problematic in the postdoctoral phase due to the fixed-term nature of project work. Is working on the basis of external funds an alternative to a regular university career or does it represent a dead-end road?

The issue of academic work on the basis of external funds was mostly discussed in the Austrian interviewees and this sub-section thus has a strong, but not exclusive focus on the situation in Austria.

First, externally funded positions seem easier to obtain than regular university positions but they are also less attractive (FILP15, AT48). This is due to the fixed-term nature and the high uncertainty and risk associated with external employment as mostly the job ends when the project ends: "The risk to lose your job at a department that relies heavily on external funds is as high as in a private enterprise if funds are running out. The risk is always higher than in a state-funded position"

(AT12MAN). Some academics remain on externally funded positions for quite a long time as they try to apply for university positions and "they are not happy. To have to finance yourself on the basis of external funds is not easy. The sword of Damocles of not knowing if you will be employed the next year is hanging over them" (AT22MAN).

Still, despite the less attractive working conditions externally funded positions seem to be on the rise, as several interviewees have noticed (among others DE0210BP, DE0127BK, AT17MAN, AT27HE, AT33). Interestingly, there is a recurring notion among interviewees that these less attractive positions are more likely to be held by women and that women are overrepresented in externally funded project positions (AT11HE, AT52).

As was mentioned above, many interviewees claim that today it is almost typical or common to start an academic career on an externally funded position in a research project (AT10, AT28MAN, AT12MAN, AT26MAN). Also many recount that their careers started through project work, that employment on a research project was their entry-ticket into academe; for example an Austrian junior in the Humanities claims that: "my professor set the course of my career with this project" (AT38, also DE0113DT).

However, the chances of switching from external positions to a regular university post are considered slim by one interviewee. She claims that it is "very difficult for externally funded project-staff to obtain a regular university or tenure track position" and that she does not know of one appointment out of a project funded position (AT46). However, a university manager states that at her institution "externally funded staff is also considered for the pool of qualification positions" (AT21MAN) and another believes that "third party funded project collaborators have the same chances as university assistants if they complete their doctorate" (AT56, also AT08). Another interviewee claims that "sometimes a university position opens up afterwards, but there are also people who work on externally funded positions for years and who are frustrated because they cannot get out", they get stuck in a "Project-hamster wheel" (AT35). Generally, career chances outside the tenure-track are considered slim and they are decreasing (AT41). "Knowledge workers in the precariate" have little chances for extended, stable employment. The majority of universities offers no career perspectives for externally funded project staff. "Most of the time project workers drop out of the system after their positions expire" (AT37).

The (current) lack of career models for these academics is deplored by several interviewees, some suggest creating a continuous career prospect for externally funded staff by creating permanent positions on the basis of external funds (AT08, AT12MAN). However, this structure implies the constant pressure of having to successfully acquire funding in order to keep staff which can also be detrimental to the quality of research as one academic argues:

> The strong focus on external funds and the required specialization is not always conducive to the quality of research. [. . .] In more strictly academic fields (basic research) academic staff should be employed by the university. (AT06)

It is also deplored that while working on a research-project it is harder to concentrate on publications and scientific performance. Working simultaneously on a project is time-consuming and leaves little room for publications or for finishing larger projects, such as the dissertation or habilitation (AT55, AT30, AT12MAN).

However, there are advantages to project work. One interviewee claims that in her current position as a university assistant she has less time for her own publications now than she did as a project worker due to her increasing involvement in the administrative affairs of the department, some also mention a certain independence as an advantage. On the other hand, this independence can translate to a feeling of isolation experienced by many project workers who are not integrated into the university structures and thus have to work alone (AT30). One interviewee feels he "lives in a vacuum", he is "on his own and gets no feedback from his professional environment" (AT02). Another interviewee – an external lecturer – deplores that "neither at my department nor on higher levels is there any interest in my career. There are no staff reviews or interviews with [. . . I] feel like a lone fighter" (AT10).

The relation or hierarchical differentiation between externally funded and regular university staff depends to a large degree on the role external funds play at the institution (AT26MAN). It seems that where a department relies heavily on external funds, hierarchies are flatter and differences less pronounced. Some claim that "there are no strong differences in roles between externally funded and university funded staff" (AT01) and many project workers who were interviewed talk about being well integrated into the departmental exchange and decision-making process (AT33). Still, one project worker mentioned that despite his being integrated into the department he still feels "like someone who is exploited" (AT10). Another project worker even claimed that "there is a two class society between externally funded staff and staff funded through the university budget" (AT55). And a university professor who works in a department with a heavy focus on externally funded staff admits while there is generally a good integration of externally funded staff, "in times of crisis the difference between university and externally funded staff becomes noticeable" (AT16MAN).

Regarding the differences of tasks between externally funded and core staff one Austrian interviewee claims that "the difference between externally funded project staff and university positions is the obligation to teach" (AT23). However, in a German interview it was repeatedly mentioned that third-party funded staff is increasingly involved in teaching and is thus taking on the core tasks of university staff as well (DE0127BK).

2.4.2   Cross-Employment

As was outlined in the previous chapters, obtaining an academic position is not easy. Even if one manages to gain employment at a university, these employment contracts are often part-time. In order to make ends meet, many academics thus have to take on additional employment. This phenomenon, which is increasingly observed, is also being conceptualised as "cross-employment" (or multi-employment) in higher education (see Campbell 2011; see furthermore Campbell and Carayannis 2013, p. 68). Having two or more jobs in different environments can also be beneficial both for the individual as well as for the involved organisations. Seen this way, "cross-employment" refers to an academic scholar or researcher who is employed (at the same time) by more than one organisation either only within higher education or across higher and non-higher education. Cross-employment offers simultaneously hybrid (parallel) academic and non-academic career opportunities to individuals (in a trans-sectoral and trans-disciplinary format). It facilitates 'parallel careers' for individuals (knowledge workers) across a diversity of organizations and sectors, "thus also a simultaneous operating in parallel in organizations with different rationales and innovation cultures" (Carayannis and Campbell 2012: 24; see in addition Campbell and Carayannis 2012). In the interviews conducted, questions about cross-employment were raised particularly in the countries of Austria and Finland. In the following, these answers are being reviewed and summarized.

In Austria, there is a certain disagreement how common or uncommon cross-employment actually is. External lecturers (socially more junior) are being regarded as one typical category of academic staff to which cross-employment applies. Complementary competences (sometimes practical competences) of external lecturers may add to their teaching qualities. Cross-employment also appears to be more common in certain disciplines, such as the medical and technical field, as well as the arts (AT59). On the other hand, there is also a need to develop cross-employment more in specific directions, for example the private industry: this still "has to be developed" (AT21MAN). Asserted advantages of cross-employment are: broader perspectives and an advancement of competences in relation to practical knowledge and practical experiences; a mutual reinforcement of complementary competences; potentials for a higher job security and a better (aggregate) salary; a dislike against only one employment form, when, for example, one interviewee underscored that she never wanted to "work only and fully for one institution" (AT60, social sciences).

Disadvantages of cross-employment mentioned by Austrian interviewees are: stressful adaptations to different environments (e.g., hierarchies outside of university can be more strict); tensions across different fields of engagement; risks of over-work; de facto a working time which is more than a mere summing-together of different part-time jobs; cross-employment may finally lead to a career-track outside of university – skepticisms raised underscored that "there is no part-time academic career" (AT44) or "this is practically impossible because research is a full-time job" (AT59).

In Finland, the assessment of the extent of cross-employment also differed. The degree of cross-employment varies across disciplines. It was mentioned that university and non-university work would have to be balanced with each other, and non-university activities should have some expression of connectedness to university activity: "Non-academic cross-employment is good for social interaction and perhaps also funding. But sometimes people do it too much, for instance some researchers who have a degree in medicine, who are full time researchers, but still work a lot as medical practitioners" (FIJW80). The rise in numbers of academic researchers implies that there is more competition for the available professorships, so cross-employment may increasingly highlight *professional non-professorial* career tracks within higher education that are more likely to be achieved.

The following advantages are being mentioned and emphasized for cross-employment in Finland: according to the opinion of some of the interviewees, cross-employment has not been regarded as being problematic so far; cooperation between universities and firms (enterprises) is being reinforced, also the successful creation of new spin-offs; the encouragement and promotion of dissemination of knowledge from higher education institutions to institutions outside of higher education; cross-employment can be the source for new ideas; through cross-employment, the academic staff creates and accesses experiences outside of universities (higher education), leading to a more realistic perception and conceptualization of trends in the "real working life" (FILP27); cross-employment can benefit the working life outside of universities; the bonus of aggregation of different incomes and sources of income; cross-employment may foster cross-institutional responsibilities within research networks; cross-employment supports the networking, network-building and formation of more cooperation between university and non-university organizations; cross-employment assists higher education institutions in their social interaction with their (social) environments and adds to the so-called "third mission" activities of universities; there are now more opportunities for researchers outside of universities to cooperate with universities.

Disadvantages of cross-employment mentioned in the Finnish interviews are: work pressures (for example, pressures to raise external funds) often do not realistically allow for cross-employment, leading, in fact, in some areas even to a decline of cross-employment; cross-employment may contribute to a further distribution of short-term contracts; reporting demands for project-based research or for the application of research money have increased, allowing for less alternative activities; a distraction from core university work, with the potential of an outward mobility of academic staff, pushing them out-of-university; university-external cross-employment may face serious constraints in some fields.

In summary, there appears to be a certain impression that a majority of the interviewees in Finland viewed cross-employment positively, whereas the responses of the Austrian interviewees were more mixed and more balanced in this regard.

2.5   Juniors and Seniors – A Hierarchical Relationship?

This section goes into particulars about the relationship between senior and junior academics and its effect on the career promotion of the latter. Firstly, some examples of the status quo in several countries are given, followed by a list of structural factors which seem to lead to a more egalitarian staff relationship. Furthermore, the role of mentorship and a structurally determined rivalry between status groups are discussed.

2.5.1   The Status Quo – A Mix of Strong and Flat Hierarchies

The tenor of interviewees' statements favours a formalised, more egalitarian senior-junior relationship over a traditionally hierarchical one. The latter is often characterized by long-term dependence of junior staff on professors. An Austrian interviewee frames the optimal senior-junior relationship as follows: "Instead of separated academic estates, there should be a faculty, and the differences and hierarchies should be evened out. Within faculty, there should be differentiation according to function, not according to traditional status criteria" (AT25). However, the translation into practice seems to lag behind. Obviously, in several countries both the traditional and a flatter hierarchical model coexist with different variations between them. In Poland, for example, where recent university reforms have still not been effective, interviewees criticise a plenitude of power and non-transparency of decisions by an "academic oligarchy" which "is not interested in changing the existing system because it benefits them and only them" (PL17). The system is described as "feudal, hierarchical and old-fashioned" (PL12). More egalitarian relationships are identified in institutions founded after the change of the political system in the late 1980s (PL30), at institutes "established in a democratic country in the spirit of freedom", where "no sharp distinction between senior and junior academics" is observed (PL18). Despite a generally critical attitude toward the system, a number of young Polish academics describe their own relationship to the professor as appropriate.

In other countries, experiences also differ. A Finnish professor identifies long-established flat hierarchies in her field, contrary to other fields with traditionally "very hierarchical structures" (FILP17, Humanities). Likewise, in some cases in Austria, personal structures are perceived as "very authoritarian", correlating with a strong dependency on professors' goodwill (AT48, Humanities). More egalitarian relationships are found, for example, at smaller institutes where "teamwork prevails" (AT57, Engineering), or at younger institutes, where the "progressive, dynamic and social attitude of the centre's head" has an impact on the relationship between team members. "Hierarchies are not set in stone" at such institutes (AT45, Physical sciences). In general, the relationship between senior and junior academics is seen as hanging on the respective department, possibly the discipline, and principally the personality of the professor – "determined by human factors", as outlined by a respondent. He can "name professors who, without any shame and hesitation, take advantage of their doctoral students [and] use them as servants in professional and private life because doctoral students have no alternative". On the other hand he knows "professors who developed a solid partnership with their junior colleagues" (PL14).

2.5.2 Structural Changes – Towards a More Egalitarian Relationship

On the basis of interviewees' considerations, structural factors which impact flatter hierarchies can be summarised.

(A) Change of generations: In consequence of changing personal structures, a new generation of professors gets promoted which takes up a more egalitarian attitude (CH1HE). The younger professors are not yet established and are therefore interested in collaboration (CH51). A Polish manager describes a new generation of professors who are "more relaxed, flexible and less hierarchically oriented" (PL1). Just having become a professor, one interviewee claims not to see "any difference between junior and senior status". (PL9, Life sciences)

(B) New career structures: Foreseeable career paths with predefined procedures and qualifying steps enhance independence of the non-professorial staff. New career models include comparative evaluations and reviews take place in a relatively earlier career phase. This allows more autonomy at a younger academic age. In the words of an interviewee, these developments are "in contrast to the chair model in Germany, and also to the Austrian tradition where someone is selected in a mysterious fashion to carry a professor's briefcase and write papers for him for ten years, then, magically, he is endowed with the aura of an ordinary academic" (AT44). In Germany, the new junior professors are more autonomous; however, they also get less support from (full) professors. "It's really nobody's business anymore. They are responsible for themselves" (0308HH). But also in increasingly meritocratic systems, dependence endures to a certain extent. Juniors' career steps require seniors' consent. In Austria, an interviewee explains that at his university "seniors in their role as mentors" write progress reports on assistant professors, "who, if they fulfil their qualification agreements, in turn receive permanent positions" (AT44). From Ireland, a "performance management and development system" is reported:

"Each increment you get, your boss has to sign off and say that you are performing satisfactorily". However, the interviewee adds that in practice the system is weakened and progression "is still automatic." (IE49)

Across all countries, the main problem seems to be the severe shortage of available tenure track positions. At Austrian universities, for example, the number of tenure track positions available depends on the commitment and the negotiation skills of the head of department in bargaining with university management. Thus, a large number of departments still do not have tenure tracks positions.

(C) Independence through international experience: During the post-doctoral phase at the latest, international experience is increasingly expected. This development is seen as another factor leading to more independence of junior academics:

> The early opportunity through scholarships to go abroad has become important, so you don't 'need to be a slave and do henchman jobs for your professor, while you are writing for your habilitation.' (0607RSK)

(D) Competition for external funding: At institutions that rely on acquisition of external funding, the traditionally hierarchical one-way dependence of junior academics yields in some way to a mutual dependence with a structured split of working tasks between seniors and juniors. Competition for national and European project funding is rising and interviewed professors report being expected from their professional environment to acquire external funding. "Academic careers have changed. Professors have to apply for funding for PhD students". (FILP4) On the other hand, it is junior staff's assignment to carry out the project work. The division of responsibilities between senior and junior academics was taken up by several interviewees: "Juniors carry out projects, while the responsibility of seniors is project acquisition" (AT60). "Project acquisition depends on seniors, they have the lead. Juniors contribute by writing, but project initiation and finalisation lies with seniors. This works well and juniors can learn a lot" (AT56). A Swiss interviewee responds in the same tenor:

> The professor manages the group, i.e. gets the funding, hires the PhDs and the post-docs, submit the papers to the journals, etc., and the PhDs and post-docs do the experiments. (CH29)

From professors' point of view, the co-operation is described similarly:

> Juniors must try to get to know relevant people and they have to learn to work scientifically. This knowledge should be passed on to them by seniors. Seniors, on the other hand, need juniors to work on scientific projects, in order to establish their research fields. (AT47)

Most of the interviewees stressed the mutual benefit from this form of cooperation and a positive effect on the senior-junior relationship.

2.5.3   Mentoring – A Steady Fundamental Element

Regardless of a more rigid or flatter hierarchy, mentoring maintains a central importance in the relationship between senior and junior academics. From the perspective of senior academics, "the most important element in an academic career is to come across the right mentor and work hard in research. This pattern has not changed very much." (PL1MAN). In the personal careers of many professors of both the elder and the younger generation, mentoring played "a very important role". Based on their own experiences, "support and promotion of junior faculty" are seen as the "most important" functions of senior academics (AT46). Support from professors' point of view consists in encouraging juniors' research and application for funding (IE34, IE22). Moreover, the status of a mentor as a role model for juniors learning how to teach was stressed (IE4). In Croatia, mentorship has recently taken on greater significance. "Every year reports on the progress of junior researchers are provided [by their mentors]; that constitutes a better system" (HR37).

From junior academics' perspective, mentors are important "to gain access to the academic system. Young academics have to create networks they can rely on during the transitional period after the PhD. Good professors pave the way for publications" (AT51). A good relationship with the supervisor is characterised as "not very hierarchical", providing good opportunities "to exchange" (CH23), to write articles together with the professor (CH41), to participate in the professor's national and international contacts (AT25) and to get relevant information concerning available university positions (PL19) and career advancement (HR45). Moreover, the involvement in – European – projects is specified (CH50).

Needless to say, so far not all interviewed academics in junior positions can share these experiences. They do not receive sufficient supervision in their doctorate (AT48). The relationship with the supervisor can be difficult when professors have a lot of projects, a lot of PhD students, and are "overloaded". The quality of the relationship suffers at times from a stagnant information flow (AT23). An Irish junior academic voices similar criticism, perceiving a

> clear division between senior and junior staff. The senior staff can hold all the information and not disseminate it; therefore younger staff, even though they have the energy and they make so many efforts to be creative, mightn't always be in the 'know how' and miss opportunities. (IE37)

It should not go unmentioned that some interviewees see a connection between egalitarian or flatter hierarchical structures and a feeling of being left alone concerning their career promotion. An Austrian junior academic describes the senior-junior-relationship at her institute, where

> collegiality is promoted by institutional structures, and even pre-docs can submit project ideas and implement them. However, due to the egalitarian structure at the institute, there is almost no mentoring for younger academics. (AT35, Social sciences)

2.5.4   Rivalry Between Academic Status Groups

Interviewees' responses accentuate classical and new forms of inner-institutional rivalry and competition between academic status groups.

(A) Supremacy of the professoriate: "There is still a clear separation between the professoriate and all other staff. Professors refuse to be grouped together with older assistants" (AT49). Repeatedly, even a strong division between habilitated academics and full professors was mentioned. "A habilitation does not automatically provide senior status within the organization. In formal terms it does, but

one must become a full-professor and gain respect by other full-professors [...] to be regarded as senior academic"; since "informal hierarchy is much more important than formal degrees" (PL5). "As a *Privatdozent* you are nothing, as a professor you get everything and you can do everything", stresses also a Swiss respondent (CH28).

(B) Lack of solidarity and "atomisation" among academic staff below the professoriate: The strong hierarchical structure at the top level is perpetuated at the non-professorial levels. "Some seniors prevent juniors from getting ahead. Senior researchers (non-professorial staff with habilitation that do not yet hold a professorship) are still working on their careers; they compete with juniors. Permanent positions relax the relationship between seniors and juniors." Only seniors in secure positions can "act as mentors" as they "do not have to concentrate on their own careers" (AT15). Due to budgetary constraints and increasing competition, individualisation and a lack of solidarity are observed. "Everyone is focused on her/his own individual career and does not care about the others. ... Instead of developing research projects some academic focus on blocking the development of others" (PL41, also AT49).

(C) Generational rivalry is dramatised by some interviewees as a "generation clash" based on a lack of available tenure track or senior positions and rising performance pressure on junior academics:

Currently two generations are 'clashing': seniors in permanent positions and juniors 'that perform incredibly well'. The old generation is slowly stepping down, the young generation is very performance oriented. (AT52, also CH30)

A higher performance level of the younger generation can upset the elders:

Lecturers nowadays tend to have more qualifications; you need a PhD or at least nearly completing one. From personal experience I see a barrier between senior lecturers who have a trade's background, and who feel threatened by the junior staff, who have qualifications, are research active and are publishing. (IE50HEP)

Summary
The road to tenure or permanent employment at a university is rocky. Young academics are faced with increasingly competitive environments as many aspiring academics compete for few available posts. In general, the PhD is the first requirement to enter an academic career. Structured doctoral programmes have recently been established in several countries. They are intended to provide a more stable working situation while completing the dissertation. However, the access to these programmes is highly selective. Many PhD-candidates who are employed as pre-doctoral assistants mention a high teaching workload which delays the completion of their thesis. Also, they are faced with the dilemma that teaching does not count equally in academic performance. Publications and conference participation as well as

(continued)

international experience are valued more. Nevertheless, interviewees are under the impression that the number of PhD-graduates has increased over the last years.

After completion of the PhD the most difficult and critical phase of an academic career begins: The postdoctoral phase emerges as a double bottle-neck in most of the EuroAC countries: at the stage of entering it after the PhD in trying to obtain a postdoctoral position and at the stage of leaving it by securing permanent, tenured employment. Interviewees clearly state that the number of available postdoctoral positions does not match the growing number of PhD-graduates. There is fierce competition for the few available posts. It is in the postdoctoral phase that precarious working conditions occur most frequently as postdoctoral positions are mostly offered on a fixed-term basis. Further, many interviewees are under the impression that there has been an increase of fixed-term employment contracts at universities in recent years. The high uncertainty and risk associated with an academic career is highlighted in the interviews. In countries with a chair-system, the only way to tenure was via a "call" or appointment to full professor, this usually took place between the age of 40 and 50. In these countries recent attempts to provide structure to the somewhat chaotic and long postdoctoral phase have been introduced, most notably in the form of a tenure-track. This model foresees a clearly outlined career path towards tenure based on the fulfillment of previously defined criteria. While the tenure-track is generally welcomed by the interviewed academics, they claim that only a very limited number of such positions currently exist. One of the most interesting and crucial aspects seems to be that the decision for or against an academic career is ideally taken earlier in the new model, around the age of 30 and shortly after the comple-tion of the PhD. On the one hand, the uncertainty and risky nature of the postdoctoral phase is thus mitigated as the long phases of precarious fixed-term employment are cut short, however, it could be argued that in this model the university closes its gates earlier as the decisive selection process takes place at a younger age: "All others are temporalized staff".

Regarding the role of university assistants, on the one hand, a trend towards earlier independence of assistants as opposed to a hierarchical sub-ordination to professors can be observed. On the other hand, old structures seem to endure in the division of labour at universities.

International mobility represents an increasingly expected qualification step during the post-doctoral phase. Especially Swiss interviewees, but also Finnish, Austrian and Croatian academics stress that longer-term stays abroad are vital requirements for career progress. Not least, the lack of post-doctoral positions and the strong competition for tenured positions force young aca-demics to enhance their profile by international experience. Often, post-doctoral mobility is only intended temporarily to advance an academic career

(continued)

in the home country. Networking and accumulating social capital are mentioned as the most beneficial effects, followed by academic independence and an increase of self-confidence, to be one's "own master". As adverse impacts of mobility-requirements interviewees mention a loss of time for completing a post-doctoral degree, the neglect of job opportunities in the home country, and, especially for women, difficulties in reconciling longer-term mobility and family.

Whether externally funded project work represents an alternative career model in academe remains doubtful as the precarity and inherent uncertainty of these positions are heightened due to the fixed-term nature of project funding. If at all, long-term careers on the basis of third-party funding seem possible only in those disciplines that rely heavily on external funds. However, for pre-doctoral researchers working on a research project seems to be an increasingly common entry point into an academic career.

Cross-employment – whether seen as an additional asset or a necessary compromise – is a reality emerging, and it seems important to closely look at the institutional and individual benefits of this phenomenon.

Taking account of the strongly hierarchical structures which generations of young academics traditionally have been subjected to, the relationship between senior and junior academics and its influence on the latters' career advancement was discussed as a last point. To sum up, the tenor of interviewees' statements favours a formalised, more egalitarian senior-junior relationship over a traditionally hierarchical one. Several structural changes prospectively favouring flatter hierarchies have been identified. A generation change of professors, new career models, international experience in an early career stage and cross-generational efforts for external project funding, little by little seem to even out older hierarchical structures. Increasing self-responsibility of young researchers is appreciated by many interviewees as long as mentoring still maintains its central importance in the relationship between senior and junior academics.

References

Ates, G., & Brechelmacher, A. (2013). Academic career paths. In U. Teichler & E. A. Höhle (Eds.), *The work situation of the academic profession in Europe. Findings of a survey in twelve countries* (The changing academy – The changing academic profession in international comparative perspective, Vol. 8, pp. 13–35). Dordrecht: Springer.
Campbell, D. F. J. (2011). *Wissenschaftliche "Parallelkarrieren" als Chance. Wenn Wissenschaft immer öfter zur Halbtagsbeschäftigung wird, könnte eine Lösung im "Cross-Employment" liegen.* Guest Commentary for DIE PRESSE. http://diepresse.com/home/bildung/meinung/635781/Wissenschaftliche-Parallelkarrieren-als-Chance?direct=635777&vlbacklink=/home/bildung/index.do&selChannel=500

Campbell, D. F. J., & Carayannis, E. G. (2012). Lineare und nicht-lineare Knowledge Production: Innovative Herausforderungen für das Hochschulsystem. *Zeitschrift für Hochschulentwicklung*, *7*(2), 64–72. http://zfhe.at/index.php/zfhe/article/view/448

Campbell, D. F. J., & Carayannis, E. G. (2013). *Epistemic governance in higher education. Quality enhancement of universities for development.* SpringerBriefs in Business. New York: Springer. http://www.springer.com/business+%26+management/organization/book/978-1-4614-4417-6

Carayannis, E. G., & Campbell, D. F. J. (2012). *Mode 3 knowledge production in quadruple helix innovation systems. 21st-century democracy, innovation, and entrepreneurship for development.* SpringerBriefs in Business. New York: Springer. http://www.springer.com/business+%26+management/book/978-1-4614-2061-3

Kehm, B. M., & Teichler, U. (2007). Research on internationalisation in higher education. *Journal of Studies in International Education, 11*(3/4), 260–273.

Melin, G. (2005). International experience. The dark side of mobility: Negative experiences of doing a postdoc period abroad. *Research Evaluation, 14*(3), 229–237.

Musselin, C. (2004). Towards a European academic labour market? Some lessons drawn from empirical studies on academic mobility. *Higher Education, 48*, 55–78.

Teichler, U. (2004). The changing debate on internationalisation of higher education. *Higher Education, 48*, 5–26.

Chapter 3
The Changing Paths in Academic Careers in European Universities: Minor Steps and Major Milestones

Marek Kwiek and Dominik Antonowicz

3.1 The Increasing Competition in the Academic Labor Market

The academic career in Europe used to be much more unstructured and much less competitive than today. Currently, as reflected in interviews carried out throughout Europe, "each step in a career is competitive" (CH_18-MAN), from doctoral and postdoctoral to junior academic and senior academic positions. There are significant variations across the European countries studied regarding the level of competition, often different in different places occupied in the academic hierarchy. But increasing competition has come to the academic profession and is bound to stay: the competition for part-time and full-time academic positions, for research grants and research funding, and tokens of academic prestige.

The academic progression today has to be made systematically, in increasingly clearly defined timeframes, and the academic career seems to be sliced into comparable time periods across European systems. Usually, the timeframes are doctoral studies, employment in postdoctoral and junior positions, employment in lower-level senior positions and, finally, in higher-level senior positions (such as traditional chair holding and/or full professorships), and all career steps have to be reached within a certain time period. The competition in academic settings means

We gratefully acknowledge the support of the National Research Council (NCN) through grant DEC-2011/02/A/HS6/00183.

M. Kwiek (✉)
Center for Public Policy Studies and UNESCO Chair in Institutional Research and Higher Education Policy, University of Poznan, ul. Szamarzewskiego 89, Poznan 60-569, Poland
e-mail: kwiekm@amu.edu.pl

D. Antonowicz
Insitute of Sociology, ul. Fosa Staromiejska 1A, 87-100 Toruń, Poland

© Springer International Publishing Switzerland 2015

T. Fumasoli et al. (eds.), *Academic Work and Careers in Europe: Trends, Challenges, Perspectives*, The Changing Academy – The Changing Academic Profession in International Comparative Perspective 12, DOI 10.1007/978-3-319-10720-2_3

41

most often measurable research outputs expected from academics for particular time periods or for particular stages of the academic career. Expectations from academics in the same stages of their careers are becoming largely similar throughout Europe. There seem to emerge an interesting combination of career progression requirements linked to age and/or specific time frames in academic careers. Increasing competition in all stages of careers is reported, and the competition is related to both employment (securing a post in the system; or retaining a post in the system; or progression up the academic ladder in the system) and securing research funding. The link between research funding and employment is viewed as strong as never before. In many cases, external funding generation actually means employment, especially for younger academics. A growing number of positions in universities are fixed-term, externally funded and project-based, especially at doctoral and postdoctoral levels. Under conditions of financial stringency felt in many European systems, the "market for academics" (Musselin 2010), the "academic labour market" (Williams et al. 1974), and especially the market for young doctoral graduates, becomes increasingly a "winner-take-all market", in particular in top research universities (Hacker and Pierson 2010; Frank and Cook 1995; Frank 1985; Brown et al. 2011). In such markets, often marginal differences in performance make the winners secure a position in the academic system, and make their marginally lower-performing competitors lose the battle for entering the higher education system. In previously, historically ever-expanding systems the competition to enter the higher education system was traditionally fierce but less of the "winner-take-all" character; with fewer new academic positions in academia today, and with systems often "frozen" due to the financial crisis, marginal differences in research performance of prospective entrants and new entrants to the system may count more than ever before, just as social networking abilities may count more. Where small differences matter, "luck", "chance", "accident" and "opportunity", historically important in academic careers, are becoming even more important.

The interviews with academics clearly show that the role of academic mentors (or academic patrons) has not been diminishing in the last few decades: the early-stage progression in the academic hierarchy is strongly linked to measurable research output and promising research achievements; but it is also linked to academic patronage: the academic progression "has to be based on scientific output, on scientific papers. But also academic networks among peers are important. A good environment for research is needed, however output is the most important criteria" (CH18_MAN). Academic mentors and academic mentorship play a powerful role in the early stages of the academic career, especially in the period of doctoral studies, the completion of which, currently, in most European systems, opens the possibility of entering the academic profession. A young academic must have a mentor "who would support him in networking and building social capital in/his research field. Good and supportive mentor is priceless" (PL27_AC).

3.2   Academic Mentors and Early Stages of the Academic Career

The first milestone in the academic career is a decision to stay in the university sector, following, in most European systems, doctoral studies. Many junior academics interviewed explained that their decision to enter doctoral studies was linked to meeting an intellectual leader. There are several channels to formalize research activities under the formal umbrella of higher education institutions which create opportunities to enter the academic profession. Among them, the most popular – since the introduction of the Bologna framework of higher education – is conducting research within doctoral study programs. The number of programs and the number of doctoral students have been on the rise in the last decade, though; in many European countries, enrollments in doctoral programs are currently reaching their historical records.

Not surprisingly, there is a feeling of increased competition among prospective academics. While the pool of doctoral students has been growing substantially, the number of academic posts available has not been keeping up with the pace of increase. Even though some programs are specifically designed to produce graduates for the business sector, in most cases in traditional universities doctoral students are inclined to consider the academic career as an important option. While the academic profession in most countries shows stagnating numbers, the pool of potential candidates seems ever-growing due to the expansion of doctoral studies. Consequently, in massified systems of doctoral education, only selected doctorate holders have a chance to ever enter the academic profession. The logic behind the expansion of doctoral education in both Europe and in the US is that "far more trained researchers than before will seek and will have to seek jobs outside academia and research institutions" (Kehm 2009, p. 155). Traditional forms of doctoral education and training do not seem to fit new government policy expectations across Europe. Consequently, based on a simple model of supply and demand, the competition for academic appointments has been growing as the number of posts available for doctoral holders outside of the university sector has also been falling behind the numbers of new doctorate holders. Part-time, project-based, externally funded and fixed term appointments seem to be entering the European academic labor market arena for young doctoral holders to a much higher degree than ever before (in a way similar to, although still at a much lower scale than in the United States, see Schuster and Finkelstein 2006; Schuster 2011, as well as Kezar and Sam 2010a, b on a related phenomenon that leads to new the stratification of the academic profession: "the new majority of non-tenure-track faculty in higher education").

In the competitive labor market for young potential entrants to the academy, the role of academic mentors, apart from the role of research achievements, emerges as an important issue. Regardless of the legal and institutional status of young researchers, they need an academic mentor who provides them with intellectual support during the entire research process leading to a PhD thesis. And they need mentors beyond doctoral studies, in a transition period potentially leading to university employment.

The interviews indicate that the cornerstone of the academic career is to be "discovered" by, and to be "invited" to work with, the right academic (institutionally, a professor and intellectually, a mentor; there is a "process of motivated search" between masters and apprentices, Zuckerman 1977/1996, p. 107). In other words, "meeting the right academic" does not have to be a random incident; for the most able doctoral students, it can be a mutual intellectual discovery based on social interactions in the academic setting, gradually leading to building partnerships in research between senior academics and most talented, ambitious and hard-working students or doctoral students with specific knowledge, skills and attitudes. A good fit in norms, values and attitudes (which can be referred to as a Mertonian "academic ethos") between mentors and their protégées is as important in view of young academics reflecting on their successful paths to the university as traditional academic achievements as viewed through the proxy of publications in competitive journals. As reported in Austria, "after graduation I was invited by my professor to work full-time on a research project as a doctoral candidate" (AT23_AC), or "for the first contract I was selected from among many, I was doing well, with high marks; it was also a consequence of my good relationships with professors" (CH11_AC).

Invitations to be employed are also important. As a Romanian junior academic reports, "the coordinating professor of my bachelor degree asked me whether I would like to follow an academic career, and thus I competed for the university tutor position" (RO55_AC). A Croatian junior academic points out that "during the hiring process, apart from the formal conditions (grade average) it was necessary for a teacher taking an assistant or a junior researcher to know the person he is hiring as his student because in this way the person had a bigger chance of being employed than someone who applied for the position from the 'outside'. For further advancement, [though], the most important criterion is a number of published works" (CR2_AC; the Croatian system is reported to be "very closed in that sense because it rarely (almost never) allows an individual outside the system to enter it", CR3_AC). Thus social networking abilities and long-term trustful relationships with academic mentors are very important to succeed in competitive academic markets for young doctoral holders (which is not largely different from the past, as reported by Logan Wilson with reference to best American universities in the post-war period (Wilson 1942/1995, 1979)).

In most general terms, little has changed since Wilson wrote in *his Academic Man*:

> entering university work as a life career is very much like entering matrimony: everybody agrees that it is an important event but so many intangibles are involved that nobody knows exactly how it happens. The candidate must choose and be chosen, and despite the indeterministic beliefs of a democratic society, chance and the pressure of circumstances are just as decisive as sentiment and rational choice. (Wilson 1942/1995, p. 15)

Many academics interviewed across Europe relate their academic careers to what they term "chance", "luck", "accident" or "opportunity" ("at the foundation of my academic career lie hard work and, last but not least, the opportunity", RO59_AC; or "but I also think luck plays an important role since there is a cap of how many academics can be promoted in a given year depending on the money available", IE55_AC).

The invitation to cooperate in research with the right academic and at the right time of the academic career opens a window of opportunity for young academics. Traditionally, promising students were approached by professors and invited to join their research groups. The criteria of choice, beside the academic merit, could be trivial but important from the point of view of interpersonal relations. As one of the interviewed academics stressed, the mentoring professor chose her "because they got along well on an emotional level" (AT55_AC). Nevertheless, the interviewed academics (mostly junior) underscored this particular moment of being an object of intellectual interest in their professional careers as a turning point that sparked their interest in research and made them seriously thinking about working in higher education in the future:

> A critical point of my academic career was a meeting with the right professor, my mentor who directs me in the right way and also who has helped me to articulate my research plans and ambitions. (PL2_AC)

Professors seem to have the power that enables them to inspire, engage and guide juniors through early stages of their academic careers. They can also, especially initially, attune their minds towards some problems rather than other problems in research, as well as determine their general ways of thinking within disciplines they represent. According to interviewees, the influence of those mentoring professors cannot be overestimated. Their intellectual imprints are left through mostly informal, indirect, sometimes even intuitively given remarks, advices or guidelines. The mentoring professor often serves as a role model for young academics.[1] These invisible but strong influences have been largely confirmed by junior academics who often declare that their personal successes in research would not be possible without the priceless and often immeasurable, both direct and indirect, contribution of their mentors. As reported, in an academic career, "the most important is the mentor who is taking care of everything. He or she is supervising and mentoring a career of a young academic, paving the way to grants, publications and fellowships" (PL1_MAN).

Meeting a good academic mentor is thus a milestone in an academic career. Academic mentorship is a difficult task to perform and requires specific personal

---

[1] As Harriet Zuckerman reported about the American ultra-elite of Nobel laureates, "as role models for the younger scientists, the masters sometimes led them to levels of accomplishment they could not ordinarily imagine for themselves. ... In part, the elite masters evoked superior performance by conveying through their own behavior a sense of how much could be achieved in scientific inquiry and what it was like to do scientific work of importance" (Zuckerman 1977/1996, p. 125).

and professional skills, mutual understanding and strong willingness to cooperate on both sides of the relationship. Undoubtedly, it is a priceless experience for doctoral candidates who require intellectual inspiration and later on seek, often tacitly, various types of direct or indirect support and intervention in finding good, preferably full-time, employment in the university or public research sectors. There is another side of the coin, too: mentorship can support nepotism and lead to the cloning in the academia (see Blackburn et al. 1981). There are many complaints expressed by interviewees about unfair procedures of carrying students further along the academic route by their powerful mentoring professors. With regard to early stages of the academic career, interviewees underscored that finding a good academic mentor was a turning point in their professional academic careers (it might imply a dead end if the cooperation fails at some point). Apart from serving young academics with their academic expertise, research experience and academic networks, mentoring professors are often able to secure external funding for them. In some countries, there is high dependency of junior academics on senior academics based on project funding provided by the latter. On top of that, mentors can provide access to their scientific networks and young academics can rely on them while creating their own networks. It will benefit them in the future, although networking of young academics is reported to be difficult without the support of a well established scholar. Doctoral students know they need to belong to larger research groups to be successful: as a Romanian young academic emphasizes, "I need to belong to a consolidated research team because I am aware that this is the only way to achieve performance in research. [. . .] To be a member of a sound research team favors publication and has a positive effect on the academic prestige of scientists and on their capacity to train new researchers" (RO19_AC). Not surprisingly thus, "an academic career is based on professionalism, individual study, research, motivation and membership in a research team showing the highest possible academic prestige" (RO20_AC).

Finally, expectations from mentors are reported to increase upon the completion of the doctoral dissertation. The advent of a transitional period following the doctoral period verifies an institutional and academic position of mentors and their intentions regarding the professional future of their apprentices, or the employment of junior scholars. The reason is that, by and large, juniors expect some assistance in getting through the transitional period and in securing employment in the academic sector. As a Swiss junior academic pointed out, she became an assistant "because of good relationship with a professor who offered me to do a master (50 %) and work at university at 50 %. I got a lot of support from this professor, with whom I also did my bachelor thesis as well as my specialization year (i.e. third year BA)" (CH_7-AC). In an academic progression path, the initial period of doctoral studies leads to a transition period which for those who wish to stay in academia means seeking part-time or full-time, university-paid or project-based employment in any part of the national (or international) system. The international mobility of doctoral students and doctoral holders in Europe has been substantially growing; one of the mechanisms used are Marie Curie Actions supported by the European Commission. The vast majority of young doctorate holders seek employment in national systems, though.

3.3   Entering the Academic Profession, Among Growing Insecurity and Increasing Instability

Following meeting the right mentor, the second milestone in the academic career comes when a decision to stay in academia after defending a doctoral dissertation is taken. According to interviewees, young academics are hold in abeyance, and have to be highly competitive in their research achievements to be able to enter the academic profession. A mass model of doctoral training leads to a substantial increase in the number of doctoral degree holders, most of whom have no option but to search for employment outside higher education. Doctoral training systems are expanding faster than higher education systems and employment opportunities they provide, though. On top of that, even more than before, in massified systems the traditional rules about selectivity in academia still hold: and traditionally, "scientific ability is very unevenly distributed" and "research is not an egalitarian profession. It is a rigorous pursuit, where incompetent performance, as signaled by persistently low achievement, eventually clogs up the system" (Ziman 1994, pp. 258–259). Traditionally, most new PhD holders in Europe are inclined to work in the academic sector. Consequently, as often reported, "I definitely think that there is very big competition among the doctoral candidates" (German, junior, female). Under these circumstances, the transformation from the status of a doctoral student to any form of research-based or teaching-based employment is a critical moment in the career development. The number of new positions in all European systems studied is much smaller than the number of doctoral graduates wishing to stay in academia. Therefore a feeling of insecurity and instability is prevalent among doctoral students, as reported by young academics throughout Europe: "universities in Finland educate such a high number of PhDs at the moment. This of course leads to insecurity especially for those who want to stay in academia." (FI72_AC). Uncertainty is also reported among young academics working on part-time contracts (IE1_AC).

Despite worsening employment conditions (see Altbach 2000, 2002), the academic profession still remains an attractive option (Enders and de Weert 2009; Enders and Musselin 2008; Musselin 2007). Despite increasing and differentiated job expectations, often increasing teaching loads, especially for recent entrants to academia, relatively decreasing salaries (compared with other professionals), changing employment relations towards less secure, less stable and more often of a fixed-term nature, despite uncertainty as to future developments of the university sector in Europe, higher education still attracts very talented people (see Kwiek 2009 on the "changing attractiveness" of European higher education sector). Higher education in Europe today is still attractive as a workplace even though it is a long way from what

Wilson described in the mid-40s as "reasonably secure tenure, public esteem . . . pleasant work and surroundings, sufficient leisure for the pursuit of personal interests, and so on", (Wilson 1942/1995, p. 21). As the result of the survey conducted in the CAP project shows, working in higher education can still offer an interesting perspective for professional path development, and job satisfaction levels in European universities are relatively high, and consistently so almost throughout the continent (Kwiek and Antonowicz 2013). As stressed before, there is an oversupply of good candidates to enter the academic profession and an undersupply of academic positions in stagnating systems. Consequently, there are increasing controversies about academic recruitment processes, for instance, as reported in Austria, "there is a 'mentality of local emperors' at this university, as heads of departments and professors have the power to decide on tenure-track positions relatively autonomously. The advertisement for an open position is an official act, but the texts are mostly tailored to certain candidates" (AT44_AC). Or as reported in Germany, "there were several candidates for this position, but through consultation with the professor it was clear that when I am applying for this job, I will get this place" (D208_AC). Some changes increasing the transparency of hiring processes for young academics are reported but they are slow; in general, both the research promise, research track record and the notion of "choosing and being chosen" matter.

In more general terms, higher education cannot be regarded as a growth industry as automatically as three or four decades ago. What was taken for granted while seeking academic employment in the long post-war period of expansion of higher education does not have to be the case anymore. As John Ziman argued, ever since science became a regular profession in the late nineteenth century, it was "a buoyant open-ended enterprise, where talented newcomers were welcome, and where they could look forward to opportunities for personal advancement right through their working lives" (Ziman 1994, p. 167). The ever-expanding higher education and research systems used to be a "growth industry" for three centuries now – but this feature does not have to be a defining one for the future. Some countries, such as Poland and several other Central European economies, face significant contraction in student numbers, leading inevitably to the contraction of university-based academic profession (Kwiek 2013a; Antonowicz 2012a). The rules of the game of entering the academic profession and of the progression in the academic career may be expected to be fundamentally different in the times of stagnation (or even contraction) from those holding in so far ever-expanding European systems.

Academic careers are linked to public universities, that is, by extension, to sustained public funding. And rationales for public funding in higher education have been evolving in the last two to three decades, as the postwar "social contract" between governments and universities, most clearly expressed in Vannevar Bush's report on Science: *The Endless Frontier* (Bush 1945; Kwiek 2013a), has been under revisions. As summarized by Martin and Etzkowitz (2000, p. 7),

> under the revised social contract there is a clear expectation that, in return for public funds, scientists and universities must address the needs of 'users' in the economy and society. Furthermore, they are subject to much more explicit accountability for the money they

receive. In addition, implicit in the new contract is a much more complex model of innovation than the previous linear model, unfortunately making it much harder to persuade politicians of the merits of increasing public spending on research!

The rules of the game may be increasingly different for different research areas because, increasingly in the last few decades, "the only arguments that now seem to carry any weight for the expansion of science are those that emphasize its promise of future wealth or other tangible benefits" (Ziman 1994, p. 85). Knowledge economy makes some types of university-produced knowledge (for instance, what Williams terms "economically useful knowledge" or "economically valuable codified knowledge", Williams 2012, pp. 20, 34; see Brown et al. 2011) much more relevant than other types. Expansion in some areas of higher education, and some areas of university knowledge production, may be accompanied by contraction in other areas of both higher education and university knowledge production (see Kwiek 2013a; 2011). The geography of study areas and, consequently, also the geography of academic posts available, has been systematically evolving. In some countries, the evolution has been clearly guided by new national strategies for higher education and innovation, and by new "competitive" research funding regimes accompanied by new science policies (Geuna 1999).

Knowledge economy changes the shape of student choices in higher education, as wage premium for higher education is increasingly related to academic fields. The impact of the growing evidence that "not all graduates are being eagerly sought by employers to contribute to a knowledge economy" (Williams 2012, p. 33) on the future differentiation of the academic profession (by academic disciplines) is still unclear; the impact of national science policies on national research funding is already perceptible, though, and often viewed as a threat to the future research funding for, especially, social sciences, arts and humanities. And research funding is used both for research performed by those already working in academia and for fixed-term positions for new entrants.

In very broad terms, so far, the history of science was that of rapid, unimpeded growth:

> Ever since modern science 'took off' in the seventeenth century, it has been a growth industry. Knowledge and technical capabilities have not only accumulated steadily: the rate of accumulation has also accelerated over time. The scale of all scientific and technological activities has continually expanded. Every measure of these activities – numbers of people engaged, resources employed, output of published papers and patents, commercial and industrial impact, etc. – seems to have been increasing exponentially for the best part of three centuries. (Ziman 1994, p. 67)

But this history may have been exceptional. The growth of science is linked to the numerical expansion of universities, and the numerical expansion of academic posts available throughout European universities. Long-term and large-scale changes in rationales for public funding for research may have a delayed impact on the academic career opportunities. The latter are a significant part of the former.

As strongly as ever before, staying in higher education after completing their doctoral dissertations becomes an ultimate goal for those who think about being full-time academics. The tenure-track is a tempting career opportunity and the transitional period following the period of doctoral studies is decisive about whether the person will stay in academia, and in which part of it. Some interviewees tend to believe (and experience) that the real selection in the academia takes place shortly after completing doctoral dissertation. "It is most critical to quickly obtain a position immediately after the doctorate, even if it is not a permanent position. It makes it possible to establish networks in the framework of regular employment" (AT50_AC). For some academics, this is the most decisive moment in their careers, a sort of "do or die" period. Reaching this milestone requires making preparations in advance. Good scientific publications, in current competitive environment, may not be enough to enter the academic profession. Also other personal assets are very useful; they include well developed social skills and social networks built during doctoral studies. As a Swiss junior academic declared "you need to be 'promoted' individually, personally, your work has to be clearly visible" (CH17_AC). Today, most of early stage career opportunities in higher education require external project funding or other external financial contribution and therefore young academics believe in getting on well with professors who have access to financial research resources and the power to distribute them. In some countries, both social networking and, perhaps surprisingly, teaching and pedagogical abilities seem to count more than ever before: "People are appointed to professorships on a strange basis. Advancing in an academic career was previously based on the quality of your research and its relevance in an international context. But now we have started emphasizing pedagogical merit more and more. Also, your social competence and your social networks are becoming increasingly important. This is of course a diffuse criterion and very difficult to measure. I am little bit worried about this development" (FI77_AC). Social networking, especially international, is believed to matter substantially in successful fundraising for research. As a senior lecturer from Ireland points out, "there is a huge emphasis now on research and acquiring research funding. But academics in the current climate cannot get funding if they apply on their own or with a couple of colleagues from their department. Instead, you bring in people from all over you know Europe or the world, different disciplines, different countries and that's how you get funding these days" (IE7_AC).

The mobility between the higher education sector and the economic sector is often difficult, especially it is hard to start academic career later on in professional career, coming from the business sector. Entering the academic profession today most often means entering it right after the doctoral or postdoctoral period, without prior experience in the business sector. In some countries (e.g. in Poland or Romania), it is very rare to succeed in coming back to the academia after early departure to the business world. It stems from the fact that the professional career development path is based on cumulative promotion and cumulative research achievements and lagging behind in measurable research output can be difficult to overcome. In addition, academic achievements are an important criterion in competitive research bids and calls for research proposals and research fellowships. The probability of getting research funding in a competitive environment without accumulated prior research achievements is low. Some higher education systems are more open to intersectoral mobility; other systems (e.g. Polish or Romanian) are almost closed for the outsiders and the mobility into the higher education sector for latecomers or for practitioners from the business world is of marginal importance for the system as a whole (as it was in the 1990s and in the 2000s, see Kwiek 2003; 2012b).

In European universities with more hierarchical institutional settings, with very limited chances for career progression for junior researchers, or with a limited (and in some countries, decreasing) numbers of senior academic posts, the intersectoral mobility is almost always in one direction: from universities to enterprises. Although full-time returns from the business world to academia seem difficult, some part-time returns (e.g. sharing practical knowledge derived from company experience) still seem possible. In general, they are still reported as rare. Most European institutions do not consider work experience outside of academia as important in their staff recruitment procedures. To the question "to what extent does your institution emphasize the following practices" (Scale of answer 1 = Very much to 5 = Not at all) – "Recruiting faculty who have work experience outside of academia" – the answers 1 and 2 varied substantially across countries, from 7 % in Italy to 39 % in the Netherlands, with the lowest scores in Italy, Poland, and Norway, and the highest scores in Portugal, Germany and the Netherlands. The cross-country variations are given below in Fig. 3.1. What it means in practical terms is that institutional norms and values, and institutional practices associated with them, do not support the arrival of new faculty from the business sector; the signal sent to doctoral students and postdocs across Europe is to start an academic career as early as possible, without delays in other sectors. Work experience gained outside of academia is reported not to be highly valued by academic institutions. The universal, direct transition between the doctoral and postdoctoral periods and the employment in the higher education sector makes the competition for jobs more fierce than it would be with the intersectoral business sector/higher education sector mobility being more institutionally accepted.

The transformation from being a doctoral student or a postdoc to being an academic means passing through a rigorous selection process; a successful passage to academic employment is a turning point. Therefore entering the academic profession in any form becomes an ultimate goal and the following statement reflects the spirit of this transitional period: "it was more important to get a foot in the door of the university than anything else" (AT46_AC). And one should not be surprised that academics interviewed declared that "in my personal career, the phase of the dissertation was decisive, not so much the phase of habilitation" (AT25_AC).

3.4 Steps Towards Full-Time Employment

Thus the next critical turning point of the academic career is obtaining full-time secure employment in the higher education or research sector. There are significant differences across European countries studied because obtaining permanent full-

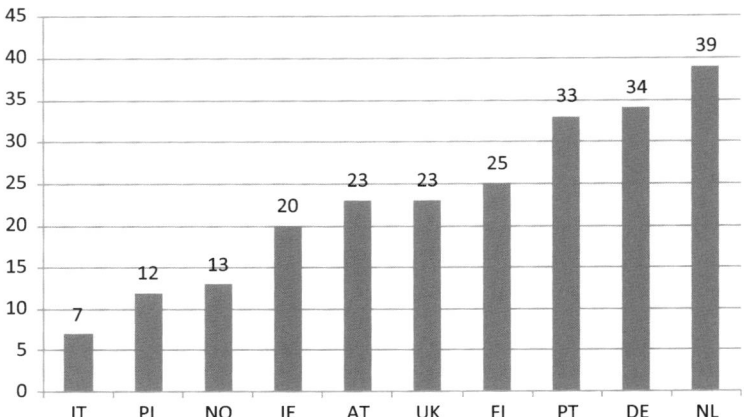

Fig. 3.1 Intersectoral mobility: faculty recruitment with prior non-academic experience (percent; responses 1 and 2 only). Question E6: To what extent does your institution emphasize the following practices? (Scale of answer 1 = Very much to 5 = Not at all): **"Recruiting faculty who have work experience outside of academia"**. Count: n(IT) = 1,622; n(PL) = 3,424; n(NO) = 871; n(IE) = 794; n(AT) = 1,113; n(UK) = 796; n(FI) = 1,173; n(PT) = 960; n(DE) = 1,001; n(NL) = 688

time positions in higher education requires meeting different formal criteria. In a few countries (e.g. Poland), the professional stability and secure employment come almost automatically with the habilitation degree. Stability and security have traditionally, throughout the whole post-war expansion period in European higher education, been crucial factors in attracting able individuals to the university; as Bowen and Schuster pointed out long ago, with reference to the US system, "the excellence of higher education is a function of the kind of people it is able to enlist and retain on its faculties" (Bowen and Schuster 1986, p. 3). Hence, in this respect, the habilitation becomes naturally a milestone in an academic career in those systems where it still exists both in theory and in practice. For instance, in Poland

the existing hierarchy resembles a feudal hierarchy and everyone knows his or her place in it. In public universities, this hierarchy is overemphasized and obtaining the habilitation degree implies obtaining a significantly different status at the university. (PL25_AC)

Or, as remarked by a Polish junior academic, "the so-called community of academics is in fact comprised of two completely different groups: senior and junior academics. The difference is not only in status in the organization, it is much more than this. Habilitation is a turning point in any academic professional career, it changes working habits, lifestyles, and sometimes also friends. There is a huge difference between senior and junior academics in Polish higher education" (PL8_AC; "feudalism in higher education is common form of relationship. And taking advantage of junior academics by senior academics is well rooted in some disciplines such as medicine" PL15_AC; see Kwiek 2014b). Nevertheless, European academics still live in what Wilson termed "an open-class society: entry into their occupation is more accessible than in most other professions, and advancement in it is closely coupled with individual capability and effort" (Wilson 1979, p. 206). Higher education working environment is tough and highly competitive – but it seems to be fair across European systems.

In Poland, representing systems with habilitation, there is a significant difference in status within the academic community between academics with the habilitation degree and those without it. In this hierarchical community, the habilitation is a dividing line between two clearly distinguished, and often not interacting, groups of academics. In interviews, academics (particularly juniors) often refer to this stratification as "a two class-society", "a caste system", a "pyramidal structure" or even more often as "a feudal society": "The relation can be very feudal – young academics are forced to write doctoral dissertation on the topic that one has neither knowledge nor interest in it. But this is the way it should be done and if one has no knowledge about a given topic, she needs to work harder to get one". (PL7_AC). Or as stressed in another interview, the relation between senior and junior academics is "underpinned by the old system [the communist system that existed in Poland 1945–1989]. Maybe there is no more 'cooking dinners and baking cakes' for professors but there are still elements of it from the past" (PL29_AC).

Regardless of which description we choose to apply to describe the relation within the academic community in Poland, they demonstrate the fundamental importance of the habilitation degree in the higher education sector in Poland. In a highly stratified community, obtaining the habilitation degree is a milestone in an academic career. It guarantees remarkable growth in both social and academic status and also (almost automatically) provides a permanent full-time university post. For many, it is the termination of a long period of professional uncertainty (traditionally in American universities, the period of uncertainty was short due to "up or out" policies: in case of instructors, the lowest rank in the academic hierarchy, "the tenure is brief or uncertain, the turnover highest, the remuneration lowest, the criteria for advancement vague or confused, the duties manifold, and the future full of doubts. . . . The mental anxiety may be prolonged by repeated short-term appointments, with the threat of eventual failure of renewal hanging over the instructor after 7 or 8 years of service", Wilson 1942/1995, p. 61). But there are also other countries (e.g. Finland, Austria, and Switzerland) in which the habilitation degree or different forms of academic seniority do not guarantee a higher academic status and secure employment. It does open more opportunities for applications for full-time permanent positions at higher education institutions but there is little doubt that there is still a long way to go to have secure employment in these countries. The Bologna structure of higher education has made doctoral schools much more accessible for young researchers. The advent of doctoral schools and a mass model of doctoral training largely dismissed the idea of apprenticeship in the academia and the selection to become faculty members have been moved up to post-doc or junior professorial level. "Competitive evaluation and selection are structured processes from the (tenure track) professor assistant on: we check for quality according to publications, i.e. research, and teaching quality, too. We ask for four to six references" (CH19_MAN).

The significance of obtaining secure employment as a milestone in the academic career is hardly questioned in contemporary academic world. There is strong evidence that there is a huge gap between academics with fix-term contracts and those with permanent ones. "At the university, there is a two-class system of those who are on permanent positions and those who know they have to leave the university eventually" (AT39_HEP). The process of marketization of higher education (Jongbloed 2003) also involves transformations of academic employment relationships. As the modernization and expansion of European higher education proceeds,

> the working life of institutions has evolved from one rooted in maintaining the privileges of a self-governing academic elite to one centered on recruiting, rewarding and managing a diverse academic workforce in ways aimed at meeting the mutual needs of both employers and academic staff in the employment relationship. (Farnham 2009, p. 212)

The direction of transformations in the last two decades most often implies less stable, less secure and less attractive working conditions in higher education. "Academic career has previously been very clear but now it is very uncertain" (FI15_AC). Some academics are employed on externally funded positions for quite a long time, they try to apply for university positions: "they are not happy. To have to finance yourself on the basis of external funds, it is not easy. The sword of Damocles of not knowing if you will be employed the next year is hanging over them" (AT10_AC). An increasing number of employees work under fix-term contracts and they can easily be dismissed if needed without extensive social and financial costs. Egbert de Weert (2001, p. 78) calls this approach a "zero-appointments" policy that leads to "invisible faculties". Therefore a transition from fix-term employment to a full-time permanent position becomes a milestone in academic career and also an ultimate goal for many academics. "Even in Germany among people with habilitation, limited term jobs have increased" (D201_AC). Fixed-time contracts may also limit effectively the access to research funding: as reflected by an Irish junior academic, "The current academic contracts are of 5 year duration which impacts greatly on an early career academic's ability to apply for research funding because most research funding requires permanency or at least that the academic will remain in that post for the duration of the grant. Moreover, the employment of post-docs is also prevented under the moratorium, so the profession of academia is actually currently suspended. The newer members that are coming in are operating in a much different role (there is a sort of 2-tier system) and I can't call that a profession anymore" (IE39_AC).

In most countries academics express their complaints about recent staff policy changes in higher education which reduce access to permanent posts. As one of Austrian senior academics stated, the acquisition of well-funded research projects makes "future fantasies of a permanent position" emerge. A secure position in a higher education institution becomes a personal goal. It is generally expected that the availability of permanent posts in higher education institutions will decrease over time and will become a subject of increasing competition between academics. "There is a huge competition for available posts. More and more is needed in order to get a post" (FI25_AC). Moreover, financial austerity plans introduced in some European countries and major cuts in public spending in higher education may foster this competitiveness of the academic working environment and make secure full-time employment more difficult to achieve. Policy changes put many academics in a very difficult professional position because at least some of them – like a Finish senior full-time academic interviewed – "has a permanent position outside university, and he will keep it because university cannot offer him a permanent position. He has achieved what he wanted, although he would like to be a docent one day" (FI14_AC).

3.5 New Pressures in Changing Organizations and Reforming Systems

Academic careers are becoming more versatile and involve a wide range of different criteria to develop, although scientific recognition, especially through internationally visible publications, are still the core of the academic career that defines academic trajectories. Interviewees report a widespread trend that might imply a departure from a career model based on a limited number of milestones (often associated with various academic "rites of passage") toward a new pattern called by one of them "cumulative promotion": "criteria for academic careers in the 1970s and the 1980s were 'not to fall out of favor with the one or two professor (s) that supported you as a young researcher', today (over the last 5 years), measurable scientific qualifications and international experience are required" (AT33_AC).

Job instability grows, causing lots of controversy inside the academia. "Academic career is based on quality work and ambition but academic career is nowadays very unstable and unforeseen" (FI4_AC). There is widespread feeling of increasing pressure to produce highly-cited publications in peer reviewed journals and to gain international experience for the academic career to progress. It is also important to publish extensively in highly respected journals. However, it has also been a commonly shared feeling that to get good publications, academics need to have to be able to acquire external funding and to be building networks in the academic community. "There is external pressure to do research, to attract funding, to update the research profile and to do the student surveys for quality assurance purposes; however, the internal pressure of self-motivation is even greater. Main challenge is having many balls to juggle in terms of teaching, research, administration, working for external bodies and helping in moving the university forward" (IE53_AC). Interviews show some concern and disbelief in modern indicators of academic performance. "Meritocracy: always too little! Also in science. Publications seem to be more meritocratic, but it is a jungle there, too. How can you measure? Publications, impact factors... quality is only linked to peer review" (CH12_AC).

According to those who welcome a new system of internationally comparable, increasingly measurable research output used for both career progression and research funding opportunities, academics from the old system (for instance, as in this case, Austrian associate professors with permanent civil servant status) still "do not have to worry about anything" (AT01_AC). A new model based on increased professional insecurity is an attempt to make them more active in research, publications and also in acquiring funding from external sources. There is growing self-motivation is securing research funding: "the pressure to get external funding comes primarily from within although it also comes from the school, the pressure comes from the university but the support comes [also] from the university" (IE54_AC). "The university careers used to be more linear than nowadays. Nowadays, a broader positioning is required" (such as foreign languages, interdisciplinary orientation, and external funding) (D120_AC). Indeed, as Schuster and Finkelstein (2006, p. 188) report in an American context, "the expectations about one's career prospects that an entering academic could have reasonably entertained a generation ago differ strikingly from current realistic expectations. The passageways have become bumpier". But, at the same time, they do not come as a surprise – the evolution of expectations from European academics have been in progress from between one and three decades, with the longest experience of reforms perhaps in the case of the UK system. European academics are functioning in universities under permanent conditions of adaptations to changing environmental settings, in different countries to different degrees. The changing social, economic, cultural and legal settings of European higher education institutions increasingly compel them to function in the state of permanent adaptation; adaptations are required as responses to changes both in their funding and governance modes. The reforming of universities does not lead to reformed universities, as examples especially from major postcommunist higher education systems studied show (in particular, see Polish and Romanian interviews). In general terms, policymakers, following New Public Management lines, tend to view universities, like other public institutions, as "incomplete"; reforms are intended to make them "complete" institutions (Brunsson 2009). Reforming is thus leading to further waves of reforms (Maassen and Olsen 2007).[2] And academics constantly need to adapt to changing institutions which are in turn adapting to ever-changing environments (see Teichler 2007; Teichler and Yagci 2009; Kwiek and Kurkiewicz 2012; and Kwiek and Maassen 2012).

A new general context for universities is that the social trust in public institutions can no longer be (automatically) guaranteed, which is a substantial change of social mood prevailing in postwar Europe, with relatively lavish public funding

---

[2] As organizational research shows, there is no surprise that reforms based on "simple prescriptive models" seldom succeed in achieving their aims: "such reforms often increase rather than decrease the felt need, and probability of, new reforms. ... it is often observed that organizations work well precisely because naïve reforms have *not* been implemented" (Brunsson and Olsen 1998, p. 30).

guaranteed and high social prestige of public universities and of the academic profession taken for granted. Traditional academic values, closely associated with the public service responsibilities of universities and science, Scott argues, "have to come to terms with a new moral context in which the superiority of the public over the private can no longer be taken for granted" (Scott 2003, p. 299).[3] This new "moral context" has been widely supported by emergent EU social policies, especially social policies advocated in CEE countries, experimenting widely with various forms of privatization of social services (Kwiek 2012a, 2013). European institutions need to continue its reliance on traditional academic values (especially academic freedom and institutional autonomy) to be attractive. As Bleiklie, Høstaker and Vabø conclude,

> [s]ome sort of contribution to society has always been demanded from the universities in return for a certain degree of autonomy and public funding. What is arguably at stake today is that a less clearly delimited definition of the nature of the universities' contribution to society pose a potential threat to their autonomy. . . . One reason for the resilience of the university institution is that universities have at one and the same time been able to sustain sweeping change and protect their core functions. However, past resilience is no guarantee against future decay. (Bleiklie et al. 2000, p. 307)

The status quo – or the current social and economic *modi operandi* of universities in Western societies – is very fragile: the multi-faceted impacts, trends, and challenges are far-reaching, long-term and structural in nature (see especially Maassen and van Vught 1996; Altbach et al. 2009; Kogan and Teichler 2007; Kwiek 2013; Antonowicz 2012b). The durability and stability of institutions, even in periods of major reforms is, however, that "institutions are not simple reflections of current exogenous forces or micro-level behavior and motives. They embed historical experience into rules, routines, and forms that persist beyond the historical moment and condition" (March and Olsen 1989, pp. 167–168). The fragility of the status quo is widely reported in all European systems studied.

Organization studies show that no matter how strong external discourses surrounding the institution are (here: global, transnational and EU-level discourses), the potential for changes and a range of possible reforms is always relatively limited, and the period for institutional adaptation – relatively long. It is therefore difficult to assume that the intentional direction of changes in the academic sector as a whole will coincide with their actual direction of changes. Often in the history of the university (see Rüegg 2004), significant scope of changes remains determined on the one hand, by redefined tradition, and, on the other hand, by sheer contingency. "Great expectations", as shown a quarter of a century ago by Cerych and Sabatier (1986), often lead to "mixed performance". At the same time, policymakers tend to view institutions, higher education institutions included, as "incomplete". Reforms are renewed attempts to make universities "complete"

---

[3] As Kezar (2001, p. 9) rightly argues from the perspective of organizational studies, "what needs to be preserved may be just as important to understand as what needs to be changed" and "balance between calls for change and tradition may be desirable".

organizations. At the level of academics, directions of changes are often unclear, rationales behind them remain often undefined, and reforms (especially in the three postcommunist countries studied) are viewed as a step in a series of reforming steps only rather than as a point of arrival. In ongoing reform initiatives throughout Europe, there is a hidden dynamics of changes in relationships between the state, or the major sponsor of teaching and research, and academics, or the major beneficiary of state sponsorship of the academic enterprise. The academic profession has a fiduciary role to play: constitutive rules and practices are not easily changeable, they take time to root and take time to change. Especially senior academics often view themselves as depositories of traditional academics rules, norms, and values, while junior academics know the traditional rules from their older colleagues but have to play according to redefined rules if they want to follow their own career steps.

Academics report to be undergoing regular evaluations that cover various aspects of their work but focus mainly on three areas: research, teaching and administrative tasks (or service, or engagement with both the university and its environment). Evaluations are often continuous and built on transparent, quantitative, measurable and comparable criteria. "The evaluation process becomes an integral part of the academic professional development from the beginning (almost) right to the end and therefore the pressure of continued evaluations is increasing" (D901_AC). It implies that the evaluation is attached to both academic degrees structure and to institutional positions in universities. It carries very concrete advantages in the academic setting: the existence of a foreseeable career path with predefined procedures.

> Nowadays even a lot of publications in A-journals is not enough. You have also to be able to raise a lot of project funds. You also have to be able to popularize your scholarly work and have a lot of contacts with your students' future employers. Sometimes it feels like measuring these academic activities has become more important than activities themselves. For instance, citation indexes have become too important in my opinion and they are not comparable enough between different subjects. (FI62_AC)

Interviewees also express a strong criticism of what they refer to as the "American model" of professional career development in higher education. They criticize "the devastating model of professional development" that is built on fierce competition, uncertainty, instability and ongoing evaluation of individual research outcomes. Each discipline or a specific field of research can develop their own unique lists of milestones. In other words, in the linear model of academic professional development, milestones are not really centrally defined, instead there is a range of opportunities to be taken by individuals and translated into milestones in their careers.

The traditional milestones of the development of academic career may increasingly be accompanied by a large number of small steps that must be taken regularly and which are regularly assessed. The frequency and regularity of evaluations make the academic career a linear and, to large extent, a predictable process. Milestones of professional development are spread over the entire length of the academic career, so that the small individual steps do not hold a critical "do or die" component. Switzerland provides a good example of this direction of changes: "elsewhere careers are established with points, so that you can plan objectives for the following years, here you only have salary increments" (CH15_AC).

Perhaps the most important element of the academic career is the tenured position. It gradually becomes nothing more than the final stage in the academic professional development, available to some. Obtaining a tenure position (if one exists in the system) is a natural culmination of the research track record and sometimes also previous teaching achievements. Interviews show that there is a strong criticism among European academics of taking a too narrow "research only" perspective of the academic promotion, in particular for tenured positions. Finland, for instance, introduced a broader approach to criteria of recruitment of professors, taking into account also other aspect of academic work (e.g. teaching) but this direction also caused some criticism.

> I think the recruitment to professorships is way too arbitrary. I could tell many stories of really talented young scholars who were mistreated in Finland and will now work abroad for good. We cannot afford that in a country with only five million inhabitants. I think a new Finnish tenure track system is completely wrong. It is a slap in the face of all those doctorate holders that aren't professors and completed their degree more than five years ago. (FI58_AC)

The academic profession is becoming increasingly competitive not only for new entrants but for all academics, at all levels of seniority. The competition for funding and prestige gets tougher and fiercer. "Because of the shrinking funding base, the academic profession will become, at least in some disciplines, extremely competitive" (CH29_MAN). In some countries (e.g. Germany), even tenured positions do not take the pressures off academics' shoulders.

> The competition is becoming a normal dimension also for the youngest, it is a daily business: by means of transparent procedures, everybody is able to understand where she stands, why she was not appointed, etc. This has to be made explicit. Then there is competition for third means, like at the SNF and at foundations. (CH26_MAN)

Even in the countries with the chair system (such as e.g. Austria and Germany) in which professorships used to be traditionally well established positions at universities, there are radical changes ongoing. As a German professor stressed, "those who habilitate got under a strong pressure because they need to do their own external fundraising, and teach on their own, too" (D118_AC).

3.6 New Demands and Mission Overload

The competition to enter the academic profession and to stay in it, especially at lower levels of academic seniority, is accompanied by growing expectations in both research output, external research fundraising, teaching, and various service missions (surprisingly, in post-communist higher education systems of Poland, Croatia and Romania, various types of third mission activities are rarely mentioned and the major divide in academics' time allocation is between teaching and research, with a frequent conclusion that the two should ideally be "in balance" (RO37_AC)). Universities under conditions of massification across Europe are increasingly expected to be meeting not only changing needs of the state but also changing needs of students, employers, labor market and the industry, as well as regions in which they are located (Pinheiro et al. 2012; Benneworth and Jongbloed 2010; Kwiek 2012b for Poland). Demands put on academics are increasingly conflicting, universities are caught in what was termed "mission overload" (Jongbloed et al. 2008). Globally, for the vast majority of academics, the traditional combination of teaching, research, and service is beyond reach anyway: as a whole, globally, the academic profession is becoming a predominantly teaching profession; gravitating toward more emphasis on teaching is also the case, to varying degrees, in both Europe and in the US (Schuster 2011). In terms of criteria for promotion in European systems, research output is a critical factor. But there are systems (such as Ireland) in which all three university missions count, and where teaching and service may weight more than research (for youngest academics). As reported, "the criteria for promotion include research, teaching, and contribution (to the department, the faculty, the university and then to the wider community). For any promotion you are judged under those three headings. For a promotion from CL [career lecturer] to SL [senior lecturer] the weighting is 40 (Research), 30 (Teaching) and 30 (Contribution). For a promotion from SL to AP [assistant professor] there is more emphasis on research so the weighting is 60-20-20" (IE7_AC).

European universities have to be able to meet sometimes conflicting, differentiated needs (see Jongbloed et al. 2008 about "interconnections and interdependencies" of higher education communities and Kwiek 2009 on the "changing attractiveness" of the academic career). These needs sometimes seem to run counter the traditional twentieth-century social expectations from the academic profession in continental Europe, though. New expectations from universities impose on universities "unlooked for, and perhaps unrealizable, roles and responsibilities", as Shattock (2009, p. 1) notes:

> Universities – endowed as they are with a long history and as important as they have been in the production of scholarship and new ideas, and for the training of elites – have not until recently been seen as such positive vehicles for economic progress. Like many other institutions they are facing pressures for change and, unlike most other institutions that have historically depended on the state for resources, their history suggests that they operate most effectively if they have a high degree of academic and managerial autonomy.

European academics are working in changing institutions, characterized by both demand overload and mission overload. What is theorized at the level of national policies across Europe, academics actually experience on the ground – where teaching, research and service missions are fulfilled. They are most often unable to term the ongoing change processes but they can clearly refer to them as they are changing their working habits, lifestyles, and job satisfaction. What we can see today as universities' missions seems to have been highly influenced by the two decades of reformulations (both in theory and in practice) of the role of public sector services. In wider terms, the university, as other public sector institutions, is increasingly viewed in the context of economic competitiveness of nations, global pressures on national economies, and global pressures on national welfare states. For public universities, these are fundamentally new contexts; and they are new to academics as well (see especially Kwiek 2006; 2013a). Never before the functioning of the university has been so important both for the economy and for the huge (and historically unprecedented) numbers of graduates; it has never been absorbing so huge (public and private) financial resources. Also the social and economic expectations regarding universities (or their "relevance", see Geiger and Sá 2008; Skolnik 2005 and Välimaa 2008) have never been so high and so widely publicly formulated. As Bonaccorsi et al. point out (2010, pp. 1–2),

> it can be said that the social demand placed on universities has increased significantly. These are great expectations of their ability to produce more education, more research, and more direct interaction with society and the economy. . . . Policymakers are devoting more attention to the workings of universities and have introduced significant institutional changes in several countries.

Current economic expectations from universities compared with those from the 1960s cannot be met, and, from a historical perspective, as Skolnik (2005, p. 120) argues,

> not since the 1960s has there been such strong and unqualified belief on the part of governments and the public in the vital importance of higher education to national economic well-being. However, in contrast to the situation in the 1960s, today the capacity of the universities to respond to these economic challenges and at the same time maintain a healthy balance between the economic and non-economic aspects of their nature is greatly jeopardized.

There is an "enormous demand overload" in European universities (Clark 1998, pp. 129–132), combined with "mission overload" (Jongbloed et al. 2008). As Clark (1998, p. 129, emphasis in original) argues,

> National systems of higher education can neither count on returning to any earlier steady state nor of achieving a new state of equilibrium. As principal actors within these systems, public and private universities have entered an age of turmoil for which there is no end in sight. Disjuncture is rooted in a simple fact: *demands on universities outrun their capacities to respond*. From all sides inescapable broad streams of demands rain upon the higher education system and derivatively upon specific universities within it.

Demands on universities, in practical terms, refer also to the demands on academics, leading to more busy academic lives. Academics report to be increasingly busy, and their professional stress is reported to be high (Kwiek and Antonowicz 2013). They increasingly work under pressure but, at the same time, pressure seems to be manageable:

> Broadly speaking, I don't know if any academic is ever in control of everything. There are always many tasks to carry out such as setting and marking exam papers. An academic is in control broadly speaking but not on a day-to-day basis. [. . .] An academic firstly feels under pressure from themselves on the research side; to conduct research, get papers published, get grants, be seen to have an active research group. Then there is pressure from the

administrative side of the role. The pressure isn't present to the extent that I am crumbling under the pressure; I can manage it so far and it peaks and troughs. (IE51_AC)

The pressure is manageable because while the professional stability is lower than in previous decades, requirements for particular steps in career ladders are more transparent and measurable today. It is perhaps easier to be planning the career based on more quantifiable, more similar across academic disciplines and across national higher education systems, indicators of academic progress. Perhaps the new rules of the academic game are tougher than ever before but at least they are advertized somehow in advance.

There is a clear difference with the past, as reflected by an Irish academic, "in order to get a promotion there are very clear criteria with regards to an academic's teaching, research/publications and service to the community. [It] was more woolly in the past, how you interpreted those criteria, whereas right now I think the criteria are very much laid down and very clear" (IE48_AC). In some countries changes are slow but unavoidable: as a Polish junior scholar reports,

> the academic professional development path is very conservative. It lacks transparency and explicit criteria of academic promotion. Instead, there is a number of informal agreements between senior academics on what is required from junior academics to be awarded habilitation. This is understandable that not all criteria can be explicitly measured and benchmarked but the existing system does not build trust around the professional academic development path. (PL31_AC)

Or as another one reflects, "informal criteria established by cliques of professors keep the process of awarding academic degrees non-transparent" (PL32_AC). As of October 2013, though, based on a new law on higher education of March 2011, massive changes in both the procedures and the criteria for awarding both habilitation and professorship degrees will be introduced in Polish higher education. The direction of changes is towards meeting measureable, quantifiable criteria to avoid blocking academic careers through the above mentioned "informal agreements" on who deserves both degrees and on the basis of what past (predominantly) research achievements (on a recent wave of Polish reforms in the context of two decades of changes, see Kwiek 2014b; and on the role of internationalization in research in Poland, see Kwiek 2014a).

Only research has been traditionally related to prestige, and prestige-seeking is the core of the academic enterprise.[4] Reputation is "the main currency for the

---

[4] There are inherent tensions between individual academic prestige and institutional prestige, though. At the institutional, rather than individual academic level, as Brewer et al. (2002, p. 147) point out (while analyzing their typology of institutions: "prestigious", "prestige-seeking", and "reputation-based"), the apparent paradox is that "prestige seeking promotes excellence on the one hand but can lead to excessive expenditures and unresponsive schools that neglect the needs of some undergraduate students and other customers who don't contribute to institutional prestige. . . . the excellence toward which institutions are striving may have little to do with the satisfaction of basic customer demands. For schools trying to build prestige, there can be a negative impact on students either because this strategy induces resources to be diverted from their basic instructional function or because the costs lead to tuition increases that exceed inflation".

academic" (Becher and Kogan 1980, p. 103; "much, then, of the driving force behind what academics do is concerned with building up, or maintaining, a professional reputation". . . . "the pursuit of a good name in one's own particular trade") and it derives from research rather than from teaching (Clark 1983; Altbach 2007). In the developing countries, research and teaching have always been separated except for national flagship institutions. Further differentiated academic profession (s) can be expected to emerge in Europe, of which small segments than in the previous decades will be involved in (usually, in the higher education sector, state-funded) academic research. In the midst of transformations and adaptations, in order to flourish, which means to be both attractive and competitive, universities need to continue to be meeting (either traditional or redefined) needs of academics. Especially since the income gap between professionals employed in the private sector and academics employed in European universities has been growing: the best performing segments of the middle classes (Richard Florida's creative class or Richard B. Reich's symbolic analysts) have less and less in common with university professors, which today in many fields of science creates a huge problem of the generational replacement. The expected differentiation-related (or stratification-related) developments may fundamentally alter the academic profession in general, increase its heterogeneity, and have a strong impact on the traditional relationships between teaching and research at European universities. These processes across the Atlantic, in the Anglo-Saxon model, are already well advanced and widely studied in both research and policy literature.

Conclusions

Major milestones of the academic career in European universities, despite huge ongoing transformations and reform packages implemented throughout European higher education systems, remain the same. In general, they include the following: entering a doctoral program and completing it with a PhD thesis defense; finding a full-time or part-time job in academia; changing academic status from a junior to a senior one; and, finally, remaining in the system in a senior academic position. These traditional milestones are increasingly accompanied by continuous, small-scale steps, almost continuously assessed by both peer and administrative bodies. The academic labor market is becoming highly competitive, at all levels, rather than as traditionally, in lower academic ranks only. While successive milestones need to be reached, they result more often than ever before from a steady accumulation of research (and also teaching and service) achievements. The academic career ladder seems ever stronger linked to fundraising abilities and research funds made available; consequently, the role of academic mentors or patrons, willing and able to provide research funding to their protégés during the doctoral and postdoctoral career periods, seems crucial.

(continued)

Research is becoming both more interdisciplinary and more collective: junior academics are increasingly either employed or doing research in collaborative research projects headed by their academic masters. On the one hand, the academic career is much less stable and secure; life-time (or even long-term) academic employment can no longer be taken for granted, especially in the case of new entrants to the academic profession; on the other, though, it may be becoming more predictable through ever-stronger processes of assessment of quantifiable, comparable (both across disciplines and across higher education systems) and internationally measurable research outputs. Through an increasing number of small assessment steps taken in between the major milestones in academic careers, the academic progression is somehow less secure but more predictable. In competitive, less stable academic environments, both small steps and requirements for moving up the academic ladder may be becoming more uniform. The interviewees across European systems stress internationally visible research achievements and fundraising abilities as perhaps most important components for a successful academic life.

Viewed from a longer historical perspective, academics need to be more aware of processes exogenous to higher education but closely linked to its future, such as changing rationales for public research funding, a revision of a social contract between universities and governments closely linked to the postwar expansion of science in Europe, changing science policies guiding national research priorities, changing perceptions of the utility of research in knowledge economy, and diversified premium for higher education in contemporary economy across different study fields (as developed in Kwiek 2013a, a book providing a panorama of "knowledge production in European universiites"). Above factors have powerful impact on the current, and especially future, academic labor market, and particularly on its expansion in some areas and contraction in other areas. More volatile, rapidly changing economies certainly mean a less stable and more competitive academic world.[5]

---

[5] The qualitative material for this chapter comes from eight European countries studied in the project "Academic Profession in Europe: Responses to Societal Challenges" (2009–2012, funded by the European Science Foundation and coordinated by Ulrich Teichler and Barbara M. Kehm): Austria, Croatia, Finland, Germany, Ireland, Poland, Romania, and Switzerland. The material consists of around 60 semi-structured interviews conducted per country. More than 500 interviews have been conducted in total by national teams and they have been transcribed or summarized in detailed interview reports (for instance, the transcription of Polish interviews conducted by Dominik Antonowicz is about 800 pages).

References

Altbach, P. G. (2000). *The changing academic workplace: Comparative perspectives*. Chestnut Hill: CIHE Boston College.

Altbach, P. G. (Ed.). (2002). *The decline of the Guru: The academic profession in developing and middle-income countries*. Chestnut Hill: CIHE Boston College.

Altbach, P. G. (2007). *Tradition and transition: The international imperative in higher education*. Chestnut Hill: CIHE.

Altbach, P. G., Reisberg, L., & Rumbley, L. E. (2009). *Trends in global higher education: Tracking an academic revolution. A report prepared for the UNESCO 2009 World Conference on Higher Education*. Paris: UNESCO.

Antonowicz, D. (2012a). External influences and local responses. Changes in Polish higher education 1990–2005. In M. Kwiek & P. Maassen (Eds.), *National higher education reforms in a European context: Comparative reflections on Poland and Norway* (pp. 87–110). Frankfurt/New York: Peter Lang.

Antonowicz, D. (2012b). Europe 2050. New Europeans and higher education. In M. Kwiek & A. Kurkiewicz (Eds.), *The modernisation of European universities. Cross-national academic perspectives* (pp. 113–126). Frankfurt/New York: Peter Lang.

Becher, T., & Kogan, M. (1980). *Process and structure in higher education*. London: Heinemann.

Benneworth, P., & Jongbloed, B. W. (2010). Who matters to universities? A stakeholder perspective on humanities, arts and social sciences valorization. *Higher Education, 59*, 567–588.

Blackburn, R., Chapman, D., & Cameron, S. (1981). Cloning in academe: Mentorship and academic careers. *Research in Higher Education, 15*(4), 315–327.

Bleiklie, I., Høstaker, R., & Vabø, A. (2000). *Policy and practice in higher education: Reforming Norwegian universities*. London: Jessica Kingsley Publishers.

Bonaccorsi, A., Daraio, C., & Geuna, A. (2010). Universities in the new knowledge landscape: Tensions, challenges, change – An introduction. *Minerva, 48*, 1–4.

Bowen, H. R., & Schuster, J. H. (1986). *American professors. A national resource imperiled*. New York/Oxford: Oxford University Press.

Brewer, D. J., Gates, S. M., & Goldman, C. A. (2002). *In pursuit of prestige: Strategy and competition in U.S. higher education*. New Brunswick: Transaction Publishers.

Brown, P., Lauder, H., & Ashton, D. (2011). *The global auction. The broken promises of education, jobs, and incomes*. Oxford: Oxford University Press.

Brunsson, N. (2009). *Reform as routine: Organizational change and stability in the modern world*. New York: Oxford University Press.

Brunsson, N., & Olsen, J. P. (1998). Organizational theory: Thirty years of dismantling, and then. . .? In N. Brunsson & J. P. Olsen (Eds.), *Organizing organizations*. Copenhagen: Fagbokforlaget.

Bush, V. (1945). *Science: The endless frontier. A report to the president on a program for postwar scientific research. Reprinted July 1960*. Washington, DC: National Science Foundation.

Cerych, L., & Sabatier, P. (1986). *Great expectations and mixed performance: The implementation of higher education reforms in Europe*. Trentham: European Institute of Education and Social Policy.

Clark, B. R. (1983). *The higher education system. Academic organization in cross-national perspective*. Berkeley: University of California Press.

Clark, B. R. (1998). *Creating entrepreneurial universities. Organizational pathways of transformation*. New York: Pergamon Press.

de Weert, E. (2001). Pressures and prospects facing the academic faculty in the Netherlands. *Higher Education, 41*, 77–101.

Enders, J., & de Weert, E. (2009). Towards a T-shaped profession: Academic work and career in the knowledge society. In J. Enders & E. de Weert (Eds.), *The changing face of academic life. Analytical and comparative perspectives* (pp. 251–272). New York: Palgrave.

Enders, J., & Musselin, C. (2008). Back to the future? The academic professions in the 21st century. In OECD (Ed.), *Higher education to 2030. Volume 1: Demography* (pp. 125–150). Paris: OECD.

Farnham, D. (2009). Employment relations in Europe: A comparative and critical review. In J. Enders & E. de Weert (Eds.), *The changing face of academic life. Analytical and comparative perspectives* (pp. 195–217). New York: Palgrave.

Frank, R. H. (1985). *Choosing the right pond. Human behaviour and the quest for status.* New York: Oxford University Press.

Frank, R. H., & Cook, P. J. (1995). *The winner-take-all society. Why the few at the top get so much more than the rest of us.* New York: Virgin Books.

Geiger, R. L., & Sá, C. M. (2008). *Tapping the riches of science. Universities and the promise of economic growth.* Cambridge, MA: Harvard University Press.

Geuna, A. (1999). *The economics of knowledge production. Funding and the structure of university research.* Cheltenham: Edward Elgar.

Hacker, J. S., & Pierson, P. (2010). *Winner-take-all politics. How Washington made the rich richer – And turned its back on the middle class.* New York: Simon and Schuster.

Jongbloed, B. (2003). Marketisation in higher education, Clark's triangle and the essential ingredients. *Higher Education Quarterly, 57*(2), 110–135.

Jongbloed, B., Enders, J., & Salerno, C. (2008). Higher education and its communities: Interconnections, interdependencies and a research agenda. *Higher Education, 56,* 303–324.

Kehm, B. M. (2009). Doctoral education: Pressures for change and modernisation. In J. Enders & E. de Weert (Eds.), *The changing face of academic life. Analytical and comparative perspectives* (pp. 155–170). New York: Palgrave.

Kezar, A. J. (2001). Understanding and facilitating organizational change in the 21st century: Recent research and conceptualizations. *ASHE-ERIC Higher Education Report, 28*(4), 1–9.

Kezar, A., & Sam, C. (2010a). Understanding the new majority of non-tenure-track faculty in higher education. *ASHE Higher Education Report, 36*(4), 1–133.

Kezar, A., & Sam, C. (2010b). Non-tenure-track faculty in higher education. *ASHE Higher Education Report, 36*(5), 1–91.

Kogan, M., & Teichler, U. (2007). Key challenges to the academic profession and its interface with management: Some introductory thoughts. In M. Kogan & U. Teichler (Eds.), *Key challenges to the academic profession* (pp. 9–18). Paris/Kassel: INCHER.

Kwiek, M. (2003). Academe in transition: Transformations in the Polish academic profession. *Higher Education, 45*(4), 455–476.

Kwiek, M. (2006). *The university and the state. A study into global transformations.* Frankfurt a/Main/New York: Peter Lang.

Kwiek, M. (2009). The changing attractiveness of European higher education. In B. M. Kehm, J. Huisman, & B. Stensaker (Eds.), *The European higher education area: Perspectives on a moving target* (pp. 107–124). Rotterdam/Boston/Taipei: Sense Publishers.

Kwiek, M. (2011). Universities and knowledge production in central Europe. In P. Temple (Ed.), *Universities in the knowledge economy. Higher education organisation and global change* (pp. 176–192). New York: Routledge.

Kwiek, M. (2012a). Changing higher education policies: From the deinstitutionalization to the reinstitutionalization of the research mission in Polish universities. *Science and Public Policy, 39*(5), 641–654.

Kwiek, M. (2012b). Universities, regional development and economic competitiveness: The Polish case. In R. Pinheiro, P. Benneworth, & G. A. Jones (Eds.), *Universities and regional development. A critical assessment of tensions and contradictions* (pp. 69–85). New York: Routledge.

Kwiek, M. (2013a). *Knowledge production in European universities. States, markets, and academic entrepreneurialism.* Frankfurt/New York: Peter Lang.

Kwiek, M. (2013b). From system expansion to system contraction: Access to higher education in Poland. *Comparative Education Review, 56*(3), 553–576.

Kwiek, M. (2014a). The internationalization of the Polish academic profession. A European comparative approach. *Zeitschrift für Pädagogik, 60*(5), 681–695.

Kwiek, M. (2014b). Structural changes in the Polish higher education system (1990–2010): A synthetic view. *European Journal of Higher Education, 4*(3), 266–280.

Kwiek, M., & Antonowicz, D. (2013). Academic work, working conditions and job satisfaction. In U. Teichler & E. A. Höhle (Eds.), *The work situation, the views and the activities of the academic profession: Findings of a questionnaire survey in twelve European countries* (pp. 37–54). Dordrecht: Springer.

Kwiek, M., & Kurkiewicz, A. (2012). *The modernisation of European universities. Cross-national academic perspectives*. Frankfurt/New York: Peter Lang.

Kwiek, M., & Maassen, P. (2012). *National higher education reforms in a European context: Comparative reflections on Poland and Norway*. Frankfurt/New York: Peter Lang.

Maassen, P., & Olsen, J. P. (2007). *University dynamics and European integration*. Dordrecht: Springer.

Maassen, P., & Van Vught, F. A. (1996). *Inside academia. New challenges for the academic profession*. Enschede: CHEPS.

March, J. G., & Olsen, J. P. (1989). *Rediscovering institutions. The organizational basis of politics*. New York: The Free Press.

Martin, B., & Etzkowitz, H. (2000). *The origin and evolution of the university system* (SPRU electronic working paper series, 59).

Musselin, C. (2007). Transformation of academic work: Facts and analysis. In M. Kogan & U. Teichler (Eds.), *Key challenges to the academic profession* (pp. 175–190). Paris/Kassel: INCHER.

Musselin, C. (2010). *The market for academics*. New York: Routledge.

Pinheiro, R., Benneworth, P., & Jones, G. A. (2012). *Universities and regional development: A critical assessment of tensions and contradictions*. London: Routledge.

Rüegg, W. (2004). *A history of the University in Europe. Vol. III. Universities in the nineteenth and early twentieth centuries (1800–1945)*. Cambridge: Cambridge University Press.

Schuster, J. H. (2011). The professoriate's perilous path. In J. C. Hermanowicz (Ed.), *The American academic profession. Transformations in contemporary higher education* (pp. 21–43). Baltimore: The Johns Hopkins University Press.

Schuster, J. H., & Finkelstein, M. J. (2006). *The American faculty. The restructuring of academic work and careers*. Baltimore: Johns Hopkins University Press.

Scott, P. (2003). Challenges to academic values and the organization of academic work in a time of globalization. *Higher Education in Europe, XXVIII*(3), 295–306.

Shattock, M. (2009). Entrepreneurialism and organizational change in higher education. In M. Shattock (Ed.), *Entrepreneurialism in universities and the knowledge economy: Diversification and organizational change in European higher education* (pp. 1–8). Berkshire: SRHE & Open University Press.

Skolnik, M. L. (2005). Reflections on the difficulty of balancing the university's economic and non-economic objectives in periods when its economic role is highly valued. In G. A. Jones, P. L. McCarney, & M. L. Skolnik (Eds.), *Creating knowledge, strengthening nations: The changing role of higher education* (pp. 106–126). Toronto: University of Toronto Press.

Teichler, U. (2007). The changing nature of higher education in Western Europe. In U. Teichler (Ed.), *Higher education systems. Conceptual frameworks, comparative perspectives, empirical findings* (pp. 55–68). Rotterdam: Sense.

Teichler, U., & Yagci, Y. (2009). Changing challenges of academic work: Concepts and observations. In V. L. Meek, U. Teichler, & M.-L. Kearney (Eds.), *Higher education, research and innovation: Changing dynamics* (pp. 83–146). Kassel: INCHER-Kassel.

Välimaa, J. (2008). Cultural studies in higher education research. In J. Välimaa & O.-H. Yljoki (Eds.), *Cultural perspectives on higher education* (pp. 9–25). Dordrecht: Springer.

Williams, G. (2012). Some wicked questions from the dismal science. In P. Temple (Ed.), *Universities in the knowledge economy: Higher education organisation and global change* (pp. 19–37). London/New York: Routledge.

Williams, G., Blackstone, T., & Metcalf, D. (1974). *The academic labour market. Economic and social aspects of a profession*. Amsterdam: Elsevier.

Wilson, L. (1942/1995). *The academic man. A study in the sociology of a profession*. New Brunswick: Transaction Publishers.

Wilson, L. (1979). *American academics. Then and now*. New York: Oxford University Press.

Ziman, J. (1994). *Prometheus bound. Science in a dynamic steady-state*. Cambridge: Cambridge University Press.

Zuckerman, H. (1977/1996). *Scientific elite. Nobel laureates in the United States*. New York: Transaction Publishers.

Chapter 4
Global Models, Disciplinary and Local Patterns in Academic Recruitment Processes

Tatiana Fumasoli and Gaële Goastellec

4.1 Introduction

Academic recruitment processes are a key dimension of academic labour markets. Not only they organise academic influxes – specifying the scientific and human composition of the academic workforce – they also testify of the configuration at play in each higher education sector (configuration they contribute to shape), and of the embedding of academic labour market in the general economy of the country.

Based on more than 500 interviews carried out in eight European countries and contextualised through national contexts' analysis, this chapter explores and analyses academic recruitment processes as a structuring dimension of both academic careers and organisations. Embedded in career structures, higher education institutions' organisation, and disciplinary identities, recruitment processes can be described as two-sided. On the one hand, a formal framework features the scientific qualifications required for each status, as well as the steps through which an application can be made, at the level of the institution and/or at national level. On the other hand, local practices are often specific, influenced by the disciplinary academic community, the available different types of resources and the position of the faculty in the national and international market, as well as the attractiveness of the private sector. In sum, the organisation of academic recruitment is to be understood with regard to the role of public authorities, of higher education

T. Fumasoli (✉)
ARENA Centre for European Studies, University of Oslo, Blindern, P.O Box 1143, Oslo 0318, Norway
e-mail: Tatiana.Fumasoli@arena.uio.no

G. Goastellec
Observatory Science, Politics and Society, University of Lausanne, Quartier UNIL-Mouline, Bâtiment Géopolis, Lausanne 1015, Switzerland
e-mail: Gaele.Goastellec@unil.ch

© Springer International Publishing Switzerland 2015
T. Fumasoli et al. (eds.), *Academic Work and Careers in Europe: Trends, Challenges, Perspectives*, The Changing Academy – The Changing Academic Profession in International Comparative Perspective 12, DOI 10.1007/978-3-319-10720-2_4

institutions, of disciplinary settings as well as of individual strategies in a broader labour market context. They are also characterised by economic relations between employees and employers. As a consequence, the higher education system can be analysed as a market (Crane 1970; Musselin 2001, 2005; Caplow and McGee 2001).

The design of the research distinguishes two sectors of the higher education systems: the university and the non-university sector. The degree of variety of recruitment processes of senior and junior academics is examined according to global trends, to national differences, to institutional settings and to disciplinary characteristics. Recruitment in academic markets has already been largely characterized (see for instance Musselin 2005). Drawing upon this portrayal, the interplay of variables affecting recruitment in a cross-national perspective is analysed.

How are recruitment processes formally organized and how are they implemented? Which actor configurations are they intertwined with? To which extent do they vary according to national settings, institutional types and disciplines? And, finally, which constraints and opportunities are available to individual academics in order to cope with recruitment processes? Particularly, the interaction of diverse models (disciplinary, institutional, national, global) is observed in order to understand how distinctive logics coexist, generating similar and different practices.

Issues have emerged in the interviews, revealing existing tensions at different levels. Eastern European countries display a break between the socialist period and the subsequent democratization. These countries encounter major financial problems reverberating in practices of recruiting and promoting academic staff. Another significant tension arises between national and international dimensions, whereby practices based locally are being, at least partially, replaced by globalized models of academic career. A shift from a chair model to a department organization (Neave and Rhoades 1987) is perceptible in recruitment practices. This has emerged clearly, although to different extents, in almost all countries observed. Internal or local careers are under strain, international staff brings new ways of understanding and practicing the academic work, while mobility becomes, almost everywhere, in academics' discourses, an important dimension of academic careers.

The reorganization of academic careers is visible through the multiple waves of reforms that have changed the regulatory frameworks (Croatia, Austria, Poland, Romania, Switzerland). Competition can be found at all stages of the academic path, not only for professorial positions but also for lecturers, researchers and postdoctoral fellows, even for doctoral students (Austria, Switzerland, Germany). The introduction, in parallel, of tenure track positions for assistant professors, with diverse intensity and scope, has put pressure on academic positions after the doctorate. Thus, postdoctoral positions are increasingly part of academic careers trajectories and more and more difficult to achieve (Finland, Austria, Germany), while international mobility is (also) often perceived as the only choice not to drop out from university. If a doctorate is not ensuring anymore an academic career, it is becoming a compulsory degree also in the non-university sector.

In order to analyse these issues, the chapter is structured as follows: in the second section recruitment is characterized through its formal frame, by a presentation of how positions are opened and funded and by the specific procedures. Then an analysis according to the status (senior, junior) in university sector and non-university sector is presented. This will take into consideration the distinctive characteristics of the various disciplines as well as the informal dimensions of recruitment. The third part relates to academics as individuals and investigates their constraints and opportunities in the different contexts of recruitment. The final section highlights the implications of the observed convergence dynamics.

4.2 Characterizing Recruitment in Academic Markets

Academic recruitment processes express both the national and disciplinary settings of academic careers and the social and power relationships at play in scientific and academic fields (Bourdieu 1976, 1984), or, to put it differently, higher education configurations.

As a specific dimension of the academic market, whose dynamics reflect the interactions among the actors involved, recruitment is a process through which the need for an academic position is expressed and constructed. Two main procedures can follow: a call can be structured and made public, or recruitment can be made "on direct call", whereby only one person is contacted, and the opening of a position is not made public or is only formally advertised. Subsequently, selection takes place, and, finally, negotiations between the institution and the candidate are conducted in order to conclude a contract (Musselin 2005).

4.2.1 The Formal Frame

Formal rules for appointment represent the tip of the iceberg. Still, they are embedded in authority relationships that can involve academic bodies, e.g. rectorate and board, and/or the state. Thus, all recruitment steps entail specific actors: academics, university management and public authorities. Academics can be observed from two different angles: as recipients of such processes, that is as professionals being hired, and as decision-makers at several stages of the hiring process. University management appears to be increasingly gaining power in personnel policies and is here taken into account as follows: rector and members of rectorate, that is vice rectors, but also, for instance, the gender delegate. Finally, the state is considered contextually: a number of recent reforms have delegated many functions to higher education institutions, however, legal frameworks still constrain much leeway, e.g. in terms of salary levels.

4.2.1.1   Changes in Legal Frameworks, in Selection Criteria, Work Activities and Career Steps Length

Legal frameworks rule a large interplay of dimensions that constrain academic recruitment: from the structure of doctoral studies, to the maximal length of temporary positions, to formal criteria to hire professors, they cover the spectrum of academic careers depending on the country and the degree of (de-)centralization, and the subsequent higher education institutions' autonomy.

In recent years, legal frameworks have changed in a number of countries (Austria, Romania, Poland, Croatia, Switzerland), weakening the public servant status. For example, in Austria, the University Act of 2002 modifies the academic status of the newcomers in the profession from civil servants to private employees (Friedrich 2013, p. 65).

Changes in legal frameworks are usually associated with alterations in the temporality and the career steps, but the pace of change has also accelerated and academics have to cope with varying requirements, so that uncertainty emerges as to the possibility to plan one's own career.

At a European level, the Bologna process has led to the restructuring of doctoral studies, as illustrated by the example of Croatia, where there used to be a postgraduate master degree for 4 years and then a doctoral stage. Now one starts immediately in a doctoral school and has a maximum of 4 years to finish his/her thesis. Enrolment in such a school is compulsory to do a doctorate. Grade average is important for potential PhD candidates as well as their integration in the department: being known by professors as undergraduate students is definitely an advantage. However, criteria for advancement change constantly, in particular criteria to become assistant professor.

> [My] mentor warned [me, that I] should keep track of advancement conditions for they change as constantly as state laws do. (HR45_AC/junior/male)

Beside changes specific to doctoral studies, the Croatian case illustrates the trend towards a shortening of the temporary positions in a career: temporary contracts are more and more limited in length. The same happens in Switzerland depending on the universities and the disciplines due to local frameworks: universities' governing bodies – i.e. rectorates and boards for management, senates and faculty councils for academics – tend to define increasingly the organisation of assistants' working time (for example, 40 % or 50 % for the doctoral work, the rest for teaching-related activities or professor's research assistance), the length of a doctorate (5–6 years as a maximum in some faculties) as well as the salary of research funded PhDs. The same applies to the fixed-term PhD holders positions.

In Austria, with the introduction of the University Law in 2002, a paradigm change has taken place and made it increasingly difficult to obtain permanent positions.

> You can have a six-year contract but afterwards you will have to leave the university. (AT12_MAN/senior/male)

This is in fact the so-called "chain contract regulation", which doesn't allow continuous fixed-term employment contracts for more than 6/8 years (AT19_MAN/senior/male). Although these contracts do not fall into the category of "tenure track" positions, they adopt the same rule: after a specific probation period, the person is either in or out of the academic career. The same rule can be found in Germany, where one cannot work temporarily for a university (in the public service) more than 12 years and, because there are not sufficient permanent positions, people have to leave university definitively (D4_ACA/junior/female, D50_ACA/junior/female).

These examples illustrate an international trend toward the formalisation of the different stages of an academic career. Intertwined with this process, evaluation procedures of the candidates are increasingly formalized. This process is reinforced by national science foundations, which have become significant actors in the academic market. Not only they fund more and more academics and research activities, they also develop formal criteria for scientific evaluations affecting universities' own processes. Furthermore, national foundations provide scholarships and grants that allow universities to overcome contingent or structural financial problems (Poland, Switzerland, Germany and Finland) and, at the same time, they influence the redefinition of the careers organisation.

The trend towards a shortening of temporary positions has ambivalent consequences: first, it potentially reduces the length of uncertainty, by offering juniors the possibility to apply for a tenured position at an earlier stage than previously. Second, it tends to support a formalisation of scientific evaluation criteria and to ask for standardized scientific guarantees others than those coming from the local space: local careers become less of a norm, while a "detour abroad" develops as a way to testify of scientific legitimacy.

4.2.1.2   Degrees and Career Steps

This common trend towards a redefinition and a formalisation of career steps is accompanied, on one side, by an increased importance given to the doctorate, on the other side, for the countries with the *Habilitation*, by a progressive decrease of the latter's weight.

The meaning of the doctorate is changing: it is becoming compulsory in every country and constitutes *de facto* the entry point to an academic career, even in the non-university sector. However having a PhD is a necessary but not sufficient condition for an academic career. The number of granted doctorates has grown in the countries observed, while the available academic positions – from postdoctoral fellowships to professorships – have not increased accordingly.

The *Habilitation*, required for access to professorship positions in countries of German tradition, is less and less required, not only in natural sciences, where in many cases it has not been mandatory for a while, but also in Humanities and Social and Behavioural sciences. In some Swiss and German universities a double career path is observable: the traditional one with doctorate, *Habilitation* and professorship and the new one with doctorate, assistant/junior professorship and full professorship. These new career paths are supported by national science foundations through the development of specific fellowships: "*Junior Professuren*" in Germany, "*Professeurs Boursiers*" in Switzerland, which somehow affect the traditional chair structure (Kaulisch and Böhmer 2010; Goastellec et al. 2007). However, there are some exceptions to these trends: in Poland the *Habilitation* is still compulsory by law in order to be granted a professorship. Furthermore, informal practices reveal that in German speaking countries the *Habilitation* continues to be a relevant title to legitimate one's academic career. Thus, even without the *Habilitation's* work, publishing a book – which is indeed the product of a *Habilitation* – is considered compulsory to get a position of associate or full professor. The scientific characteristics of the *Habilitation* (i.e. writing a book) are thus translated into a scientific requirement detached from certification. The social transactions behind the use or the demise of degrees such as the *Habilitation* in the career structure reflect disciplinary as well as generational issues, and, more widely, an understanding of what science and scientific practices are about.

In Finland the career steps are called a "four – stage model": assistant (doctoral student), researcher (possibly postdoc by means of external funding, working abroad or funded by the national academy), lecturer, and professor. With respect to universities of applied sciences, a double path is observable: as a teacher, from senior to principal lecturer (for this position a PhD is needed), then the highest title is head of educational matters. Otherwise a career can be based on research. The term "horizontal expertise" is used by a respondent to describe the different types of expertise one can acquire both in teaching and research, without a formalized (vertical) climbing up in the academic hierarchy (FI27_ACA/senior/male). A career in administrative positions (e.g. head of training division) is also possible and seems to represent the highest achievement in terms of non-academic internal career.

In Germany, the position of student assistant is described as a good entry point for the academic career, therefore this can start already during the master program. Then one becomes PhD student (assistant), a postdoc either in the same university or abroad, then assistant professor, associate professor and full professor. The *Habilitation* is not compulsory anymore but it can be still required (for instance in educational sciences D41_ACA/junior/female). A respondent academic reported that he could substitute the *Habilitation* title by practical experience and scientific publications (D48_ACA/senior/male). However, the classical model with doctorate, *Habilitation* and professorship persists, even though there is a perception of a change with the introduction of assistant professorships. While in universities of applied sciences industry experience is important and relevant in order to get professorial positions, the doctorate is indicated as a compulsory title to make a career in such institutions.

In Austria a career starts with a position as doctoral student ("predoc") and a part-time contract, then research collaborator and assistant, as well as postdoc with a full time contract, followed by professorship (assistant, contract, associate, full professorship). In the non-university sector career trajectories go from junior to senior researcher with project leadership, senior researcher responsible for research areas and strategic development and, finally, to department leadership. In some cases a lapse of time is defined to conclude one's own studies: 4 years for the doctorate, 6 years for the *Habilitation*. A doctorate within 4 years would allow for a position as tenure-track assistant professor. However, these positions are rare. In all other cases, one gets a "rotating position", which comprises maximum 4 years plus 4 years (AT11_HEP/female). Only then, by competitive call, one can obtain a permanent position either as senior scientist/lecturer or as full professor. According to our interviews, there is no clear career path outside the tenure track which allows for a fixed-term assistant professorship, then a tenured associate professorship and, in the end, a full professorship. Yet, this progression is still sporadic due to cost reasons. Hence, for instance, external lecturers find themselves in a vacuum, for they depend on their teaching contract to work in the university but they are not able to build a concrete path of advancement, as they do not have enough time for research activities.

In Irish universities of applied sciences, after the position of senior lecturer, the only possible promotion is becoming head of department, head of school, head of faculty, assistant registrar, and registrar. These positions are administrative and provide increasing managerial responsibilities (IE59_ACA/junior/female). The doctorate is becoming more and more important and many lecturers work to get this title in order to offer a more academic profile.

Poland presents one of the clearer career paths: research assistant, assistant professor, associate professor, full professor. This advancement is regulated by law and is framed by getting the necessary degrees in due time.

In Romania an academic career starts with a position of tutor (however this position will be abandoned soon), then of assistant, lecturer, assistant professor, associate professor, professor. Doctorate adviser is an additional title that is granted to full professors and allows them to supervise doctoral theses. According to some respondents, it is the legislation that establishes criteria to measure career progress (RO4_AC/senior/male, RO22_AC/junior/male).

In Switzerland an academic career can start by becoming student assistant, then assistant (which covers both PhD students and postdocs); the title of assistant professor depends on the higher education institution and on the discipline. In parallel or afterwards one can be associate professor and then full professor.

Finally, diversity between and sometimes within countries remains important when it comes to the polymorph structure of academic careers. The career steps, which entail also the different entry points for building an academic career, are more or less similar in the first stages: becoming a PhD student and working as a teaching, research and/or administrative assistant. After the doctorate, opportunities bifurcate into two main paths: first, as already mentioned, in countries of German tradition, work as assistant continues in order to complete the *Habilitation*, to become a *Privatdozent* and wait for a professorial position. Second, a series of postdoc positions follows, mainly in a different university and/or abroad and the passage to a professorial position is not clearly defined, as it can happen after a couple of years or several more. In this case, a position of tenured track assistant professor can exist as an in between. In all, both paths have the same effect: they provide the institution with a "screening period" allowing the evaluation of the academic *in situ* before hiring him or her definitively.

Countries also differ regarding the degree of co-existence of research-only positions and teaching and research ones. A general trend seems to be characterised by the development of research-only positions at the level of doctoral studies as well as of post-doctoral studies. This phenomenon may be interpreted as a consequence of an increased number of PhD students but it also illustrates the development of external academic labour markets where internal markets used to be the rule. The development of these research positions in the early stages of a career is connected to the internationalisation of the academic careers.

The analysis of the eight countries underlines the complexity of careers organisation, as career paths are manifold, so that an academic may have different alternatives (internal vs. external career, postdoctoral positions vs. tenure track) which can be or not be permeable, implying path dependency in choice or opportunity.

Beside the classical structural diversity of academic careers, in the end, three main nexuses appear to be structuring academic career path: the possibility or the constraint for internal or external career; the research and teaching activities distribution among faculties, and the academic – administrative potential articulations (see Table 4.1. hereafter).

4.2.2   Hiring and Funding: Two Sides of the Same Coin

Investigating the funding of academic positions grasps the interplay between institutional and third party funding as well as the research-teaching work division.

While professors are generally recruited permanently on institutional funding, PhD students and members of the non-professorial academic staff are increasingly hired on non-permanent contracts based on third party funding. On the one hand, temporary positions are often developed to meet teaching needs: in Austria and Germany, teaching – whether or not based on third party funding – is more and more devolved to the lower levels, accordingly professional requirements and salaries for lecturers are decreasing. On the other hand, in other countries, like Switzerland, an increasing number of PhD students and assistants do exclusively research on the basis of third party funding – and in some cases administrative tasks. Both models coexist, to different extent, in our various countries.

As some interviews schematically depict:

> There are new patterns of career, whereby people do only research for a long time, then come to teaching and do not have enough experience. The double career teacher/researcher doesn't exist anymore and it is not any more important in order to do an academic career. (CH25_ACA/senior/female)
>   ... [young scientists] are not connected to the chair, because this generation of new scientists' doesn't teach and then possibly becomes an assistant professor, without knowing responsibilities of the chair. (D2_ACA/junior/female)

Table 4.1 Career paths in eight countries

Switzerland		Finland		Germany		Austria		Ireland		Poland	Romania	Croatia
University	Non university	University	Non university	University	Non university	University	Non university	University	Non university	University sector only	University sector only	University sector only
Student assistant	Student assistant			Student assistant								
Assistant, PhD student	Assistants (new category emerging)	Assistant	Lecturer/ researcher	Assistant	Assistant (doctoral student)	Predoc	Doctoral student		Assistant lecturer	Research assistant	Tutor (to disappear)	Junior researcher/ Assistant
Assistant/MA postdoc abroad/ PrivatDozent	(Industry experience)	Researcher		Postdoc (abroad)	(Industry experience)	Research collaborator (wissenschaftlicher Mitarbeiter – 4 years)	Junior researcher	Lecturer			Assistant	Higher assistant
Maître d'Enseignement et de Recherche	Lecturer/ researcher		Senior lecturer/ Senior researcher			Assistant (6 years)		Senior lecturer	Career grade lecturer			
Assistant professor		Lecturer	Principal lecturer	Assistant professor	Professor	Contract Professor (*Vertragsprofessor* 7 years)	Senior researcher		Senior lecturer	Assistant professor	Assistant professor/ lecturer	Assistant professor
Associate Professor						Assistant professor (tenure track)		Associate professor		Associate Professor	Associate Professor	
Ordinary professor	Professor or management position	Professor	Head of training division	Professor	Management position	Professor	Department leader	Professor	Management position	Professor	Full professor	Full professor

This table identify, for each country, the different types of academic status existing in the university sector and in the non-university sector, going from the first type of available position to the highest status existing. This allows to compare the complexity of the academic careers depending on the national and sectorial contexts as well as to identify potential structural homology lying beside status named differently

In Finland, Poland, Germany and Switzerland there has been an increase in externally funded scholarships, so that postdocs have the opportunity to finance their own position through a grant by the national science foundation. This is not without consequences: in Finland the increase in the numbers of PhD students is linked to the development of externally funded positions. According to a junior female academic, getting external funds is a long process and besides these cannot always cover the whole duration of studies (FI15_ACA/junior/female). This puts doctoral students as well as their supervisors under pressure. Even worse is the situation of postdoc positions, which are structurally problematic: because there is little funding, they are frequently part-time. However, tenure track assistant professor positions have been introduced to consolidate careers (FI20_MAN/senior/male).

In Austria, too, positions can be funded externally or by the university. The first appear as more vulnerable, for they usually focus only on research and have time limits according to the project and not according to the necessities of the assistant, e.g. publishing, finishing his or her thesis. Hence, those who are funded externally would like to change to a post funded by the university. But the context is not necessarily favourable: the board/ministry imposes 40 % permanent positions and 60 % fluctuating positions in a university, while not respecting this rule implies a cut in funds (AT19_ACA/senior/male). As a result, the number of externally funded PhD has increased. Those are hired on shorter terms than the traditional doctoral assistants, and have to articulate their PhD within the constraints of a collective research project.

In Croatia and in Romania there are currently serious financial problems, due to the recent economic crisis: a Romanian senior academic reports on the government having barred advancement to higher academic positions (RO27_ACA/senior/male). In the same vein, in the Croatian case, the opening of new job positions has been restricted: very few positions for junior staff have been created, while a large number of new PhD is produced.

The general trend towards the development of third party funding positions, essentially for PhD students and post-doc, is intertwined with the development of research activities. More widely, one could argue that the first period of higher education massification has led to the recruitment of a large number of academics, mostly on permanent positions, to face teaching needs. In a less dynamic economic context and with changes in the governance of higher education, the last decades have seen the development of non-permanent positions: mainly based on internal funding for teaching positions, on third party funding for research ones. This diversification blurs the traditional professional boundaries and the division of labour within the profession.

4.2.3 *Recruitment Procedures*

Procedures of candidate selection reveal who contributes to decision-making and by which prerogatives, that is from the selection of files to the last rank where one candidate is proposed.

Determinants of actors' involvement in recruitment depend on the status of the opened position and on the funding source. The higher the status of the person recruited, the more formalised the process by the higher education institution's governing body, be it faculty, rectorate or university board. Depending on whether the position is permanent or not, the degree of formalisation differs. Thus, recruitment implying an important and long-lasting financial investment (e.g. full professors) tend to be governed at university and faculty level through increasingly formalised processes, while short-term recruitment based on third party funding (e.g. for PhD students and scientific collaborators) are more prone to individual academic appreciation. Accordingly they are also less formal in their implementation.

However, a trend towards recruitment processes to come closer to those implemented for the professoriate is observed for the other stages of the academic career. Promotions, too, are increasingly concerned with the formalisation of the procedure and criteria, particularly when assistant professors are granted a tenured position. *De facto*, the procedures are the same as in recruitment.

4.2.3.1 Recruitment of Professors

Professorship is mostly granted permanently from associate to full professors (with the exception of Finland and Austria, where not all professors have permanent positions), while assistant professors may be with or without tenure track (in the last case, assistant professors are usually hired for 6 years).

In Switzerland most respondents describe standardized procedures: opening of an official and public call; establishment of a recruitment commission comprising dean, internal and external professors, a delegate of the intermediary body, a representative of the rectorate, and the delegate of the equality office (the latter without voting right); selection of the best candidates; organisation of interviews; possibly a trial lecture; production of a ranking – usually a short list of three names – by the commission; validation by the faculty council; validation by the rectorate or the board. Lastly, while before the status of full professor was often perceived as the retribution of a long career, a trend towards an early recruitment of strongly internationalised academics with sound research records is now observed in some disciplines. In some fields, hiring of professors is standardized in its formal selection process, evaluation and required criteria depending on the national higher education system or on regional, institutional or disciplinary arrangements. In Switzerland, professors have historically decided and influenced this process, but major differences among institutional types emerge: while in universities job descriptions and positions are decided by the concerned faculty with its dean, in federal institutes of technology and universities of applied sciences president and board control key phases of the process and decide on final candidates with a veto right.

In Poland some respondents called professorial recruitment a *"façade* exercise", where loose criteria, centrally defined by the state, are easily shortcut by senior professors within faculties (see Sect. 4.2.3.6). The Polish system has been criticized by many interviewees: allegedly it is based on inbreeding, often there is no open call and potential candidates are not aware of new available positions. It is centrally organized by the ministry or a special central committee for academic degrees and titles, setting formal requirements for each degree. Departments can set their own requirements, which are usually more demanding. However, the *Habilitation* as well as all the other promotions are said to be awarded in a "non-transparent way", to be "a fiction" (PL44_ACA/senior/female). Even open calls are called a *façade* (PL1_ACA/senior/male, PL4_ACA/junior/female, PL44_ACA/senior/female, PL48_ACA/junior/male) *a* legendary joke (PL54_ACA/junior/male) because of the opacity of the procedures. Professors offer positions to their assistants, selections are conducted in a way that everybody knows who will win. In any case, internal candidates seem to be favoured, for criteria are extremely specific in order to select a predefined applicant. Academic calls do not require interviews but only documents (PL23_ACA/junior/male), while the process is usually very lengthy (PL55_/ACA/junior/female).

Profiles of candidates also depend on the discipline. In this perspective, for instance, engineering and life sciences can favour industry experience. A German junior male academic relates that in the Natural Sciences and in Engineering, practical experience is well accepted and people can go back to university (and get a professorial title) after 3 years training (D55_ACA/junior/male). A German senior male academic reports how attractive life sciences are nowadays: in the last years, the domain has been expanding (D27_ACA/senior/male) and competition for attracting scientists has become fierce: in Germany universities contend themselves the best researchers. This has brought to a high turnover, contracts may be broken before they expire, as scientists migrate to other universities in order to profit from better facilities and laboratories.

In Croatia the National Science Council has established formal criteria for career advancement based on time frame and number of publications. Although advancement criteria vary depending on the disciplines, and papers are differently classified according to the type of journal they have been published in (international, national, with foreign reviewers or national ones, if the journal is indexed, in which databases, etc.), in average three papers in peer-reviewed journals are required to become assistant professor, then six such publications are needed for tenured professorship. According to Croatian junior female academic this constitutes a "minimum common denominator" for quality in recruitment (HR6_ACA/ junior/female). Hence, even though also class work and international experience are taken into consideration, quantitative measurement of publications seems to be the basis of progress in academic career, whenever an opening is at hand (HR16_ACA/junior/male).

In Austria procedures are equally perceived as non-transparent, while some interviewees consider that the rectorate has a corrective function in order for recruitment to be more uniform (AT01_ACA/junior/male). As in Switzerland, a member of the equality commission is active in recruitment processes (AT09_ACA/senior/female).

In Switzerland, as well as in other countries to different extents, a certain convergence of criteria concerning full professors can be observed, like for instance negotiating the number of assistants per professor and the teaching hours. The formalisation of the evaluation processes to access tenure seems to be negotiated between faculty and university. Other instruments are salaries, working conditions such as offices, number of assistants, research budget, sabbaticals, teaching hours. With respect to academic status and tenure track, the university defines the range of possibilities while faculties and departments decide how to use them.

4.2.3.2   Assistant Professorship and Tenure Track

In Germany, tenure track has been introduced as a way of providing a foreseeable career path with predefined procedures and to counteract the fact that an assistant used to work for a professor for up to 10 years. It is advertised by an official act, but then processes are allegedly not transparent, texts are tailored to certain candidates.

In Switzerland, from assistant to full professors recruitment procedures are standardized and follow the same rationale: international competition, research-based reputation (publications are required and reviewed by a scientific committee). These procedures have been introduced quite recently and have been imposed by the rectorate (e.g. at History) or agreed within the faculty (Business Administration and Chemistry), thus reflecting different disciplinary identities on the one hand, different positioning in the academic market on the other hand. Planning of professorial positions has been formally introduced, however, only at the faculty of Business Administration this seems to be implemented thoroughly: in Chemistry full professor titles are still favoured, in History assistant professors are usually recruited without tenure track, they are funded by the national science foundation or by private foundations. In the first case there is little involvement from the faculty and from the department, as it is the individual getting the scholarship from the national foundation that decides in which university she or he wants to work.

> I don't know of any expectation of my university. I am free to do as I like it. I am a researcher [an assistant professor funded by the national science foundation] and I don't feel like I am connected to this institution. (CH21_ACA/senior/female)

In the second case, the inclusion of a representative of the private foundation changes the actors' configuration: the rectorate manages the relationship with the foundation and intervenes significantly in case of conflict between the foundation and the faculty, for instance on the selection of a candidate (CH24_AC/senior/ male).

Tenure track exists only in the university sector, but disciplinary differences in its use according to discipline can be detected. According to a German junior male academic, in Economics, the minimum age to get a tenure track assistant professorship has been lowered to 27 years (D21_ACA/junior/male). Careers go faster in Life Sciences, while in the Humanities, scientific maturity is advocated at a later age, what can also be analysed as a rationalisation for preserving the chair-based organisation.

> Especially in jobs in the Humanities educational field, where personal maturity is very important, I do not want to imagine a 30-year old professor teaching 20-year old students. (D33_ACA/senior/male)

The tenure track instrument allows the hiring of younger academics for professorship positions, however, its concrete use appears to depend upon disciplinary fields, e.g. economics seem to comply more thoroughly.

4.2.3.3   Intermediate Body Recruitment

With the exception of Ireland, Romania and Switzerland (in the case of *Maîtres d'Enseignement et de Recherche*), where lecturers and researchers may be granted permanent contracts, lecturers, researchers, assistants and scientific collaborators are characterized by fixed-term employments. Periods may be decided by the duration of research projects or the need for educational activities, by the timeframe provided institutionally in order to carry out a doctorate (from 5 to 6 years) or a *Habilitation* (from 3 to 10 years). In the case of senior assistants, limited time is accorded as a rule (e.g. in Switzerland 6 years). After the *Habilitation*, *Privatdozenten* have to wait until they are granted a professorship in Germany, Switzerland and Poland. Nevertheless this position should not be overestimated, as it funds only minor educational duties (and not research) providing little financial support.

Standardization of recruitment procedures can be found in most universities, where rectorates try to impose transparency and competition also at the lower levels. In this perspective, the introduction of doctoral schools is functional to the formalization of PhD student hiring. In general, however, professors remain in charge of selecting academic staff in a flexible way, in order to respond to contingent needs of research, teaching and students' supervision. Spontaneous applications for a doctorate continue to be made by prospective students and, as many respondents all over the countries observed, previous acquaintance with professors, in spite of open calls and numbers of competitors, represents the greatest advantage for recruitment (see Sect. 4.2.3.6). In sum the intermediate corps is somehow oppositional to the professoriate, in that particularly in the chair model, it holds a very different status, accordingly gets very different type of contracts and exercises diverse professional functions.

In Germany the recruitment process has not changed a lot

Now there is more expert advice but there has always been international cooperation. (D31_MAN/senior/male)
   Overall performance is taken into consideration. (D49_ACA/junior/female)

In Ireland appointments have become more professional: criteria are precise and relate to teaching, research, contribution to the institution and to the community. Internal and external committees review applications and panel interviews are conducted. According to a senior male academic one needs a minimum of 3 years in a position to be promoted (IE45_ACA/senior/male). A trend is visible in the hiring of young staff who are offered part-time contracts and who are very active in research. This creates a gap with the existing academic personnel and pushes the latter to build more scientific profiles, for instance by doing a doctorate. A senior male academic details how promotions are evaluated: from career lecturer to senior lecturer 40 % research, 30 % teaching, 30 % contribute onto the institution and the community, i.e. community service. From senior lecturer to assistant professor 60 % research (peer reviewed articles, book chapters, conferences), 20 % teaching, 20 % contribution (IE7_ACA/senior/male). According to another senior male academic also involvement in administrative tasks is considered (IE55_ACA/senior/male).

In Austria the role of professors in hiring assistants (predoc, postdocs towards the *Habilitation*) is underscored: a female junior academic testifies that those who are mentored get a predoc position (AT30_ACA/junior/female). In other words, assistants depend on professors for changing their position and moving upwards in the hierarchy. Nevertheless, formal procedures are in place for the recruitment of predoc: a letter of application is required and 1-h interview is carried out. One has to show experience in research projects, the appropriate age, and publications. An Austrian female junior academic feels enormous pressure to comply with certain expectations (AT37_ACA/junior/female), another complains about writing research proposals, while the professor agrees to take on the formal leadership (AT38_ACA/junior/male). In case of (already) funded research projects, recruitment is more informal, without application and the candidate is approached directly by the professor.

Assistants are recruited through a quite formal process in Switzerland: publication of the position on the Internet, selection of the applications. This said, informal discussions between the professors hiring their doctoral students – whom often had already met at Master level – and postdocs, bringing the candidate to be hired, are frequent. Depending on the departments (thus, it is the level of the disciplines that is concerned), the procedure differs: in some a PhD commission decides on candidates, while in others, students are hired by single professors. In both contexts, spontaneous applications may be taken into consideration. Although assistant recruitment takes place through a call, these positions can be obtained also by replacing someone else (maternity leave, sabbatical or scholarship abroad as in the case of a History department). Given the importance of being assistant to a full professor and the requirement for the *Habilitation* after the doctorate in the German speaking part of Switzerland, these positions are often occupied by postdocs, who thus hamper many PhD students from climbing the hierarchy. The latter are often recruited on research projects, i.e. on more precarious positions without teaching activity. In this case recruitment is related more to the professor's choice and his/her necessity. According to a Swiss senior male manager (CH19_MAN/senior/male), university management wants to introduce transparency and competition of recruitment processes also at lower level and discusses nowadays the possibility to select the best master students. This is somehow already implemented at a History department, which can select PhD students for its doctoral school, while young graduates are invited to work for a limited period of time in order to get their PhD research funded. Although this is reported as a positive novelty and an opportunity to enter the academic career (CH24_ACA/senior/male), it should be noticed that these students are recruited with a lower salary than assistants, their contract is limited to 1 year, after which they may be selected out if they do not receive funds for their PhD proposal.

The hiring of the intermediary body suggest that the chair-based organisation, characterised by the power of full professors on hiring assistants and defining their tasks, resists the implementation of a more departmental based one. The latter is implemented formally, but informally professors maintain their structuring power.

4.2.3.4   The Non-university Sector

In the non-university sector a professorship is granted through different procedures and processes. Professors are appointed after some years of activities in teaching and research. It is an internal procedure disconnected from disciplines, as the title of professor is not related to a chair, it is not even mandatory in order to be institute director and research leader. In Switzerland, the committee (professors, representative of the council, externals) as well is unrelated to the specific disciplines: the candidate is proposed by his department head, then the school board decides.

> Professors: everybody applies spontaneously, this title is unrelated to disciplines. (. . .) The commission for evaluating professorships is made of traditional university professors. How can they really assess? I have never applied to become a professor because I don't want to be assessed in this way. (CH8_ACA/senior/male)

The evaluation procedure relates to studies (doctorate is favoured), applied research with regional scope and competitive projects, quality and number of scientific publications, quality of education, institutional activities, possibly activities and acknowledgements in other universities, "exceptional performance" in arts. This can be explained by the universities of applied sciences' history as educational institutions, with former professors and teachers constituting still an important part of the staff. Moreover, teaching activities can be extremely intensive (e.g. in Switzerland up to 22 hour a week), under these conditions, it is not surprising that part of the staff is mainly involved in teaching and cannot take up significant research tasks.

At universities of applied sciences career paths and recruitment at non professorial level appear to be distinct from those of traditional universities. Career stages are more differentiated, first because they are organized separately according to teaching and research. Even though in order to become professors both activities are required and only the so-called teachers/researchers have access to these positions (Switzerland). In fact, procedures to hire teachers/researchers are more formalized than for the other levels and include various steps (public call, evaluation committee, interviews) similar to the professorial position in universities.

Hence, entry at universities of applied sciences depends more on research activities and experience in industry than on teaching, which is seen as a task that can be taken up successively, once someone has demonstrated to be proficient in managing research projects and acquiring external funds. Positions of researcher and senior researcher are mainly granted at the level of the department (i.e. faculty), while the relevant professor or institute director is in charge of the whole process.

Even if universities of applied sciences may grant permanent positions to their staff, researchers, lecturers and assistants are increasingly hired on a temporary basis and paid through external research funds. This means also that a candidate may have to get his research funded before getting a contract. The same is true for PhD students, who are affiliated to a university, as universities of applied sciences usually do not grant doctorates. Assistants are usually selected by professors among the best students at bachelor and master level and fulfil coordination tasks within research projects.

Finally, a distinctive characteristic of academic careers is the rise of the research manager profile, who has to be skilled both in management (strategy, funding, staff) and administration (accounting, controlling). This has been indicated often as a mandatory competence for career advancement, for instance in order to manage research projects, teams and budgets as well as for coordinating educational programs.

Industry-related working experience is necessary as well. To make a career in universities of applied sciences one has to assume responsibilities and show command in management skills, commitment to the institution, pedagogical expertise. Cooperation with stakeholders, foreign languages, project management, teamwork and student supervision are also mentioned by respondents.

In three countries (Germany, Ireland and Switzerland) elements of academic drift are observed. In Germany and Switzerland more research and publication outputs are required, as well as international networking and, accordingly, the use of foreign languages.

> Careers are becoming academic: degree, PhD and postdoc, young people are doing academic careers, there are now professorial councils, they are getting important but they do not manage anything. (CH10_ACA/senior/male)

A German senior male academic confirms that the PhD has become an important requirement (in Engineering, D57_ACA/senior/male). In Ireland, increasingly the doctorate figures as a necessary requirement to advance, together with research activities and outputs, and acquisition of research funding. However, an Irish junior female academic states that promotions are still ruled by in-house politics, seniority instead of meritocracy (IE37_ACA/junior/female). Finally, in Finland, and Austria, indications of academic drift couldn't be detected from the interviews.

4.2.3.5   Some Disciplinary Features

Criteria for advancement are not identical in all disciplines. In the Natural Sciences research is central and depends upon facilities, groups and science dynamics. Accordingly, progress in the academic hierarchy is affected by some boundary conditions: first, publishing is harder and slower, because work in the laboratory requires time and patience (HR17_ACA/Physical Sciences, Mathematics, Computer Sciences). However, a Romanian academic in Mathematics also argued that empirical sciences are more favoured than theoretical sciences, for the latter it is more difficult to publish, given the requirements of most scientific journals. Secondly, being part of a team is the only way to achieve performance in research, then to publish. Thirdly, in Physics, a researcher must be ready to switch to different groups (thus change research topics) in order to remain in academia. He or she therefore has to be flexible and not too much specialised. In general, doctoral students in these disciplinary fields are primarily active in research. Even if PhD students are funded through the institutional budget, they rarely teach in courses (although they often coordinate exercises in laboratories).

In Medicine there is a strong division between clinical work and basic research. This structures four different types of careers: to become a clinical doctor, to get a professorship and do basic research, to be active in industry research, and, finally, to do research in fields belonging to the natural sciences (e.g. life sciences). Moreover, for an academic path, international experience in the US has been mentioned by several respondents as a significant advantage.

In the Humanities, being attached to a chair is still considered important in order to get a higher position. In History the assistant position is deemed important for career prospects, for both postdocs and PhD students. Being an assistant means being connected to a full professor, or to a chair, and be able to do teaching, research and administrative tasks related to student support. However, in Switzerland, this position is limited to 50 % part-time, hence some interviewees (maybe already in their 40s) have found complementary professional activities outside the university.

Disciplines constitute still an important space of constraints and opportunities. In engineering, if one is specialised in a specific topic, he/she risks not to have an opening for a professorial position (FI3_ACA/Engineering, Manufacturing and Construction, Architecture). Moreover, disciplines affect differently academic career paths (RO10_ACA/Physical sciences, Mathematics, Computer Sciences) and modify them constantly, through their own evolution (RO29_ACA/Business Administration and Economics).

Poland has been described as a system heavily based on disciplines, where professors are able to rule almost without control. According to a manager in Business, Administration and Economics, this has been criticized and characterized as one of the reasons why the Polish system is rather immobile and difficult to reform (PL49_MAN/Business Administration, Economics). It doesn't come as a surprise that interdisciplinarity is considered an advantage by some (FI9_ACA/ Medical Sciences and Health Care). On the one hand it is considered a way of doing research that is becoming more and more relevant, in this respect academics have to adapt themselves. On the other hand it is perceived as a way to overcome disciplinary silos defended by senior professors.

4.2.3.6 Recruitment: Balancing University Missions, Social Competences and Personal Attributes

In Croatia, recruitment and advancement are enhanced if one works for the benefit of his or her own institution (e.g. attracting funds, working in committees), is active in relation with curriculum activities and is able to manage websites. Networking includes personal acquaintances, which can make a person advance in spite of not fulfilling formal criteria or in addition to them (HR60_ACA/senior/female).

In Finland, beside publications, career is said by the interviewees to be based on scientific autonomy after the doctorate, passion for research, success in getting research funds, building international networks, ambition and persistence as well as "insecurity tolerance", adaptability, profiting from a good supervision. Internationalization in early career is also underscored together with cherishing the informal social side of a career, or, as a Finnish respondent puts it: "to be part of the in-crowd" (FI65_ACA/senior/female).

In Austria our respondents mentioned establishing international contacts early on, gaining insight into the research field, enjoying mentoring through senior professors. Moreover, project acquisition and leadership, proposal writing, risk taking, internal and external networks, own project ideas are mentioned. From a more personal perspective, a junior academic should have a partner with a fixed income in the first 3 years as a postdoctoral fellow, be ready to compromises, be accepted by students and contribute to their professional future, obstinacy. A significant change is claimed:

> Before one had not to fall out of the favour of your professor, now [there are] measurable scientific qualifications and international experience. (AT33_ACA/senior/male)

Working independently in one's own research area and acquiring a broad knowledge of the field while specializing on a certain area is also seen as an obligation in early career. Postdocs have to publish but also develop their own ideas. Dealing with norms, competition, academic habitus and hierarchies "without taking it personally" (AT15_ACA/junior/female) is fundamental in order to be academically successful.

In Germany, career advancement is also based on the ability to raise external funds, expertise in committee work, fruitful link between research and teaching, networking internationally and with "relevant" professors. Subsequently perseverance, discipline, strong personal interest, language skills, teaching quality are also considered important characteristics. Advanced education to get management skills has become more and more a requirement for career advancement. Even though formal applications are the rule at all levels, many interviewees recognize that acquaintance with professors and with the university structures is important.

Requirements for career in Poland, besides getting the relevant academic degrees on time, are the following: having the right ("known and likeable") mentor, be successful in research and accordingly publishing more and more, be known and agreeable by senior academics, being aware of the informal hierarchy. Social networks within one's own discipline and department are relevant in order to be awarded degrees by associations of peers and to be introduced to key people. From a personal point of view, an academic should be ready to abandon large parts of his/her social and family life and to develop some "egotism and assertive attitudes".

In Romania requirements for academic career are: receiving a formal recommendation upon graduation based on good academic results, being able to exploit the various institutional and financial opportunities, carrying out research intensively, possessing good communication, psychological and pedagogical skills. International experience in research projects and in conferences, in professional associations, participation in scientific events and being a reviewer in international journals are also considered very important responsibilities for one's own and students' development. Furthermore Romanian interviewees also indicate teaching and third mission as relevant dimensions of involvement.

> Teaching talent as a passion to convey to the younger generation the desire and instruments to investigate the new (RO51_ACA/senior/male).

This is followed by interest for students, cooperation with all parts of the national educational system, contribution to community affairs life, being interested in society dynamics.

In conclusion, three categories of characteristics appear as being differently articulated in recruitment: those related to university work – research (mainly), teaching and third mission – those featuring the social competences needed to cope with academia – often related to an international dimension – and, finally, the personal attributes – passion, tenacity, risk-taking – necessary to be competitive enough to remain and progress in the academic career.

4.3   Applicants' Constraints and Opportunities: Some Insights

Recruitment is often looked at from the institutional side. But what about the applicants? This section attempts to link recruitment characteristics to individual leeway in balancing advantages and disadvantages in order to be hired. In doing so, it illustrates how individuals deal with recruitment processes: how they select the positions to which they apply and how they try to comply with existing conditions and requisites.

Models of external versus internal academic careers entail different strategies for advancement. Moreover, affiliation to specific disciplines – more or less dynamic and "fashionable" – as well as requirements of degrees – such as doctorate and *Habilitation* – may modify individual positioning in the academic job market, influencing one's opportunities to apply for the most favoured opening.

Besides fitting the structural requisites for the academic position, job seekers actively position themselves within their national, disciplinary and institutional community. This is relevant in order to understand the dynamic relationships between the different layers of the academic profession. It is important to observe how (potential) candidates connect to their colleagues in order to position themselves appropriately and how they carry out such networking.

Relating to the uncertainty and precariousness characterizing the first stages of the academic career, two trends are detected: on one side, fragmentation and conformity of junior academics and assistant professors, who try to comply with the requirements of "research excellence". In the department model junior academics and assistant professors express their feeling to be more on their own in organizing their career paths. This means that they do not have (anymore) a senior professor advising and guiding them. In fact their acquired autonomy makes them more loosely coupled in relation to the institutional setting. On the other side, in the chair model, persisting for instance in Poland, compliance with perceived powerful professors is very strong. However conformity is also a pattern among junior professors in the department model: they do not want to take a risk by profiling themselves in research too much, particularly in the beginning. Accordingly, it can be argued that pressures for conformity vis-à-vis senior professors persist in both models, while requirements for research excellence are usually defined by the number of publications in international journals.

> Today young academics have to publish and do public relations to become visible. (. . .) one has to create bubbles by highlighting achievements and developing a broad portfolio. This leads to a fragmentation for the individual and the university. Also, profiling takes place through the successful acquisition of external funds, thus a "Me Inc." is founded. (AT25_ACA/senior/male)
>
> Now junior professors are autonomous in their career, no support from senior professors, no structure anymore. (D26_MAN/senior/male)

Yet, as we have seen, professors continue to be important for many junior researchers' careers. Strategic positioning and networking with perceived "powerful" professors are instrumental to obtaining support along the different career stages.

> [Old professors] preserve the feudal system and openly block careers of many young academics just because they are too young and too independent and too critical. Many professors are scared of their younger colleagues who speak foreign languages, are more internationally recognized and research active. They use their institutional power to postpone their development. (PL40_ACA/junior/male)

In other cases, a Croatian senior male academic argues, professors choose their junior researchers and educate them in order to prepare them for an assistant professor position (HR11_ACA/senior/male). Mentors have become very important to guide doctoral students, who often find themselves out of institutional affairs and thus need to be oriented.

Mentors help to gain access to the academic system, professors pave the way to good publications. (AT51_ACA/junior/female)

These two trends are visible across all countries, institutional types and disciplines, at different intensity according to the adherence to standards of research excellence and talent promotion and to the traditional chair model, where patronising relationships continue to be in place. According to the discourse of our interviewees, it is possible to contend that these two opposing conditions – junior autonomy in research and junior dependence on senior professors, produce the same outcome, that is decreasing the variety of scientific (and human) profiles.

Since academic career is nowadays unstable people change careers and broaden their expertise, which is good but confusing and decreases effectiveness. (FI4_ACA/senior/male)
A broader positioning is required: languages, interdisciplinary orientation, external funding. (D28_HEP/senior/female)
No administrative tasks anymore, but focus on scientific performance. Involvement with the organization and cooperation in teams are not conducive to advancing one's curriculum vitae. (AT41_ACA/junior/male)

Internationalization in its dimensions of research, publications, and fellowships push academics to position themselves increasingly outside their institution (Austria, Germany, Switzerland). In Eastern European countries, international experience is valued but long term mobility is not required, however academics have to participate in international conferences, projects and as reviewers for international journals. At the same time, in many cases, remaining in the targeted institution seems to be the best solution (if available) to finally apply for the desired position.

People stay more in Finland after their PhD, because people have noticed that working abroad is not necessary in progressing in academic career and they keep active their contacts in Finland and are ready to apply for posts when they become available. (FI7_ACA/junior/male)
Going abroad can mean not to return any more because of the closed nature of certain disciplines (e.g. Humanities). (AT41_ACA/junior/male)

As many respondents observed, mobility can be a temporary solution to unemployment on the one hand, it is also expected from young researchers on the other hand. Postdocs are becoming more and more international, there is pressure for mobility coming both from competitive dynamics and from the impossibility to find positions in the home country. The other side of the coin with respect to this mobility trend can be observed in traditionally nationally oriented countries: in Poland researchers go abroad and acquire "Western standards", which they bring back, building up

A new generation of senior academics who are more internationally oriented and less feudal. (PL13_ACA/junior/female)

Precariousness and uncertainty can influence personal decisions, in terms of family planning for instance, and professional decisions, e.g. in relation with mobility. On the one hand, academics underline that fixed term contracts (typically each one up to 2-year duration) entail a tension between the working framework and timing of publications, which usually take longer. On the other hand, the *Habilitation* appears not to be a secure path anymore and under such conditions it becomes difficult to plan a career. The compression of the duration of studies is visible also in medicine, where traineeship used to be originally 10 years and has now been decreased to 5 years (D16_ACA/senior/female). Along the same line, increasing requirements of internationalization – in form of fellowships, research projects, publications – may influence individual trajectories and preferences with regard to the different positions offered.

Conclusion: Convergence and Divergence Through Standardization Pressures and Local Practices

The interviews reflect the reshuffling of the academic profession from an academic system based on a chair organisation and implicit knowledge towards an organisation based on a network organized around an open market and the competition processes that come along. These models and the type of careers they bear in embryo can coexist not only within one higher education system, but also within a single institution, or, even, sometimes, within a faculty.

In the framework of the Bologna Process, doctoral studies tend to become harmonised both regarding their length (average duration) and their content (through the implementation of doctoral schools), although these trends have to be considered as a general movement occurring unevenly depending on the type of institution and on the discipline. We thus discern a diversification process, from the once unique classical model of doctoral student characterised by the status of teaching assistant and belonging to a professorial chair, to its coexistence with a doctoral student working in a collective research project. In the first model, PhD candidates and supervisors select themselves mutually on the basis of individual interactions. The supervision and the integration into the broader community of researchers are highly variable and the time devoted to the PhD is usually long. In the second model, the PhD candidate is more often hired on the basis of a national or international competition, often centred on criteria such as "early talent". In this model, the candidate is allegedly more integrated to the scientific community through a shared supervision by a group of professors (Enders 2005). This new model, favoured by the Bologna process and the implementation of doctoral schools, tends to increase the workload of PhD candidates during the first years of the doctorate and to accelerate the building up of the PhD project. The thesis thus becomes an exercise in order to get an entry ticket into the academic career. Though, these changes also come with a progressive formalisation of the rights and duties of the doctoral students: the funding limitation reduces the thesis time but is accompanied by a more precise

(continued)

definition of the work to be dedicated to the doctorate (40–50 %), which is a protection for the PhD student.

The same can be observed regarding senior researchers, lecturers and professors: as of the first group, senior researchers and lecturers working on a non-permanent basis, their contracts have often been reduced to a specific number of years, after which a professorial position (or another permanent position) has to be achieved.

Two general comments can be made. First, although recruitment procedures tend to converge at professorial level through standardization, they can be loosely coupled with practices, while at lower levels, though some standardization is detectable, professors continue to maintain their control on who is hired and for what activities. Indeed, behind the on-going standardisation, different informal practices can be detected depending on the discipline and its degree of internationalisation (Fumasoli 2014).

Second, individual strategies in the aggregate display a trend towards decreasing diversity among young scientists, on one side induced to conform to standardized research evaluation and, on the other side, encouraged to reproduce senior professors (research) activity orientation. However this trend is mitigated by the increasing influence of national foundations: these fund postdoc and junior professorship positions, allowing young academics to develop their own – more or less original – research agenda.

Finally, the analysis of the interviews shows that a European trend can be spotted: regulated internal academic markets have emerged, whereby career progression increasingly follows explicit rules and incentive mechanisms (Musselin 2005), while external markets have developed, since national and international performance is progressively required.

References

Bourdieu, P. (1976). Le champ scientifique. *Actes de la Recherche en Sciences Sociales, 2*, 88–104.

Bourdieu, P. (1984). *Homo academicus*. Paris: Editions de Minuit.

Caplow, T., & McGee, R. J. (2001). *The academic marketplace*. New Brunswick/London: Transaction Publications.

Crane, D. (1970). The academic marketplace revisited. *American Journal of Sociology, 7*, 953–964.

Enders, J. (2005). Border crossings: Research training, knowledge and the transformation of academic work. *Higher Education, 49*(1–2), 119–133.

Friedrich, P. (2013). University autonomy and professorial recruitment. A case study at the Department of Economic and Social History at the University of Vienna. Master thesis, Oslo: Faculty of Educational Sciences, University of Oslo.

Fumasoli, T. (2014). Strategic management of personnel policies: A comparative analysis of Flagship universities in Norway, Finland, Switzerland and Austria. In F. Ribeiro, Y. Politis, & B. Ćulum (Eds.), *New voices in higher education research and scholarship*. Advances in Higher Education & Professional Development, IGI Global.

Goastellec, G., Leresche, J.-P., Moeschler, O., & Nicolay, A. (2007). *Les transformations du marché académique suisse: évaluation du programme Professeurs boursiers FNS*. Ecublens: Fonds national suisse de la recherche scientifique, Observatoire science, politique et société.

Kaulisch, M., & Böhmer, S. (2010). Inequality in academic careers in Germany. Indications from postdoctoral careers. In G. Goastellec (Ed.), *Understanding inequalities in, through and by Higher Education*. Amsterdam: Sense Publishers.

Musselin, C. (2001). *La longue marche des universités françaises*. Paris: PUF.

Musselin, C. (2005). *Le Marché des universitaires*. Paris: SciencesPo.

Neave, G., & Rhoades, G. (1987). The academic estate in Western Europe. In B. R. Clark (Ed.), *The academic profession: National, disciplinary and institutional settings*. Los Angeles: University of California Press.

Chapter 5
Changing Employment and Working Conditions

Timo Aarrevaara, Ian R. Dobson, and Janne Wikström

5.1 Introduction

The academy in Europe is adapting itself to the diverse demands of society and higher education markets in a knowledge economy with contradictions between traditional research sector working conditions and rapidly growing open source practices (Marginson 2009). This adaptation is not limited to Europe; change is a global phenomenon. As many of the newly acquired responsibilities of academics are in addition to their previous workload, in one sense they are unfunded. This has become a major burden for academic staff to bear. Evidence has shown that although academics in many countries report overall job satisfaction, across Europe the proportion of academics claiming to be very satisfied or satisfied ranges from 77 % down to 47 % (EuroAC 2011). In addition, relatively few European academics perceive that working conditions have improved. Fewer than 20 % of academics in most countries perceived improvement, but by way of exception, 60 % of Croatian academics thought things to be better now than in the past (EuroAC 2011). These are important matters, because the academic profession's work has traditionally been based on professional autonomy, socialisation, affiliation, status and identity.

Several internal factors have caused a change in the work conducted in the academy, as increasing external stakeholder influence is evident in European higher education governance (Aarrevaara and Dobson 2012). Among the many changes in

T. Aarrevaara (✉) • J. Wikström
Higher Education Governance and Management (HEGOM), Faculty of Social Sciences, University of Helsinki, Unioninkatu 37, PB 54, Helsinki 00014, Finland
e-mail: Timo.Aarrevaara@helsinki.fi

I.R. Dobson
School of Education and Arts, Federation University Australia, University Dr, Mt Helen VIC 3350, Australia

© Springer International Publishing Switzerland 2015
T. Fumasoli et al. (eds.), *Academic Work and Careers in Europe: Trends, Challenges, Perspectives*, The Changing Academy – The Changing Academic Profession in International Comparative Perspective 12, DOI 10.1007/978-3-319-10720-2_5

higher education in recent years has been the rapid expansion in the number of students able to attend universities and other higher education institutions. Higher education has moved from its previously elite status to one in which institutions have become purveyors of teaching to the masses, via a process generally described as 'massification' (Trow 1999; Teichler 2008). Rarely has there been a commensurate increase in the number of academic staff to teach them. For example, studies in Australia (where detailed national statistics are available) have shown that a doubling in the number of full time equivalent students had been matched by an increase of only 44 % in the number of teachers, and that nearly 59 % of that increase had been effected by hiring 'casual' staff on extremely short and usually precarious contracts (See, for example, Dobson 2012; Coates et al. 2009).

Even if governance models are unique to each country, some generalisations are possible from the eight countries examined here. This chapter is based the opinions of academic staff from Austria, Croatia, Finland, Germany, Ireland, Poland, Romania and Switzerland. In the text, higher education institutions have been described either as 'universities' or 'polytechnics', with the latter term being used to represent non-university higher education institutions.

Data sources from which academics' opinions were obtained are twofold. First, summary quantitative information on the differences of opinion between academics in the countries has been obtained from the EuroAC data set. This has been done in order to demonstrate the broad parameters of the academic profession in Europe. Second, an extension to the EuroAC data set is available in the form of a series of in-depth interviews undertaken with selectively-representative samples of academics in the countries examined here. In all eight countries, around 60 interviews were conducted and a summary of each was written up to improve the transferability of the information. Coverage of the interviews varied according to each interviewee's areas of interest, although the thematic structure for the questions was similar for all interviews. Highlights or summaries of the interviews were translated into English for purposes of reporting and in order for the results to be available for use in international comparisons. A typological selection was made among disciplines, gender, types of higher education institution and career stages of the academic interviewees as recommended in the guidelines of the EuroAC Consortium described elsewhere in this book.

This chapter includes a review of previous research on working conditions and academics' affiliations. This review and the information presented from EuroAC statistics is intended to be a foundation for analysis of the EuroAC interview data. The interview data were analysed using content analytical methods, such as using keywords.[1] The diversity of academic work between the eight countries has been

---

[1] Key words used to analyse interviews: formal working conditions and contracts; promotion; institutional autonomy and academic freedom; control of work; support and administration; influence in institutional governance; collegiality; performance based salary components; seniority; the binary divide between polytechnics and universities and the teaching-research nexus.

considered according to work time, academics' preferences for teaching and/or research, and the infrastructure available for work in the academy (Teichler 2012).

5.2 The Work and Affiliations of the Academic Profession

Individual academic staff members work in a profession based predominantly on teaching and research, with other activities pertinent to higher education institutions, such as community service and administration, also being involved. At the same time, the same academics affiliate themselves to differing degrees with their academic department, their institution and their scholarly discipline. These matters are considered in this section.

Looking at teaching and research, there are academic departments within institutions that undertake both functions, but there are also departments that conduct (predominantly) either one or other (Leisyte et al. 2009). In binary systems of higher education, it is possible, even likely, that one of the binary sectors will have a greater focus on teaching or research. This is the case in Finland, for example, and many of the academics in departments in polytechnics are predominantly teaching-focussed, and teaching is therefore the predominant activity of the academics in those departments (Aarrevaara et al. 2013). In the Finnish case, this tendency is particularly strong because the polytechnic sector of higher education is a new one, with the first institutions opening in the early 1990s. The centuries of tradition that saw universities evolving as researching and teaching institutions is not present in the novice polytechnics, the establishment of which was instrumental in the massification of higher education in Finland (Aarrevaara et al. 2013).

An extension of the teaching vs. research nexus can be found in the many studies on academic work time conducted over many years, and the recent study by Tight (2010) is among these. Tight (2010) compared the hours of work reported in a number of British surveys over about 60 years, and noted that the total number of hours increased until the 1960s, but since then the number has stabilised. The distribution of hours between teaching and research in British institutions varied between older and newer universities/polytechnics, and much of the increase in total hours had been an increase in the amount of administration required (Tight 2010).

Among the results identified in the EuroAC survey, the proportion of hours spent on teaching (during teaching periods) within Europe varied from about 25 % to over 40 %, whereas the proportionate range of time spent on research varied from just over 25 to 45 %. Administration took up one-third of academic time in some countries (EuroAC 2011).

Members of the academic profession in higher education institutions have several entities with which to be affiliated, typically including (at least) their academic department, their university and their scholarly discipline. Academics are affiliated with academic departments in a range of ways (Brew 2008), and the weight of these affiliations can vary. For example, a full time academic working a single job for a single institution is likely to feel a stronger affiliation to their department than a part-time academic who might have employment arrangements simultaneously with departments at more than one higher education institution or a contract outside academia. From the higher education institutions' point of view, this can be important, for example in terms of which higher education institution reaps the rewards of the research output of multi-employed academics: which institution should the research be linked to? It is not possible to establish an unambiguous definition of affiliation, because the work of the academic profession is partly connected with finance, research infrastructures and research networks outside the academy.

Although higher education institutions in the eight countries examined for this chapter have much in common, they also have strong traditions that are based more on national practices. Academic departments' gravitas is based on the knowledge and understanding of members of the academic profession that work there and is loosely or tightly based on the understanding of this knowledge. In higher education institutions, it is not possible to determine affiliation solely on the basis of employment, and the significance of discipline must be taken into account (Locke et al. 2011; da Zilva 2010).

The concepts of academic freedom and institutional autonomy are also important in the discussion about affiliation. In principle, when a person's affiliation to their academic discipline is strong, their desire for academic freedom might also be strong. In addition, perhaps their affiliation to their academic department will therefore be relatively weaker. In other cases, strong affiliation to the formal organisation is a necessity in order to protect academic freedom. In some countries, such as Germany and Finland, the right to academic freedoms is firmly established in the legislation (Karran 2008). There is an inherent and inevitable tension between institutional autonomy (in which management, funding and supervision functions are to the fore) and individual academics' freedom (in which unimpeded rights to individual-driven research and teaching are paramount) (Slawek 2012). From this perspective, institutional autonomy and academic freedom can present somewhat contradictory pictures in the academy, and this was one of the matters respondents identified in the EuroAC interviews.

From this brief consideration of academic work and the affiliations under which members of the academic profession conduct it, we move to a consideration of the changing academic profession, and academics' impressions of the shifting sands of working conditions.

5.3   Changing Working Conditions in Eight Countries

Researchers are aware that academics perceive that there has been change in higher education. The main issue about 'change' is whether or not it is change for the better. The EuroAC database reveals the views of European academics on this matter. For example, about 62 % of Austrian academics held the opinion that the situation has deteriorated, and nearly 55 % of German academics were of a similar opinion. However, in some countries perceptions were less pessimistic. The proportions of academics reporting deterioration were Croatia 20 %, Switzerland 27 %, Poland 29 % and Finland 34 % (EuroAC 2011).

Building on these observations by using the interview data from the eight countries, one concept stands out from the contextual change of employment conditions: there has been on-going *incremental change through a transition and transformation of the management* of higher education. Higher education institutions themselves or the organisations who act as employers of members of the academic profession have introduced result premium and other salary incentives and stronger managerial power e.g. in recruitment. The power of collegial bodies has clearly diminished when it comes to recruitment. In some countries these decisions have been made wholly incrementally by the higher education institutions themselves and in other countries these decisions are based on legislative changes prepared by the government.

Implications of a change due to this concept can be found in the interview data by studying some of the key variables. For instance the degree of seniority, in other words the division between junior and senior academics, is a hot topic in some countries in the discussion about obtaining a permanent or long-term position under the new employment legislation. This has been the case especially in Austria after the introduction of new employment legislation for university staff between 2002 and 2009 (EuroAC Context papers 2012). In addition, the more incremental power regarding employment conditions, for instance recruitment and result premiums, and seniority is heavily debated in Austria, as it is in Germany and Poland, which also apply the habilitation model that divides junior and senior academics. Seniority connected to old cultural layers is experienced as a hindering factor for better employment conditions by some interviewees from the newer member states of the European Union (EU) in this study.

Relative seniority has a major role in the conduct of the academic profession's work. This is because more senior members influence the recruiting of staff to undertake academic work, the training of those appointed to those positions, and evaluating their academic competence. Therefore senior academics carry the responsibility for the quality of work, enjoy high social prestige, and enjoy a profession based on a complex body of knowledge, regulatory mechanisms and ethics (Light 1974; Dill 1982).

Regarding differences between disciplines, the interviewees representing the humanities and social sciences seemed to be more concerned about the stronger influence of result premiums. Some of these disciplines have a national character and they cannot publish and participate on an international level and cannot therefore receive additional kudos for publishing in international journals. Interviewees in the humanities were also concerned about the increasing importance of external funding, since they find it difficult to attract external funders. Gender is another variable that stands out as a dividing line in employment conditions in some countries. At a general level, the academic profession reacts strongly on both rapid and incoherent legislative change (arguably the case in Romania) and too stable and conservative structures regarding employment conditions (arguably the case in Poland). Another interesting dimension is the implications of recession in the local economy. This has affected employment conditions in higher education, especially in Romania and Ireland.

5.3.1 Working Conditions and Employment Contracts

Working conditions are a crucial link between academic freedom and institutional objectives. The expression refers equally to the working environment as it does to employees' terms and conditions of employment. Good working conditions are often reported as being important for those (senior) academics who are actively involved in research and teaching, and less often for those academics with a research-only orientation (Teichler 2010). Also, public higher education institutions are increasingly adopting a model based on economic rationalism, 'product-orientation', individual productivity in research outputs and flexibility resulting in a loss of job security (Santiago and Carvalho 2008).

One of the issues raised by some interviewees was their dissatisfaction with employment relationships in countries with temporary public service contracts. Fixed-term employment contracts and increasing workloads are related (Germany, junior, female, university). In these eight countries and based on the interviews with junior academics, the early stages of career are based on project work and fixed term contracts. For most academics, seniority brings an opportunity for permanent employment, placed into context by a Swiss junior academic:

> Almost all contracts here are based on a specific project. The only way to maintain people within the group is to find funds. At the moment, I don't have a permanent contract. Only after several years is it possible for a person to have the opportunity to have a permanent contract. (Switzerland, junior, polytechnic, female)

Similar patterns were noted in Germany, where the trend is that positions in the career chain from postgraduate research posts up to post-doctoral posts are provided on fixed-term contracts. This is also where the major teaching load is carried in Germany as higher education institutions try to achieve more with less and in an environment of declining working conditions (Germany, junior, male, university). Another example of changing practices was identified:

> I have the feeling that when employees retire, they aren't 'replaced' properly. Sometimes a position will be split into two part-time jobs or even abolished. The employees are very important, but they get too little attention. (Germany, junior, female, polytechnic)

5.3.2 Promotion

If there is a clear academic career path, it is likely that the academic profession will be perceived in a positive light is. In some ways, this is an extension of the discussion on employment contracts. Many interviewees expressed a clear opinion on this matter. There are also reasons to worry about the attractiveness of the academic profession. Clear rules and procedures for employment and equivalent working conditions based on career stage are important. It was also reported that students believe that employment is still based on 'relationships', and that competence was of less concern (Romania, junior, male, university). That is, who you know is more important than what you know.

Other academics discussed the concept of multi-disciplinarity, and its potentially negative effect on career paths. Of course, this flies in the face of the rhetoric one hears from most universities, about their support for multi-disciplinary activities. One Polish colleague mentioned his disappointment about the narrow disciplinary paths of academic development. His view was that the existing system largely kills off interdisciplinary research efforts, because Polish science in general and higher education is dominated by a silo disciplinary structure of academic degrees followed by the tunnel vision of the academic oligarchy. Crossing disciplinary borders in social and behavioural sciences seems "to break existing tribal disciplinary hierarchies" and can cause problems in the process of academic promotion because the promotion is always in one specific discipline (Poland, junior, male, university).

In another case, the interviewee was an Irish polytechnic lecturer, who observed that there had been changes in what had been the typical career path. Criteria used increasingly in recent times for new appointments required applicants to have a PhD, and have a background in research and bringing research money to the School. In the past, a PhD qualification and involvement in research had been considered 'desirable', but now it had become virtually mandatory. This interviewee found this to be a controversial change because

> ... the last senior lecturer was (appointed)... with little or no teaching experience but they were heavily involved in research and immediately used that research money to buy out their time so they could concentrate entirely on research so really we (the School) didn't gain any expertise coming in. (Ireland, junior, polytechnic, male)

A similar increasing emphasis on research at the expense of teaching was noted by Leisyte, Enders and de Boer in their study of university researchers in the Netherlands and the UK (2009).

However, the same interviewee that also was of the opinion that the handling of appointments had become more professional in recent years. In the past "there was sort of a crony society" (Ireland, junior, male, polytechnic), in fact contrasting observations of a Romanian colleague (see earlier).

The fact that an academic future is harder to foresee is a challenge to academics in some countries. In Ireland, for example, some academics are resigned to the fact that promotion may never come, due to the economic climate. Consideration of early retirement therefore becomes more common. Such matters have an impact on overall job satisfaction. The general feeling is that things have worsened which has had a deleterious impact on enthusiasm (Ireland, junior, male, polytechnic).

The biggest challenge according to one Irish interviewee is the moratorium on employment being experienced in Irish higher education, due to the adverse national economic situation. First, if some programmes rely heavily on one or two staff members and if those members retire, those programmes are in danger. Second, the declining number of academics means a greater lecturing burden for the remaining staff. As one academic put it, "the profession of academia is actually currently suspended"; if academics don't engage in research then they are effectively "glorified teachers and our salaries will probably fall to match that", whereas just doing research isn't an option either because there is a need to train the next generation of students (Ireland, junior, male, polytechnic).

A Croatian interviewee was clearly concerned about career uncertainty. The next step after acquiring a PhD would be to advance along the career path. However, criteria have been changing in recent times. His mentor warned him he should always keep track of constantly changing advancement conditions and the relevant legislation. Considering all that, the interviewee concluded that there is no real certainty (Croatia, junior, male, university).

However within the same country but a different discipline, opposite views on the stability or uncertainty of conditions for advancement were expressed. This interviewee claimed that conditions for advancement to higher positions in her field of study had not changed for the past 20 years. She stressed that the quantity of research published was still what counts (but not their quality). Based on her personal experience, she also mentioned how committees for advancement based their assessments on subjective criteria, such as personal acquaintances (Croatia, senior, female, university). This theme was also noted by interviewees from Romania and Ireland.

One of the Polish interviewees described the pursuit for seniority in the Polish higher education system. The university management favours scholarly publications and good work with students. In particular, there is a form of growing pressure to deliver publications to academic journals. If junior academics do not achieve this, they can face serious consequences, including being laid-off (Poland, junior, male, university).

Polytechnics are newer institutions and lack the history and ballast of academic traditions, and therefore they do not offer a traditional academic career. According to a Swiss interviewee there are very few career possibilities (Switzerland, senior, male, polytechnic):

> Once you become a professor, which is only an acknowledgement, not a status, you can remain so for many years. This title is worthless outside.

The only possibility is to become head of department, meaning becoming part of the executive management.

> Besides, I don't even know if it is a reasonable ambition: you are a manager overwhelmed with administrative work making up 90 % of the job. Hence, there are different titles and positions, but you always do the same thing.

The interviewee said that there is a huge gap between polytechnics and universities.

> How can you publish if 95 % of the projects with industry are confidential? The only way is to apply to the Swiss national foundation.

Polytechnics' structures are hierarchical, and promotion and higher salaries are available for those occupying management positions but not for those in teaching positions. A Finnish interviewee mentioned a similar issue:

> Academic career opportunities are not that good in polytechnics. Most of the higher positions are administrative. Also, the salary incentives [for academics] are poor. Polytechnics are not for academic careers. To advance as a teacher here requires that you get satisfaction from your work and that you develop yourself and to have a PhD. I do not have one, so my chances to advance are grim. (Finland, junior, male, polytechnic)

Many of the interviewees from these eight countries feel that there is an increase in unfair practices in the changing academy. This significantly affects the attractiveness of an academic career. Changes in higher education structures means the co-existence of a variety of promotion systems, for example, based on traditional seniority and length of service or tenure-track. A traditional merit-based career including tenure is not a plausible option for everyone in these eight countries.

5.3.3   Institutional Autonomy and Academic Freedom

Institutional autonomy has had important implications regarding the formal status of the employees especially in Austria and Finland. According to the latest relevant legislation in these countries, university employees are no longer civil servants, but are now employed under ordinary employment contracts and their employment relationship is directly with universities as autonomous legal entities under public law. The findings from the interview data report that the Austrian interviewees are more worried about this than the Finnish ones. This might be partly because of the differences in implementation of the model in these countries and partly because in Austria new higher education legislation was under reform 2002–2009, in Finland much shorter period of 2008–2010. Fewer academics are now eligible for permanent positions in Austria. In Finland, this type of change was scarcely noticed by the interviewees. Both Finnish and Austrian interviewees stressed the importance of personal lobbying for better employment conditions in these new structures.

There are however also positive notions on individual academic freedom from each of the eight countries: "I have responsibilities that I need to meet. When they are done, one can have 'academic freedom' and pursue one's own ideas" (Germany, junior, male, university).

An Irish interviewee from a polytechnic acknowledged that he enjoys and appreciates academic freedom but at the same time the institution lacked ambition in that there is no pressure for academics to do research or to publish; therefore "I have freedom, but I wouldn't call it empowerment". The institution provides him with considerable creative freedom but it has created a workforce with relatively low motivation (Ireland, senior, male, polytechnic).

A Polish respondent identified a strong notion of autonomy at her institution. She finds the relationship between senior and junior academics in her department to be 'perfect'. She admits to enjoying a certain degree of professional 'freedom' in research and receives all the help she needs. But at the same time she observes relationships of different kind in some other departments of the university (Poland, junior, female, university).

A Swiss interviewee expressed her satisfaction with the freedom she had to undertake research of her own choosing although she was concerned about not having a permanent contract:

> We work together in the project. I have enough academic freedom, but if there is a problem I can ask for advice and help. I don't have a permanent contract at present. It takes several years before a person can have the opportunity to get one. (Switzerland, junior, female, polytechnic)

An Irish interviewee also stressed her academic freedom but she also stated that it varies from person to person and case to case. She believes that she has total freedom due to her line manager, but that isn't the case for all her colleagues (Ireland, junior, female, university).

A Croatian interviewee believes that as the amount of administration increases, the extent of academic freedom decreases, and that academic work is becoming strongly 'formalised' (Croatia, senior, female, university).

There are natural tensions between institutional autonomy and academic freedom. The modern trend in most higher education systems is for increasing institutional autonomy through so-called new public management. The fact that academics perceive an encroachment on their academic freedom can be seen from their responses to the CAP/EuroAC survey. For example, the proportion of academics perceiving a top down management style varied from 76 % of Irish academics to 42 % of Croatian academics. The proportion of academics that agreed that there was collegiality in decision making varied from 18 % in Ireland to 37 % of Croatian academics. There are clear differences between countries, but it could be argued that these responses indicate the reciprocal nature of institutional autonomy vs. academic freedom.

5.3.4   Control of Work

An extension of the discussion about the impact of top-down management and academic freedom can be seen in views about the control of work. The perception of academic freedom comes from having the right and ability to control one's own work schedule. Some of the interviewees find it difficult to set the limit for their teaching preparation, so there is a need for leadership in teaching. Still, there are differences between the countries. In the Finnish interviews, there was evidence that interviewees shared teaching (two or more teachers working together for the same class), and the expansion of online learning was causing increased pressure.

Many of the interviewees, but especially senior academics from every country, stated that they have good control of their *academic work*, that is research and teaching, but in recent years it has become more and more difficult for them to control their *administrative workload*. Regarding academic work, there is a general notion shared by most interviewees that teaching is a bit more institutionally regulated than research. However, there were also notions of increasing institutional strategic profiling of research areas. Some interviewees also stated that individual research profiling is increasingly important, e.g. regarding publishing and networking.

The general trend of accountability and indicators regarding control of work is described in detail by an Irish interviewee:

> the managers of his unit are engrossed with performance indicators and score cards because they have to quantify certain elements. Higher education professionals at his institution are not actively following up on their graduates' professional progress. So it begs the question: '...what are they measuring at the managerial level?' ... I sometimes wonder if they are measuring the right things.

He says that the problem stems from a lack of professionalisation of roles. Managers in the administration are seen as people in roles with grandiose titles who lack professional experience. The interviewee says he is seeking out ways to acquire new skills becoming but finds that there is a lack of drive in his unit. The interviewee acknowledged that he has considerable academic freedom which he enjoys and appreciates but at the same time the institution lacks ambition and drive due to the fact that the working environment is free from preasure to be successful. The institution provides him with a lot of freedom in terms of being creative but on the other hand, it has created less motivated people with low work ethic (Ireland, senior, male, polytechnic).

Another Irish interviewee said that the individual capacity to influence time planning has diminished, and this will have an impact on academic freedom. Insofar as the Irish academic year has been divided into short, tight modules, academics' work span is now over a shorter period of time and the year is mapped out more than before. The interviewee suggests

> there isn't the same time to work with the class and develop ideas as you had before, you are literally watching a calendar ... and there is another assessment due and before you know ... it is the end of semester... I don't like modularisation at all, it doesn't suit the students well, it certainly doesn't suit the lecturers well.

On a positive note, learning outcomes were introduced for the first time according to him. There is more direction in one's teaching and less need for interpretation which is subjective. The lectures delivered are becoming more homogenous as a result (Ireland, junior, male, polytechnic). A German interviewee stated that more restrictive working conditions also mean heavier workloads and this reduces academics' opportunity to contact employees other than those in their own academic department (Germany, junior, male, university). A Swiss interviewee noted that their university required everybody to work well, fast, reliably and autonomously (Switzerland, senior, female, university).

Another Swiss interviewee said that the administrative workload for academics has increased:

> I feel like I am controlled [by management] and I have no direct opportunities to change anything. In general I work more than 100 % and since I started working here, my workload has increased by 20 %, but this has gone all to administrative tasks. Research has diminished, proportionally. I was working in Austria before, and I had much more time for research. I can't say that pressures come from the dean's office, they come from what is decided in the administration and it is forwarded to me through the dean's office. Once decisions are taken, they cause pressure. (Switzerland, senior, male, university)

Some interviewees talked about the rapid changes and expansion of managerialism in the academy. At the same time, interviewees provided information about their declining influence in governance matters. However, this is only one side of the coin. The interviewees also showed clearly that the culture of the disciplines is still very strong, and that academic cultures continue to regulate conditions of employment as well as institutional structures.

5.3.5 Support

Support for those undertaking academic work is also needed due to the increasing obligations for academics to be 'accountable'. This is seen, for example, in documentation and reporting. Those who know the services and how to use them feel that service and support have increased at the same time as the demands have increased (Austria, junior. female, university). In many Romanian interviews it was also stressed that scholarly results are dependent on support services and some scholars feel that they lack such support. This may be due to fact that the selection of Romanian interviewees is focused on the natural and life sciences. However, similar attitudes were also reported in natural sciences in Finnish cases (professor, female, engineering), as some in the polytechnic sector also reported support services had improved in last 20 years (academic, junior, female, polytechnic). In the university sector, support services and management are in the middle of criticisms partly because they are associated to the reforms in management (e.g. increased self-reporting and reward-based salary negotiations) and have led to an increased workload for senior academics (Finland, senior, male, university).

In Ireland the financial crisis has weakened support services, according to a number of interviewees:

> A quality assurance person has come on stream in the recent years. When she initially joined the department there were several people working in support services whom had a positive impact in the institution. Unfortunately the financial crisis meant that they became part-time staff on limited contracts. (Ireland, junior, female, university)

5.3.6 Academics' Influence in Institutional Governance

In terms of influence, there are considerable differences between academic units. Levels in the capacity to influence are in decline due to stratification and top-down models of management. It is partly because influence is not necessarily a personal issue, but an issue for an academic unit or research team (Finland, junior,, female, polytechnic). Some Romanian junior academics reported a lack of influence in institutional decision making, which seems to be a consequence of stratified management. In the Finnish case, this does not necessarily depend on status but rather on management:

> My time use and planning is influenced by both external and internal issues. At the moment, for instance, we are evaluating all the salary tables and salary negotiations. There is a lot of reporting to the Ministry of Education and a lot of statements about degrees and dissertations. (Finland, senior, female, university)

Measuring student satisfaction and also measuring the research performance of individual academics has been are cent phenomenon at the university. In the last 4 years expectations have become more explicit. Another important factor is associated with the arrival of the information technology. Electronic administration and accounting systems such as SAP must have an impact on management. A Polish respondent admitted to having little influence on managerial decisions taken either centrally or at the departmental level. The interviewee saw this situation as a direct result of the fact that he is a member of neither the university senate nor departmental board (Poland, junior, male, university).

Another Polish junior academic reported university governance as being traditional and is based on collegial bodies such as the university senate or departmental boards. Senior academics are in the majority and have the authority to propose new initiatives. Therefore, they are the really influential players in these collegial bodies. The respondent had no influence on university governance, institutional policy and admits to have weak and indirect impact on her university department. Her influence on the department depends on the leader of her academic unit who often listens to the opinions of his junior fellows and passes other senior scholars during the meeting of board of department (Poland, junior, female, university).

A German interviewee sees the increasing amount of evaluation conducted at universities as diminishing the influence of academic staff (Germany, senior, male. polytechnic). Similar notions on relatively weak institutional influence were made by interviewees from every country, whether from a university or a polytechnic. Even department heads felt their influence on institutional issues to be limited.

However, there are also views from every country that there actually is a possibility to exert influence on the institutional governance, especially for senior academics, but they do not like to use this option because it reduces the time they have for academic work. This view was expressed, for instance, by an Austrian senior academic: The interviewee played an active role in strategic development processes, but despite being involved at many levels, these were not necessarily the areas that he wanted to influence: "More participation does not make you happier; it depends on the content" (Austria, senior, male, university).

5.3.7   Collegiality

Socialisation is a means of understanding the norms and expectations of an academic community (Clarke et al. 2012). Collegiality, in its turn, is a form of governance that leaves academic staff free from direct external interference (Elton 2010). According to Tapper and Palfreyman (1998), collegiality is more than a question of buildings, space and shared functions. It also embodies ideas, university governance and the relationship between academic colleagues. Lack of collegiality can affect academics' morale (Finland, senior, male, university), and weakening of collegiality can lead to stronger political involvement in the academy (Austria, senior, male, university). Collegial decision making has decreased. There is some kind of democracy, but the decisions are made by those from the upper levels. This affects the atmosphere, and there can be more frustration (Finland, junior, female, university).

Under these circumstances, joining and being part of the academy is a complex process, and some interviewees described that stage as: "I had no manual, nobody told me what to do and invariably something happened and I had to react to it and fix it" (Ireland, junior, male, university). Similar views came from Croatia:

> Formally there is an opportunity to discuss anything at the college level. Most people, however, do not use that right, and in almost 100 % of cases what management suggests is what is eventually accepted. Of course, people in management are not the only ones responsible for [the situation]. Uninterested staff members, lack of criticism and the principle 'I'll scratch your back, you scratch mine', which is deeply rooted, lead to opportunism. People have become used to it and don't think about it anymore. Their only goal is to make council sessions as short as possible so that they can go home. (Croatia, senior, male, university)

A German interviewee noted a weakening of the collegial body, but not necessary as a negative phenomenon. In the interviewee's opinion, there are set boundaries to wheeling and dealing and stagnancy in decision processes. This respondent was content with the faculty's management. The last 3 years have brought out a strong faculty structure, which he considers to be a positive attribute. As a representative of the institution, the interviewee can influence some of the structures, but this falls outside his priorities. The interviewee can organise his own time, but he is subject to restrictions by appointments with the committee, which he can mark out himself, too (Germany, senior, male, university). A junior academic German interviewee said that it was possible to exert collegial influence but it was time consuming. Employees who work full time have more opportunities to participate in collegial decision-making processes. Working at the university is perceived as self-discipline oriented. There is no committee work because he lacks the time.

Colleagues working in full time positions or working more time at the chair have better opportunities to work in committees (Germany, junior, male, university).

An Irish interviewee believes more restrictions are now placed on academics and that there is less collegiality. In the past "there might have been a view that there was sort of benign chaos...but there was a level of trust". Now there is a lot of paperwork involved and managers who will only correspond by e-mail, "these passive-aggressive e-mails" (Ireland. senior, female, university).

However, in countries like Poland, which has gone through few legislative and governance changes during the last 15 years, university governance is still based on collegial bodies which are dominated by a range of interest groups. If one is a member of a ruling interest group, then s/he has wider access to resources. This is a major mechanism for the distribution of research funding in some departments (Poland, junior, female, university).

In some of the countries, the interviews tell us that an academic can become a full and respected member of the academic community when he or she has been awarded the so called habilitation degree (and therefore gains the possibility to apply for a permanent position as a post-doc.) A Polish interviewee said that representation of junior academics in various boards has only symbolic meaning and in fact they are powerless. But on the other hand, the respondent admitted that he would have no time for attending meetings. Therefore, even if there is such an opportunity he would not like to be involved in governance processes (Poland, junior, male, university).

A Swiss interviewee stressed the anonymous institutional character of collegiality:

> I can't say that pressures come directly from the dean's office; they come from what is decided in the administration and it is forwarded to me through the dean office. Once decisions have been taken, there is pressure for conformity.

The interviewee cited the example of an 'anonymous' decision that required all professors and institutes to have a website (Switzerland, senior, male, university).

A number of interviewees also spoke of senior academics attempting to avoid serving in collegially elected academic manager positions. For instance a Swiss professor noted the rotating process, such as it being professors' duty to act as the head of the department for 2 years. But the professors don't seem to like it. Few take up the option of serving for a second term because nobody wants to give up their research to focus on governance and management issues. Having a practice of rotation for this position of head of the department also allows them to keep the consensual aspect of their decision they make on research or hiring. This interviewee emphasised the collegial aspect of their organisation (Switzerland, academic, senior, male, university). An Irish senior was also of this view. The head of department who is a professor is obliged by her or his contract to take the post up for 6 years and then it will be passed to another member of staff on a rotation system (Ireland, senior, female, university). Similar phenomena were also reported from most of the other countries.

Another Irish interviewee reported similar views on academic freedom and collegiality. He has been on the academic council for a number of years, and was of the opinion that the academic council simply ratifies decisions made by the governing authority. He feels restricted by timetabled duties such as lectures and practical classes, but in terms of research "I am my own boss; in terms of my interaction with industry I'm given free rein" (Ireland, senior, male, university).

5.3.8 Performance Based Salary Components

There has been constant incremental change in governance modes of higher education institutions that affect the employment conditions both financially and through merit systems. Most of the countries examined show trends towards offering result premiums at least for some sections of the academic profession. The required attributes for permanency, especially tenured professorships or long-term contracts are becoming higher due to international competition. Interviewees from some countries point out the contradictions between the academic grass-roots (for instance departments) and central administration of higher education institutions or the government regarding this. This scenario was especially evident among a number of Austrian interviewees, and two of the foreign-born academics from Finland noted the gap between reality and rhetoric, particularly in human resources matters.

One of the Austrian interviewees had been involved in the introduction of a performance based salary system. According to him it was based mainly a database system of records of academics' 'performance'. He described a general difficulty in measuring scholarly and didactic achievements. He was convinced that this kind of quality management has an effect on academics through personnel decisions such as promotion and salary increases, because those decisions become increasingly dependent on the basis of performance records in the quality management database. This database is now accepted by most academics. As a result of the introduction of performance measurement "departments have become more active as a group" and reporting duties have also led to an increase in competition between institutes: who/what institute has more publications, entries in the database (Austria, male, university).

A Finnish professor observed the following about the performance based salary system at Finnish universities:

> Salary incentives for those who have achieved good results were introduced in 2005. But we have not always managed to take that into account in our budget. So being fair to everybody with this problematic situation doesn't necessarily mean that you are fair to each individual in each salary negotiation. This is a very difficult situation. (Finland, Senior, male, university)

5.3.9 *Seniority and Employment Conditions*

Older interviewees from countries from the newer EU member states (Croatia, Poland and Romania in this study) noted a general Europeanisation of the structures, employment conditions and content of their academic work. They exemplify this by participation in European projects and networks in research and in curriculum development according to the Bologna process. According to one Croatian interviewee, the strong bonds with the government are still there, especially among the university administration:

> People see themselves as civil servants who register and take notes on what they must report to government. There is not enough of managerial spirit in university administration. (Croatia, senior, male, university)

In the Romanian case, the employment conditions are turbulent because of rapid political change and incoherent higher education strategies during the past 20 years. Many Romanian interviewees stated that there had been too many legislative changes. Most Romanian interviewees were stressed because of the lack of a coherent personnel policy for higher education. In addition, the public sector in Romania suffered from an economic crisis in 2008–2010 which led to a cut-back in the salaries for the academic profession by an average of 25 %. In Poland, the case was the opposite. There have not been any major reforms regarding employment conditions since the early 1990s. Poland is perhaps the country among these eight to have undergone the least number of governance changes in its higher education institutions during the last 15 years (OECD 2008; 2011).

Quite a few Polish interviewees mentioned the habilitation system as causing a too strong dividing line between the junior and senior academics in the Polish university system and noted that it conserves existing governance structures. University governance is the subject of national legal regulation and many respondents do not expect rapid changes in this matter.

The habilitation is a strong dividing line also in the German-speaking university systems of Austria, Germany and Switzerland. According to many interviewees from these countries, habilitation creates a glass ceiling for junior academics and makes their chances to gain better employment conditions grim. The previously reported legislative change in Austria has worsened the possibilities for long-term contracts for non-habilitated academics. Most of the Austrian junior academics interviewed strongly opposed this. On the other hand a number of older Austrian interviewees also criticised the older model where almost 100 % of the academic staff had permanent contracts and some of them ceased to be productive.

Conclusions

Change in higher education in the eight countries analysed for the purposes of this chapter has been derived from a range of sources. For example, in six of the countries, vertical diversification, via the introduction of a polytechnic (or equivalent) sector has been a major driver of change. The structure of higher education was changed in Austria, Croatia, Finland, Poland, Romania and Switzerland through legislation when these countries established their respective polytechnic sectors during the 1990s. Germany and Ireland established their polytechnics earlier, and in these two countries, the binary model was institutionalised before the new public management trends of the 1980s and 1990s.

According to some of the interviewees in the countries in which the binary model was not introduced until the 1990s, the polytechnics have come to symbolise new public management, managerialism and stakeholder values. As an example, a number of Finnish interviewees from both sectors stressed that the polytechnics never established a collegial culture that could be compared with the traditional decision-making in universities. This affects the conditions regarding recruitment, for instance. In polytechnics, many of the employees were hired by managers but in many European universities, the collegial bodies still have their say in recruitment decision, although their power is diminishing. Teichler's (2008) article presents an analysis of vertical and horizontal diversification of European higher education.

Legislation other than that to introduce a new higher education sector has also been important in some countries. In addition to the introduction of a binary system, legislation in Austria and Finland sought to provide some institutions with more autonomy than they had enjoyed in the past. The quest for institutional autonomy and new financial structures were undertaken through legislation in the early twenty-first century (Austria 2002 and Finland 2010). The most important change in legislation in these two counties regarding the autonomy of universities has been their transition from being governmental institutions under direct budget control to becoming autonomous legal entities under public law.

The general autonomy of institutions from the state is regarded with mixed feelings by academics. According to some interviewees, it gives higher education institutions a chance to create and focus on their own strategic priorities. On the other hand, some interviewees think that this will increase the risk of arbitrary management even at the macro-level. Some interviewees (mostly the same ones that made the previous observation) stated that the risk of arbitrary micro-level management has increased because of the decrease in collegiality.

Among the many changes noted by interviewees has been the expansion of 'administration' and bureaucracy in general. This change in the composition has been noted by Tight (2010). By way of example, according to one Finnish

(continued)

respondent, her university is hierarchic, and there are now many non-academic ways of action, and it is more school-like than the university at which she studied and subsequently worked. She described her current university as being more like a polytechnic than a university; students now have to enrol and be assessed in many compulsory courses (Finland, senior, female, university).

In all eight countries it is evident that institutional level strategies promote interdisciplinary research, and the international research funding seems to favour this trend. The interviews provided clear information about the difficulties of academics who work in interdisciplinary research and teaching. In addition, there is evidence of vertical diversification of working conditions and the research/teaching nexus between universities and polytechnics. This seems to be the case regardless of the age or maturity of the binary system – Ireland has had polytechnics for decades while they were introduced less than 20 years ago in Finland, Austria and Switzerland. Many of the interviews with university sector employees in the EuroAC project and previous research (Leisyte et al. 2009) confirm that successful research is better promoted than successful teaching within many European universities. This can be seen as a part of the vertical diversification trend (Teichler 2008).

The formal organisation is still relevant for supporting work itself, but the strong stratification can lead to dissatisfaction with working conditions. The control of work and time does not necessarily arise with seniority. For junior academics, pressures to publish and internationalisation create pressure and restrict the 'freedom' of work. For senior academics and those in management positions, working conditions are limited by administrative duties and responsibilities of the wider disciplinary networks.

The changes in the type of work (public/common contract) do not necessarily exert any relevant influence on the work conditions. In the longer term, it might affect the selection of the academic profession and, above all, those who agree to operate in teams and accept limited academic freedom. At the same time, the ability to acquire academic freedom by their own work is separated from organisational structures.

Competition and pressure are part of academic work, so many interviewees did not speak much about their personal views. The existence of pressure seems to be a general feeling, but some attitudes came out of interviews quite often. For junior academics, the most evident source of pressure is having short, fixed-term positions, including tenure track in the countries in which it exists.

The second highest source of pressure concerns publishing, which is a source of pressure, but is also a source of individual appreciation. For many scholars time is very tight, and it is a challenge to work under pressure to meet the many dead-lines (Austria, junior, university, male,). It seems that the

(continued)

pressure for junior academics to publish is greater than for senior academics, but there did not seem to be any obvious differences based on gender. For Austrian senior academics, the most important source of pressure is that they have to undertake administrative tasks not closely connected to their work as academics. For Romanian interviewees there is slightly different angle with frustration caused by bureaucratic activities and an increase in the pressure from management (professor, male, natural sciences). Many Romanian interviewees also mention the frequent changes in governance modes as a stressful factor. Other sources of pressure mentioned by respondents from several countries are international mobilisation and measurement of performance.

References

Aarrevaara, T., & Dobson, I. R. (2012). Movers and shakers: Academics as stakeholders – Do they control their own work? In U. Teichler & E. A. Höhle (Eds.), *Work situation, views and activities of the academic professions: Findings of a survey in twelve European countries* (pp. 159–181). Dordrecht: Springer.

Aarrevaara, T., Dobson, I. R., & Postareff, L. (2013, in press). The scholarly question in Finland. To teach or not to teach. In A. Arimoto, W. Cummings, J. Shin, & U. Teichler (Eds.), *Teaching and research in contemporary higher education: Systems, activities and rewards* (pp. 135–152). Dordrecht: Springer.

Brew, A. (2008). Disciplinary and interdisciplinary affiliations of experienced researchers. *Higher Education, 56*, 423–438.

Clarke, M., Hyde, A., & Drennan, J. (2012). Professional identity in higher education. In B. M. Kehm & U. Teichler (Eds.), *The academic profession in Europe: New tasks and new challenges* (pp. 7–21). Dordrecht: Springer.

Coates, H., Dobson, I., Goedegebuure, L., & Meek, V. L. (2009). Australia's casual approach to its academic teaching. *People and Place, 17*(4), 47–54.

da Zilva, D. (2010). *Academic units in a complex, changing world – Adaptation and resistance.* Dordrecht/New York: Springer.

Dill, D. (1982). The structure of the academic profession: Towards a definition of ethical issues. *The Journal of Higher Education, 53*(3), 255.

Dobson, I. R. (2012). *University staffing: Do we have the right blend?* Paper presented at the Tertiary Education and Management Conference, 16–19 September. Adelaide, Australia. Retrieved from http://temc.org.au/documents/49-TEMC2012-Stream-Resized.pdf

Elton, L. (2010). Complexity theory – An approach to assessment that can enhance learning and – More generally. *Assessment & Evaluation in Higher Education, 35*(5), 637–646.

EuroAC. (2011). *Tables by country* (0). Unweighted data. INCHER, University of Kassel.

EuroAC. (2012). Context papers.

Karran, T. (2008). Academic freedom in Europe: A preliminary comparative analysis. *Higher Education Policy, 20*(3), 289–313.

Leisyte, L., Enders, J., & de Boer, H. (2009). The balance between teaching and research in Dutch and English universities in the context of university governance reforms. *Higher Education, 58*(5), 619–635.

Light, D. (1974). The structure of the academic professions. *Sociology of Education, 47*(1), 2–28.

Locke, W., Fisher, D., & Cummings, W. K. (2011). Comparative perspectives: Emerging findings and further investigations. In W. Locke, W. K. Cummings, & D. Fisher (Eds.), *Changing*

governance and management in higher education. The perspectives of the academy.
Dordrecht/New York: Springer.

Marginson, S. (2009). The knowledge economy and higher education: A system for regulating the value of knowledge. *Higher Education Management & Policy, 21*(1), 39–53.

OECD. (2008). *Education at a glance 2008. OECD indicators.* Paris: Organisation for Economic Co-operation and Development.

OECD. (2011). *Education at a glance. OECD indicators.* Paris: Organisation for Economic Co-operation and Development.

Santiago, R., & Carvalho, T. (2008). Academics in a new work environment: The impact of new public management on work conditions. *Higher Education Quarterly, 62*(3), 204–223.

Slawek, T. (2012). Autonomy, education, debt. In C. Koscielniak & J. Makowski (Eds.), *Freedom, equality, university.* Warsaw: Civic Institute.

Tapper, T., & Palfreyman, D. (1998). Continuity and change in the collegial tradition. *Higher Education Quarterly, 52*(2), 142–161.

Teichler, U. (2008). Diversification? Trends and explanations of the shape and size of higher education. *Higher Education, 56,* 349–379.

Teichler, U. (2010): The Diversifying Academic Profession? European Review, Vol. 18, Supplement S 157–179.

Teichler, U. (2012). Diversity of higher education in Europe and the findings of a comparative study of the academic profession. In A. Curaj et al. (Eds.), *European higher education at the crossroads: Between the Bologna process and national reforms* (pp. 485–509). Dordrecht: Springer.

Tight, M. (2010). Are academic workloads increasing? The post-war survey evidence in the UK. *Higher Education Quarterly, 64*(2), 200–215.

Trow, M. (1999). From mass higher education to universal access: The American advantage. *Minerva, 37,* 303–328.

Chapter 6
Academics' Perceptions of Their Professional Contexts

Marie Clarke, Jonathan Drennan, Abbey Hyde, and Yurgos Politis

6.1   Introduction

The role of the academic is recognised internationally as comprising teaching, research and administration, however the concept of an academic profession is relatively new and includes a mixture of profiles. This is due to the move to mass higher education, the development of international markets for students, the establishment of quality assurance systems increased competition between universities and other organisations in the knowledge economy (Johnson and Deem 2003). The diversity within the profession suggests that it cannot be viewed as one where traditional divisions within the role are clear-cut. The findings from the eight country EuroAC study presented in this chapter interpreted within Bourdieu's sociology of academia (1988) highlights the tensions academics experience in their professional roles, teaching, researching, managing, writing and networking (Blaxter et al. 2006). The authors argue that academics experience significant challenges between the scientific capital (or prestige) routes and the academic capital routes within their roles and the demands made by the institutions where they work.

M. Clarke (✉) • A. Hyde • Y. Politis
School of Education, University College Dublin, Roebuck Castle, Belfield, Dublin 4, Ireland
e-mail: Marie.Clarke@ucd.ie

J. Drennan
Healthcare Research, Centre for Innovation and Leadership in Health Sciences, Faculty of Health Sciences, University of Southampton, Southampton, UK

© Springer International Publishing Switzerland 2015   117
T. Fumasoli et al. (eds.), *Academic Work and Careers in Europe: Trends, Challenges, Perspectives*, The Changing Academy – The Changing Academic Profession in International Comparative Perspective 12, DOI 10.1007/978-3-319-10720-2_6

6.2   Theoretical Framework

Bourdieu (1988) uses the concept of habitus to explain the sociology of academia. Habitus refers to persistent outlooks (perceptions, appreciations, behaviours), which are internalized by particular social groups. The habitus of academics incorporates many assumptions, beliefs, and behaviours surrounding the question of what it means to be an academic (Bourdieu 1988). Habitus is what forms opinions and expresses much of the socialisation that individuals of particular groups have undergone. In each social field agents struggle to accumulate and maximise forms of symbolic capital. According to Bourdieu (1988) there are two routes for academic careers, the scientific capital (or prestige) route and the academic capital route. The former emphasises research, with research funding, research projects and publications the main forms of capital, the latter focuses on teaching, academic networking, leadership and the protection of disciplinary boundaries. These routes impact on the five elements of the academic role teaching, researching, managing, writing and networking (Blaxter et al. 2006). Teaching is viewed as the facilitation of learning through a variety strategies in different contexts (ibid.). The research role involves working as an individual or as part of a team. Managing within this framework comprises administrative, developmental and political roles, which involve running programmes, departments, faculties, institutions, societies and professional bodies (ibid.). Writing is identified as reporting academic work to different audiences, those with a general interest in the area and those who are experts in the area. Publications from this process can include books, articles, course materials, reports, memoranda or other forms of presentation (ibid.). The final role in this categorization is networking which focuses on using personal and professional contacts (academics and non-academics), to maintain and develop academic careers and research initiatives. This is not institutionally based and can extend beyond disciplinary boundaries. It may take place within, between or outside departments and institutions, and may or may not be confined to a particular subject area or their role (ibid.).

6.3   Academics Perceptions of Their Professional Roles

Many changes have been identified in the role performed by the professional academic. Teaching has become a more diverse activity. The changing student profile also impacts upon academics. Rolfe (2002) found that lecturers viewed students' approaches to their university education as instrumental and expressed disappointment that present-day students seemed uninterested in their chosen degree subject and required more instruction and guidance. For some lecturers, this devalued the teaching experience (Rolfe 2002).

The research role has changed from being closely associated to the researcher. Research groups; temporary grant-funded research centres, clusters and alliances now dominate the discourse (Mittelstrass 2010). Academics are expected to be research active and publish in journal articles (Murray and Cunningham 2011). However, there are only a certain number of journals and there is a limited amount of research funding. The pressure to publish (Wellington and Torgerson 2005) has been accentuated in a context where securing research funding is dependent on research publications (Murphy 1998). The perception of research as a high status activity is a common theme across the literature. Promotion to posts requires not just evidence of academic writing, but also the capacity to lead research teams and organise the activities of others (Hyde et al. 2011). Securing research funding is regarded as a key component of the academic role. Lepori et al. (2007) using data from universities in 11 European countries (Czech Republic, Denmark, France, Germany, Hungary, Italy, the Netherlands, Norway, Spain, Switzerland, UK), found that in the period 1995–2003 almost all of the institutions in the study increased their share of grants and contracts in total revenues.

McInnis (2006) suggests that an issue of major concern within higher education is the nature of the relationship between academics and administrators, which can generate difficulties for both sides. Academics have expressed dissatisfaction with administrative burdens, which have increased their workload. Cheng (2010) found that changes in the higher education system produced more administrative workload, but there were fewer administrators at the departmental level to do the work. Consequently, academics were required to take on more administrative roles, even though their teaching and research workloads were not reduced. Many of the issues that have emerged in other studies are also present in the findings from the current study.

6.4 Results

The data from the semi-structured interviews conducted in the eight countries participating in the EuroAC project highlights the significant challenges faced by academics within the specific elements of their roles.

6.4.1 Teaching

Within the teaching role a number of issues emerged in relation to recent changes in pedagogical approaches; time constraints; diversity of student populations with varied expectations and greater emphasis on quality procedures.

6.4.1.1 Changes in Teaching

Change in pedagogy was a common theme among participants. The following comments reflected the general views:

in the past 20–25 years teaching methodology changed. Content didn't change as much as the way it is presented changed. Teachers are expected to teach in a new, contemporary way, which wasn't the case 25 years ago. (Croatia, Male, Uni)

lecturers must nowadays be facilitators of learning, not only transmitters of knowledge. The content of teaching is changing here. Progressive teachers do not give ordinary passive lectures any more. They try to teach the students by letting them do things by themselves. We should talk more of learning than teaching. I think enabling learning is more demanding than teaching. (Finland, Male, Polytech)

Some academics expressed concern that the number of direct contact teaching hours with students was decreasing. One participant explained:

contact hours in teaching are decreasing all the time... This requires new teaching methods and use of social media. Pedagogy should be developed to reach the goals set for teaching and learning. Especially new modes for teaching in addition to face-to-face teaching are needed. (Finland, Male, Polytech)

The decrease in contact time was perceived to impact negatively on student experience. Participants reflecting this general view commented that:

we aren't able to show the students how much fun specialization can bring, because they have too many things to do. (Germany, Male, Uni)

there isn't the same time to work with the class and develop ideas as you had before, you are literally watching a calendar ... I don't like modularisation at all, it doesn't suit the students well, it certainly doesn't suit the lecturers well. (Ireland, Male, IoT)

The associated tasks with new approaches to teaching, such as continuous assessment, small group teaching and the development of new programmes were also viewed as very time consuming. Participants' views were characterised by such remarks as:

it is necessary (to spend) more time for the new commitments and responsibilities such as tutorial activity, the assurance of the continuous learning, the promoting of the new academic programmes. (Romania, Fem, Uni)

teaching requires much more service than before E-learning, email communication. (Austria, Male, Uni.)

Some participants raised concerns about the absence of a clear rationale for changes to university programmes. The following comment was illustrative of the general view:

introducing changes to modules for instance should reflect student evaluations, changes in teaching practice and/or changes in society. It is important to have a rationale for why you are changing something, why you are introducing something new (Ireland, Fem, Uni).

Participants in the study also reflected on the diversity within the student populations that they were expected to teach.

6.4.1.2   Diverse Student Populations

The changing nature of the student profile posed a number of challenges for participants. Participants commented on the fact that lecture settings now included many different age groups with varied experiences, who were in pursuit of different qualification. This general view is reflected in the following comment:

> there are more and more students and the number of formalities has increased, because the students often study in different conditions (e.g. master/diploma). Furthermore the student (cohort has) become more and more heterogeneous: There are more career changers or from other vocational education. (Germany, Fem, Uni)

This diversity impacted upon teaching performance.

6.4.1.3   Teaching Performance

The institutional emphasis on teaching performance emerged as an important issue for participants. Many referred to the issue of quality. The following comment illustrates the general view:

> in teaching more attention will be paid in its quality, and if someone is considered to be a weak teacher, their actions will be watched more closely. (Finland, Male, Uni)

The complexity of quality assurance with reference to teaching performance was also referred to and this impacted negatively on delivering quality teaching:

> new study programs are being accredited the quality assurance system is increasingly complex. (Romania, Fem, Uni)
>   everything related to the quality management sabotages even the process quality itself. (Romania, Male, Uni)

The evaluation of teaching also emerged as a significant issue for participants in the study. That general view was reflected in the following comments:

> teaching is more professionalised because there is pressure to evaluate. (Ireland, Fem, Uni)
>   you have to be sure that the quality of teaching is adequate and the student evaluations are reasonable and all that and if you can do that it is ok. (Switzerland Male, Uni)

It is clear from the data that academics from the EuroAC study countries faced a number of new challenges in their teaching role. This was also their experience when they discussed their role as researchers.

6.4.2   Research

Participants offered a range of perspectives with reference to their role as researchers. They focused on the institutional emphasis placed on research output and productivity, the emphasis on securing funded research and time constraints related to pursuing research.

6.4.2.1 Institutional Emphasis on Research Activity

Participants had noticed that a greater emphasis was placed on research by their respective institutions. The following comment reflects the general view:

> mainstream research is expected if you don't do it, they look at you, as if you're stupid. (Germany, Male, Uni)
>
> there certainly also external pressure because there is a matrix that the university wants to use to determine how much funding every unit deserves there is external pressure to do research, to attract funding, and to update the research profile. (Ireland, Male, Uni)

Reference was also made to an increased monitoring of research performance. Participants suggested that higher education institutions reorganised their own structures in order to actively pursue a research orientation. The following comment illustrates a general perception:

> in 2008 the entire Management system was redesigned. The emphasis has shifted to research. (Romania, Male, Uni)

The efforts made by higher education institutions to monitor research outputs was referred to by participants as captured in the following comment:

> the university management expects research outcomes and invest lots of resources to monitor research performance of departments research performance is evaluated in details by special committee on departmental level. (Poland, Male, Uni)

It also emerged that institutions also emphasised research activity by using non-formal approaches:

> there is a flow of unofficial information and raising pressure on individual academics to deliver more research outcomes publish or perish. (Poland, Fem, Uni)

It was generally felt that this approach had influenced the views of younger academics the following comment captured that view:

> most junior staff worship of work is focussed only to produce publications and relationships to go abroad in order to obtain large financial profits from various projects. This mentality leads to de-professionalisation. (Romania, Male, Uni)

According to a number of participants the prominence accorded to research activity has changed the focus within higher education institutions where less time is now given to teaching. This general view is reflected in the following comment:

> if you look at recent years research has been viewed as more important, stronger, so it also means very concretely that our activity ratio, our educational activity decreased. (Switzerland, Male, Uni)
>
> One participant viewed his university as an institution akin to an industrial park with a range of companies though this was a minority view:
>
> a big collection of small companies. Each research group is relatively independent. (Switzerland, Male, Uni)

For those participants who had teaching contracts in institutions which had changed their focus to prioritise research this was quite challenging. The following comment illustrates a general perception:

there is a greater demand on us these days to be more research intensive. My job description is quite focused on teaching. So if I want to do as much research as is expected for being successful in academia I have to raise external funds and take periodic leave from my ordinary job if I want to do more research. (Finland, Fem, HEI)

It emerged from the study that changes in institutional culture also impacted upon academics capacity to become involved in research.

6.4.2.2   Institutional Culture

Those participants who were employed to teach found it very difficult to get the time to engage in research. The following comments illustrate this view:

university teachers do not have time to pursue their research work. (Croatia, Male, Uni)
    research-professorships were shortened. Instead university professorships were established, which mainly engaged in teaching. It is not possible to research any more. (Germany, Male, Uni)

For participants working in institutions where teaching was the main activity, lack of time, lack of ethos and lack of mentoring support to engage in research emerged as significant challenges:

Academics have 16 contact hours a week, which doesn't leave much time for research. There isn't an ethos for research. . . I didn't publish because really there was nobody to talk about publishing. (Ireland, Fem, IoT)

Many participants referred to pressure of time with reference to research engagement. It was the general view that more time was spent on the administrative side of research than engaging in the research itself. The following comment reflects this general view:

less time to engage in research work and increasingly occupied with administration around research. (Croatia, Male, Uni)

Securing funded research presented a number of challenges for academics in higher education.

6.4.2.3   Securing Funded Research

Funded research played an important part in participants' perceptions of their research role. The importance of external funding, relationships with industry, the constant requirement to secure funding streams, the short-term nature of such funding and the lack of institutional support were issues that participants raised. External funding was considered critical to higher education institutions due to the cut backs in public funding. This general view is reflected in the following comments:

the basic funding will not increase anymore. (Finland, Male, Uni)
  the financial situation at university has worsened. (Germany, Fem, Uni)

Some participants considered that political influences and the development of close relationships with industry had resulted in universities placing more emphasis on funded research. The following comment is illustrative of that general view:

External funding or industry partnerships are now a political aim. Today, however, certain external funding quotas are required by the professors. (Germany, Male, Uni)

In order to sustain research participants felt pressured to access funding streams frequently. This view was reflected in the following comments:

within institutes you have to obtain research funds that help financing the institute, provide new competences, resources, knowledge. (Switzerland, Male, Uni)
  every researcher acts as a manager: searching for funds, conceiving projects. Every person is made responsible for research and management, depending on the size of the research unit. (Switzerland, Fem, Uni)

Much of the funding is short term and for many participants this was perceived as having a negative impact on the quality of the research:

the short-term funding provided for research will influence quality of research. (Finland, Male, Uni)

The support structures required at institutional level in relation to securing funded research were not considered adequate though improvements were acknowledged:

I am disappointed with our administrative staff. We have to work more and more with funding applications. (Finland, Fem, Uni)
  Incompetence. (Austria, Male, Uni)
  administration is gradually changing, demonstrating more positive approach to new research initiatives. (Poland, Male, Uni)

For participants many of the demands placed on academics in their research role centred on the ability to network and engage in collaboration.

6.4.2.4   Networking and Collaboration

Networking and collaboration was identified as being an important element of the academic role. Participants in the study referred to the importance of being active in international networks and engaging in collaborative research activity which often was outside their own subject specialism. This view is reflected in the following comments:

the funding allocation and sources have changed some projects are co-funded with researchers from the US. (Ireland, Fem, Uni)
  there is more collaboration with other scientists in other countries nowadays, and more orientation towards research and broadening of the scope from own subject to others as well. (Finland, Fem, Uni)

The traditional role of the academic researcher working on their own has changed:

> research has professionalised in a way, that there is no anymore individual research, but instead bigger research groups. (Finland, Fem, Uni)
>   the old model of the academic who gives classes, does research and almost works solo, as an independent agent is contrasted to the academic arena as it has transformed, especially in the research front where more and more research is thematic and collaborative. (Ireland, Male, Uni)

Key to these developments is the ongoing requirement to develop new skills and competencies.

6.4.3   Acquisition of New Skills and Competencies

For a number of participants the acquisition of new skills and competences was considered very important. The following comments illustrate that general view:

> an academic needs to be this blend of specialist/administrator/HR/finance/Head . . .seems to be this conglomerate person. (Ireland, Fem, IoT)
>   I notice huge quantities of knowledge are expected of researchers, knowledge no one could possibly have acquired during their official education. (Croatia, Male, Uni)
>   new roles, tasks and professional obligations, which engage academics to train and develop new skills and competences. (Romania, Male, Uni)

Participants in the study identified a number of areas where new skills and competences were required as a result of changes that had occurred in their roles. With reference to teaching the majority of participants referred to the need to secure qualifications in the area:

> new staff are required to get their certificate in teaching and learning. (Ireland, Fem, IoT)

Supervising students was also considered to be a more professional activity. One participant's comment reflected the general view:

> competence requirements have increased, at least in professorships. For example, supervision is more professional and you have to keep on track of several things constantly. (Finland, Fem, Uni)

In the research area it was clear that participants considered the acquisition of new skills and competencies to be very important. The following comment illustrates participants' views:

> a relatively new phenomenon is that in order to get research grants academics must learn how to manage research projects, to plan research budgets and also get to know a number of regulations as to spend public money. (Poland, Male, Uni)
>   administrative competences are also necessary: reporting to institutions, preparing funding requests, managing databases. Public relations with companies and media are also carried out. (Switzerland, Male, Uni)

It was generally agreed that greater international collaboration necessitated the acquisition of new skills in a range of areas such as funding applications and the development of different attitudes to work:

> new source of funding, projects and culture of work has arrived with European projects. They require different standards of work, different skills and competences and also attitudes. (Poland, Male, Uni)
>   in addition to specialized knowledge and skills there are required management and communication skills, teamwork capacity and foreign languages proficiency. (Romania, Fem, Uni)

The development of competencies in foreign languages was also considered necessary by many of the participants. This general perception was reflected in the following comments:

> co-operation skills and networking has gotten more important. Also internationalisation has increased and language skills are important. (Finland, Male, Polytech)
>   internationalization leads to increased demands on the language skills. (Germany, Male, Uni)

In addition to the development of language skills, information technology skills are also considered necessary:

> the requirement for developing new competences manifests through learning new languages and through acquiring new skill in the field of information technology. (Croatia, Male, Uni)

Participants indicated that they found it difficult to set aside time to attend training courses and relied on the support of colleagues in order to avail of such provision as reflected in the following comments:

> missing training for the management tasks, problems to stay up to date, especially in technical things. (Germany, Fem, Uni)
>   would need to be relieved by another staff member. (Germany, Fem, Uni)

Participants also indicated that training initiatives were not sufficiently supported in their higher education institution. The following comment is illustrative of that general view:

> there are many training courses on offer from the computer centre, HR in terms of mentoring and then the graduate studies office in terms of supervising PhDs, but not many staff attend them, [I] attend courses on my own initiative but the Heads of Department should encourage their staff more. (Ireland, Male, Uni)

Tensions existed between the development of new skills within the academic role and the requirement to remain up to date in their professional areas. Many felt that in order to pursue an academic career, practice based commitments had diminished in importance. These views were reflected in the following comment:

> new academic staff are pursuing an academic career and therefore have been told to abandon their practice commitments one challenge is to manage to stay in touch with developments in your subject, because the longer you are here, the more institutionalised you become. (Ireland, Male, IoT)

Participants in the study considered that many of their roles now generated extra administration, which they viewed as another challenge in their work.

6.4.4   Administration

Participants experienced increased levels of administrative responsibility in many aspects of their professional lives.

6.4.5   University Central Administration: Impact on the Role of Academics

Many participants referred to increased levels of reporting expected by central administrative units in the higher education institutions. This is reflected in the following comments:

> documentation and reporting has become more important, also service and support for academics have increased. (Austria, Fem, Uni)
> reporting duties have increased. (Austria, Male, Uni)

Respondents were in general critical of university administration. This perception is illustrated in the following comments:

> A blown up central administration wants to prove its right of existence – the result is 'paper shooting'. Management meddling has increased, everything has to be put down on paper. (Austria, Male, Uni)
> Negative attitudes, lack flexibility and hierarchical thinking are main sins of the central university administration. (Poland, Fem, Uni)
> Stiffness of structures and roles can affect the quality and diversity of educational services offered by universities. (Romania, Fem, Uni)
> Most academics feel that universities are over-bureaucratic organizations overwhelmed by extensive number of detail regulations that consumes time. (Poland, Male, Uni)

6.4.5.1   Increased Administrative Workload

Participants offered a range of views concerning the impact of increased administration within their role. The following comment highlighted the general view:

> the demands are increasing, but more or less you have no time. (Germany, Male, Uni)

Other participants suggested that increased administrative workload took time away from teaching and research and required a lot of energy. The following comments reflected the general perception.

the new professional role includes automatically new administrative tasks. Any increase of
the assignments in one direction leads to diminishing the performance in other directions
such as teaching and research. (Romania Male, Uni)
      administrative work takes a lot of energy. Even though there have been reorganizations
in order to improve efficiency, academics waste too much time. (Switzerland, Fem, Uni)

Greater involvement in research activities also brought increased administrative
responsibilities. The following comments are indicative of the general view:

There is perceived increase in duties of project application and reporting. (Germany, Male,
Uni)
      Up to 50 % of my work are administrative tasks, then the rest is for teaching and
research. As director of an institute I have to take care of budget, funds, different functions
within the faculty and in different other university bodies. Broadly speaking the structures
have become more complex and diverse. There is evaluation, measures, you have to acquire
funds. (Switzerland, Male, Uni)
      What was once considered dominantly the job of an academic, teaching and research, is
now being enriched by new jobs such as writing projects, project managing, class admin-
istrating, managing numerous administrative tasks that were once completely outside the
scope of academics' duties and were performed by other employees. (Croatia, Fem, Uni)

Many participants referred to the lack of administrative support available to
them with reference to their teaching and research roles. One participant reflecting
the general perception commented:

previously there were more administrative staff, but now their work has been distributed to
teaching and research staff. (Finland, Fem, Uni)
      the biggest changes can be seen in the increase of administration and requirements that
are in that respect expected of academics. (Croatia, Fem, Uni)

Participants also referred to unwillingness on the part of administrative staff to
adapt to changes that were taking place. This general view was reflected in the
following comment:

in the department the same administrative staff has been already working for thirty years
and it is difficult to learn old dogs new tricks. (Poland, Male, Uni)

6.5   Discussion

The findings from this study when examined within Bourdieu's sociology of
academia (1988) suggest that academics who participated in this study find it
challenging to reconcile a number of tensions within their professional role.

   With reference to the scientific (prestige route) many of the participants
recognised the importance of being research active, securing funded research and
engaging in academic publishing. This was regarded as the institutional priority and
the key to acquiring symbolic capital. For participants this message was conveyed
through the monitoring of research outputs and was a result of institutions being
dependent on external funding. Where a culture of research had not previously
existed in some institutions, this caused problems for participants who were

expected to adjust to changed circumstances without the benefit of mentoring or support. Their working environments had changed and the emphasis was now focused on research groups, temporary funded research projects and research clusters (Mittelstrass 2010). The increased pressure to publish in academic journals, which emerged as a theme in other studies (Wellington and Torgerson 2005) and Murray and Cunningham (2011) was an important issue for academics in this study. Participants felt pressurised to secure funding on a continuous basis due to the short-term nature of research contracts and expressed concern about the quality of the research produced as a result of this. The scientific (prestige route) brought additional responsibilities, which included the management of large-scale projects, working in diverse teams sometimes going outside academic disciplines and often engaging in complex administrative tasks (Hyde et al. 2011). Data from the study suggests that participants did not have sufficient administrative support in order to carry out their roles successfully.

There was little institutional support for the academic route (Bourdieu 1988). Participants in this study attributed changes in their teaching roles to mass higher education; the diversity of the study body and the introduction of quality assurance systems (Johnson and Deem 2003). While participants acknowledged a greater emphasis on quality teaching and performance, they considered themselves inadequately prepared for the diverse teaching roles that they were expected to perform. They felt that different approaches to teaching brought additional administrative tasks in terms of assessment for which they did not receive adequate support. They taught students who had different profiles and attitudes and they found this challenging (Rolfe 2002).

Participants perceived their administrative work-load to have increased. For many, the extra administrative duties generated by changes in university structures, and new approaches to teaching and research impacted negatively on their professional contexts (Cheng 2010). Few participants commented on preserving disciplinary boundaries another aspect of the academic route, but in the context of research many acknowledged that they were expected to go beyond their academic disciplines in order to participate in research teams and secure funding.

While Bourdieu (1988) included academic networking as part of the academic career route, participants in this study were clear that it formed an important part of the scientific (prestige) route. Engaging in collaboration and networking in an international context was perceived as an important route to gain additional social capital. In addition to the five roles performed by academics as identified by Blaxter et al. (2006), a sixth emerged in this study, which was the acquisition of new skills and competencies. The emphasis on this area was prominent among participants in this study. Securing additional qualifications, developing competencies in foreign languages and becoming proficient in information technology were perceived as ways of increasing social capital within the academic role. However, it was also acknowledged that they did not receive sufficient support to avail of such opportunities and as Blaxter et al. (2006) found in their study many invested their own time and money in order to develop these skills and competencies.

6.5.1   Implications of Findings

The preceding analysis has important implications for the academic profession. It is clear that the elements which comprise the scientific (prestige) route identified by Bourdieu (1988) with reference to academic careers is not discipline or area based, but extends across institutions with reference to research, funding and publications. The strategies used by academics to manage this context require them to accumulate symbolic capital through additional investment in additional qualifications and the development of new skills and competencies. This has become an acknowledged aspect of their academic role.

Equally important is the nature of the research funding that exists. Generally it is short term, requires academics to work outside their own disciplines and there is continued pressure to secure additional funding. This has serious implications for institutional contractual obligations and career development pathways. The pressure to publish in order to secure additional funding has implications for the way research is conceived and conducted.

The prioritisation of research over teaching by institutions impacts upon the teaching and learning experiences of academics and students. Quality review and teaching performance focus on outcomes as opposed to providing the necessary inputs for academics to meet the needs of diverse student populations and to engage with a range of appropriate pedagogical approaches.

This is an important study in a European context as the findings suggest that academics are dealing with a variety of areas within their professional roles. The study highlights fragmentation as academics try in different contexts to meet their professional obligations across the different areas of teaching, research, administration, academic writing, networking and acquiring new skills and competencies. In many ways the profession is not structured and consequently academics try to address a range of areas simultaneously without adequate institutional support.

This chapter argues that it is only through the analysis of these tensions that insights can be gained about the needs of academics in the context of institutional priorities and their individual efforts to reconcile different aspects of their professional role. The implications of such analysis are of fundamental importance not only for the academic profession itself but also higher education systems more generally.

References

Blaxter, L., Hughes, C., & Tight, M. (2006). *How to research*. Maidenhead: Open University Press.

Bourdieu, P. (1988). *Homo academicus*. Stanford: Stanford University Press.

Cheng, M. (2010). Audit cultures and quality assurance mechanisms in England: A study of their perceived impact on the work of academics. *Teaching in Higher Education, 15*(3), 259–271.

Hyde, A., Clarke, M., & Drennan, J. (2011). The changing role of academics and the rise of managerialism. In B. M. Kehm & U. Teichler (Eds.), *The academic profession in Europe – New tasks and new challenges* (pp. 39–52). London: Springer.

Johnson, R. N., & Deem, R. (2003). Talking of students: Tensions and contradictions for the manager-academic and the university in contemporary higher Education. *Higher Education, 46*, 289–314.

Lepori, B., Benninghoff, M., Jongbloed, B., Salerno, C., & Slipersæter, S. (2007). Changing models and patterns of higher education funding: Some empirical evidence. In A. Bonaccorsi & C. Daraio (Eds.), *Universities and strategic knowledge creation. Specialisation and performance in Europe* (pp. 85–110). Cheltenham: Edward Elgar.

McInnis, C. (2006). Academics and Professional Administrators in Australian Universities: Dissolving boundaries and new tensions. *Journal of Higher Education Policy and Management, 20*(2), 161–173.

Mittelstrass, J. (2010). The Future of the University. *European Review, 18*(1), 181–189.

Murphy, P. (1998). Journal quality assessment for performance based funding. *Assessment & Evaluation in Higher Education, 23*, 25–31.

Murray, R., & Cunningham, E. (2011). Managing researcher development: 'Drastic transition'? *Studies in Higher Education, 36*(7), 831–845.

Rolfe, H. (2002). Students' Demands and Expectations in an Age of Reduced Financial Support: The perspectives of lecturers in four English universities. *Journal of Higher Education Policy and Management, 24*(2), 171–182.

Wellington, G., & Torgerson, C. J. (2005). Writing for publication: What counts as a 'high status', eminent journal? *Journal of Further and Higher Education, 29*, 35–48.

Chapter 7
Academics and Community Engagement: Comparative Perspective from Three European Countries

Bojana Ćulum, Marko Turk, and Jasminka Ledić

7.1 Introduction

Modern university environment is characterized by a significant number of stakeholders whose requirements and expectations change and increase. As a result, universities become complex and multidimensional organizations, inseparable from the environment in which they operate (Jongbloed et al. 2008). Of course, such a context has implications on academics also. Academics are no longer expected only to achieve excellence in teaching and research, but they also have to develop numerous connections with the external environment and community they live and/or work in. It becomes clear that the interaction of universities with various stakeholders presents a major challenge for modern universities, with respect to various pressures and expectations that come from inside and outside the university settings, thus shaping the landscape of higher education development. Those kinds of pressures and expectations for the increasing relevance of universities in the development of society and knowledge economy (Brennan 2006) have opened an area of research on university third mission that seeks a better understanding of the university-society interaction.

Most research in this area (on university third mission) examines the role of the university and its contributions to local, regional and national (economical and social) development (Goddard and Chatterton 2003; Arbo and Benneworth 2006; Benneworth and Hospers 2007). Such research is, among others, rooted in the idea on universities being morally accountable to society in general (Cooper 2005), through teaching, research and engagement with the communities, which they serve; on the idea that universities should be engaged in the process of social transformation as well

B. Ćulum (✉) • M. Turk • J. Ledić
Faculty of Humanities and Social Sciences, Department of Education, University of Rijeka, Sveučilišna avenija 4, Rijeka 51000, Croatia
e-mail: bculum@ffri.hr

© Springer International Publishing Switzerland 2015
T. Fumasoli et al. (eds.), *Academic Work and Careers in Europe: Trends, Challenges, Perspectives*, The Changing Academy – The Changing Academic Profession in International Comparative Perspective 12, DOI 10.1007/978-3-319-10720-2_7

as the performance of the university's functions of instruction/teaching and research Schleicher (2006); on the idea that universities are the most important source of knowledge in society and that, as a social institution, have a responsibility to extend their core academic activities and to apply that knowledge in the community in order to contribute to the improvement of living conditions (ACU 2001).

Such researches on university third mission examine the relationship between higher education and society that goes beyond pure teaching and research – they analyze the dual role of universities as (I) a holder/agent of positive changes that contribute to the social and cultural development, and as (II) an entrepreneur contributing to economic development at local, regional and national level.

The existing concepts of university third mission, in a broader sense, discuss the university contribution to the development of society through a number of economic, political, social and cultural networks with various stakeholders. However, the importance of particular stakeholders and these networks in different concepts of university third mission is differently interpreted. One might find this as oversimplifying. However, academic debate clearly reflects a conflict between the two dominant paradigms of the third mission: one of which emphasizes the social and the other one the economic dimensions of university-community interaction.

Many current analyses of higher education role in the society revolve around discourses about the knowledge society and related notions of knowledge production, transmission and transfer. Within this frame of reference and university third mission notion, higher education's role is described predominantly in terms of its (research) applied functions and the potential for knowledge generation and transfer in supporting innovation, and dominantly (national) business and industry development (Singh and Little 2011). This expected role of universities as the 'brain' behind economic development is well explained within the national, European and international policies, as well as in strategies and relevant reports.[1]

However, it seems that within these overarching knowledge society discourses on HE responsiveness to socio-economic problems of society, little attention was given to the academics' public engagement in the community/society. Even less emphasis is placed on how academics engage and interact with the non-economic local community. That kind of community engagement has been established to benefit and enhance the place of higher education by bringing forth new knowledge (Hudson et al. 2007), through research and improving the teaching and learning process through various activities in local communities (Wynsberghe and Andruske 2007; Persell and Wenglinsky 2004; Vickers et al. 2004; Butcher et al. 2003).

---

[1] Lisbon strategy (2000), EU Communication *A new partnership for the modernisation of universities*: the EU Forum for University Business Dialogue (2009), EU Communication *Delivering on the modernisation agenda for universities: education, research and innovation* (2006), EU Communication *Mobilizing the brainpower of Europe: enabling universities to make their full contribution to the Lisbon Strategy* (2005), EU Communication *The role of the universities in the Europe of knowledge* (2003) OECD reports like *Higher Education and Regions: Globally competitive, locally engaged* (2007) and Public-private partnerships for research and innovation: an evaluation of the Dutch experience (2004) are only some of the examples.

Singh and Little (2011) accentuate that investigating this kind of relationship between higher education and community/society could be greatly enriched through greater attention being given to the public engagement dimensions of academics' role within the knowledge society discourse. Along the same line, Correa Bernardo et al. (2012) indicate that there is a need for research on the ways in which community engagement is implemented by higher education institutions.

The aim of this chapter is therefore to contribute to the ongoing discussion on community engagement by focusing on the nature, extent and the evaluation of academics' community engagement[2] in three European countries – Croatia, Germany and Ireland – and their different social, cultural, political and economic contexts. Differences in contexts can be reflected in differences in the involvement of the university with wider community. A qualitative inquiry was deemed appropriate for the research which was designed to examine the (I) the nature and extent of academics'/participants' public engagement in the community/society with non-economic stakeholders (other than business and industry) and (II) the status of their community engagement in the frame of institutional commitment to value that kind of activities and academics' public engagement.

Primary data was obtained through 180 conversational interviews about key elements of academics' community engagement. In this part of the EuroAC study there were around 60 participants included from each of the country mentioned above, juniors and seniors from various institutions and disciplines. Research results and discussion in this chapter will take place at the level of comparing subjects from different countries from which they come, given that the analysis of the data revealed little differences between other characteristics of respondents (academic title and status, discipline, institution, age and sex).

Particularly, different dynamics in how widely or narrowly academics interpret and enact community engagement, whom they target for knowledge production and transfer partnerships networks, what activities they find themselves engaged with, and various incentives for their involvement will be observed in order to understand if there are country specific models, as well as institutional strategies in communicating the importance of academics' community engagement.

7.2   Nature and Extent of Academics' Public Engagement – The Roles Academics Play in the Community

Community engagement in higher education is often described in terms of a cluster that includes a spectrum of activities, among others, service-learning, various educational programs and research that address specific social, economic and

---

[2] Authors find this notion of community engagement only as one aspect of the entire complex relationship of the university with the community.

political needs (Hall 2010). When talking about community engagement, Macfarlane (2007) presupposes academic expertise in the interaction with wider non-academic community: the representatives of the government and local authorities, business and professional associations, non-profit sector, civil society organizations and civic initiatives in the community and the media. The examples of activities include public lectures, professional cooperation with the media on important and current issues, advisory activities for the government and local authorities, cooperation and help in strengthening the capacity of local civil society organizations, the development of cooperative relationships with the representatives of community, opening educational opportunities for students to acquire experience through business opportunities and encouraging learning through their community engagement etc.

When reporting on community engagement in Australian context, for example, Winter et al. (2008) presented nine dimensions of community engagement in higher education: engagement through teaching and learning, curriculum design, policies, research, external relations, social and cultural engagement, partnerships with school and educational providers, economic engagement and organization and participation of students. In a report by the Russell Group of Universities (2004) on Higher Education Community Engagement Models for the United Kingdom, motives for community engagement can include responding to a specific need of the community without any return to the university, investing on a particular interest in the community which can be mutually beneficial to the university and addressing the core needs of the university but structured in a way that also benefits the community.

It is important to note that much of the literature addressing the issue of community engagement is developed from countries such as the United States of America, the United Kingdom, Canada and Australia. As Correa Bernardo and her associates stand, in many of these developed countries, institutional networks have been established among universities, which are actively pursuing community engagement as an area of scholarship (Correa Bernardo et al. 2012).

The participants of the EuroAC research in Croatia, Ireland and Germany were asked about the role of academics in the context of contributing to the development of community and society, and about the activities in which they engage in order for them to contribute to community development. Based on the analysis of the obtained responses, we can define the activity groups in which the respondents engage, the description of stakeholders in achieved interactions, the ways and methods of their own actions and the status of academics' community engagement in their institutions.

Academics from all three countries involved in this part of the research participated in various activities which served the interests of the communities in which they work. The study shows that the majority of the respondents from Germany, and about half of them from Ireland, participated in some kind of community engagement activities. In Ireland and Germany, academics have identified over 20 different activities and events in their communities in which they engage. Although to a lesser extent, similar activities were also recognized among the academics from

Croatia. In various community engagement activities, academics cooperate with many stakeholders – public institutions, kindergartens, primary and secondary schools, museums, civil society organizations and civic initiatives, charities, local authorities and the media.

The analysis of the data obtained by interviews gives six different categories of academics' community engagement, i.e. the activities that they engage in[3]:

(I)   Academic service-learning and students placements
(II)   Community- based research
(III)   Outreach activities
(IV)   Volunteering and pro bono work
(V)   Service organized by an institution (university, faculty, department)
(VI)   Political engagement

(I) Academic Service-Learning and Students Placements

The integration of academic serving-learning, as a model of experiential learning, into basic academic activities – teaching and research, rests on two ideas: first one is that the current needs and problems of a local community and society are an essential component of (higher) education in a democratic society, and the second one is that planning, creating and implementation of activities which would contribute to solving these needs and problems are approached in collaboration with relevant stakeholders in the community (public sector, lower levels of education, civil society organizations, civic initiatives, healthcare and social welfare institutions, local and regional authorities). In doing so, one should take into account the specific characteristics of a university and a local community in which it operates.

---

[3] The order of operations/categories is not random, but it should be noted that it is not related to the quantification of the respondents' answers or their perception of the importance of certain activities, given that the research questions were not directed towards such analysis. This section first highlights the activities that are associated with the integration of engagement activities into regular academic activities (teaching and research), and then those activities that take place outside the traditional academic framework. This way we tried to further underline the importance of interconnection of academics' community engagement activities with teaching and research, the very perspective that we support. In fact, a growing body of research systematically suggests the benefits which the integration of academic service-learning model brings to the academic growth and development of students, the development of their social skills, as well as their personal and moral development. The results of the research emphasize the positive changes in students' critical thinking, their analytical skills, comprehension, and greater commitment to academic work, the perception of greater usefulness of the contents they learn, greater satisfaction with their course and study, and a greater likelihood of staying in the formal education system (Astin et al. 2000; Eyler 2000; Root et al. 2003). Students who participate in such designed community activities, show a positive change in their field of communication skills, are more willing to work with diverse groups of people, show greater confidence in their ability to promptly detect problems in the community, to organize and take the necessary steps for the development of problem solving approaches and stronger civil engagement and dedication to the community (Myers-Lipton 1996; Osborne et al. 1998; Eyler and Giles 1999; Kezar and Rhoads 2001). Engagement in such activities allows students to develop leadership skills, a better understanding of racial and cultural issues, and it strengthens their sense of social responsibility (Howard-Hamilton 2000).

It is a multi-dimensional educational experience that enables students to participate in a well organized and planned activity in a community, which is associated with a course (academic and/or professional field) and responds to the identified needs of the community, and, after the implementation of the agreed activities, it encourages students to analyze their own experience in a way that allows them a deeper understanding of the course content, the appreciation of the contributions of the (scientific) discipline and a stronger sense of their own social responsibility (Bringle and Hatcher 1996). There is a consensus among experts that the integration of the model of academic service-learning represents an intentional integration of curriculum and students' community engagement, and thus allows connecting theory and practice (profession), while, at the same time, students gain valuable experience, knowledge and skills on social responsibility towards the community in which they live and work. Thereby, numerous researches show that academics often achieve better results in their discipline (e.g. better academic productivity) and in the community (e.g. recognition in the community, cooperation) thanks to the integration of roles (Linton 1995; Reardon 1998; Benson et al. 2000; Peters 2000; O'Meara 2002).

The EuroAC research shows that the interconnection of teaching and community engagement, regardless of the affiliation to an academic discipline, is recognized mainly among academics in Ireland, in rare instances among respondents in Germany and it is entirely absent when it comes to the respondents from Croatia. Irish participants' opinions on this approach to teaching were characterised by comments as:

> Environmental health students are active in community based learning with visits to nursing homes and talks about hygiene practices. Environmental health officers have programmes with schools such as safety in road crossing. (IE_17-ACA, Ireland, Agriculture)
>
> The university is committed to service to community and I think it's a really important aspiration. School has service learning as a module, where students talk to managers in the community about problems in the workplace; this is beneficial for both the students because they like to learn about the workplace and real problems and it exposes the community to some of the things the students are learning. People don't really know what an academic does; therefore I think we need to put in place ways for academics to effectively contribute and ways for academics' contribution to be accepted. Academics are committed to an ideal of service and the research they do isn't really for profit, rather it is intended to generate more knowledge for the world. (IE_46-ACA, Ireland, Social and Behavioural Science)
>
> Besides academic service-learning, academics in Ireland and Germany also recognize the 'institution' of students' placement, as a model which successfully connects students, the university and the community itself – "The Institution sends students to do their placements on human resource projects, for example in hotels, or on development plans in the local community." (IE_15-ACA, Ireland, Social Sciences and Humanities);
>
> By connecting students with the community, we teach them how to read critically, thoughtfully and analytically, how to be able to express themselves, regardless of their orientation towards teaching, civil service or journalism, and, ultimately, how to make a great contribution to society. (0125TT_AC, Germany, Social Sciences and Humanities)

Through academic service-learning programmes planning and implementation, students and academics from Ireland established partnerships with various stakeholders in their local community – e.g. schools, museums, healthcare and social welfare institutions – with whom they share interests in a particular field of science. Through the organization of students' practical work, some respondents have established close connections between the courses they teach and the associates in non – academic community, in order to provide a quality support to their students in a future job search.

(II) Community-Based Research

In contrast to the described model of higher education teaching, which strongly encourages students' community engagement, rarely are there scientific and professional articles on the model of research, which has similar goals. Strand (2000) writes that community-based research involves collaboration between academics and community representatives in the process of creating, and then implementing a research project the aim of which is to respond to the defined needs and problems of the community. Stoecker (2003) introduces into the definition the dimension of student participation, and states that participating researches based on the community's needs connect the active involvement of students in the research with their civic efforts in the community and the development of specific knowledge and skills. Strand et al. (2003) define this research model as cooperative research oriented towards the changes in the community which are based on the active engagement of academics, students and representatives of local community in a research project that corresponds to the needs and problems defined by the community representatives. Community-based researches are designed with the purpose of an equally significant impact on the development of students and the community, the integration of teaching and research, and the promotion and strengthening of students' engagement in various domains of the community in which they live and in which one day they will be active as educated professionals.

This research suggests that academics are far less involved in the community-based research than it is the case with their involvement in planning and implementation of academic service-learning model. Although the respondents from Ireland and Germany present their (modest) experience in this model of research planning and implementation, the respondents from all three countries warn more strongly that many studies in academic community are conducted in still closed, in their words – intellectually isolated state – which often makes them insufficiently perceived by the public and very poorly orientated towards the community:

> We are an overly closed community, little is known about what we do, people are barely interested in what we have gained in our researches because it is boring to them. In this sense, we should present our work more; we should be more concerned for ourselves. (HR_8, Croatia, Social Sciences and Humanities)
>
> Academics in Social Care are not as involved in issues in society as they should be; professionals notice the absence of an academic voice and they ask "where are the academics, why aren't they talking?" People have a respect for academics and it is important that we use our knowledge and research in particular, and lend these voices to help the profession. (IE_13-ACA, Ireland, Health)

> There is much research in the "ivory tower", which is not sufficiently perceived by the public. Academics have a strongly scientifically oriented career but they do not have as many contacts with other social sectors. (0113DT_AC, Germany, Geography)

As in the previous example, Croatian respondents have no experience in this form of academic research work.

(III) Outreach Activities

Current literature (in the context of the analyzed topic) shows how these activities are mainly related to the activities of cooperation between universities, i.e. academics, with civil society organizations and community initiatives, educational institutions (especially those of previous educational level), and often to planning and implementation of socially-oriented projects with socially delicate groups of citizens in the community. Some authors associate outreach activities with various projects and activities that have a social, socially sensitive character in the broad sense of the word (Göransson et al. 2009), while some describe them through heterogeneous connections of universities and academics with civil society (Krücken et al. 2009).

The EuroAC research shows that students and academics from all three countries, more than in two previously described activities (academic service-learning and community-based research), are involved in (various) outreach activities. We found more short-term activities and community engagements of academics lasting one day and/or one night than long-term activities and significant partnership networks establishments with various (relevant) community stakeholders. Academics state that these activities are usually not associated with teaching and research and are performed additionally, on top of the basic academic activities, as one of Irish respondents said "this activity leads you to a different area and requires you to provide additional time and energy." (IE_45_ACA, Ireland, Natural and Technical Sciences)

Outreach activities, which respondents from all three countries emphasize, consist of public lectures and (incentive) conversations of academics with children and young people in kindergartens, primary and secondary schools, and their participation in various workshops, panel discussions, lectures, presentations and other events that promote science in general, especially among children and youth. Respondents thus point out a number of activities, particularly those associated with the popularization of science, such as the *Day of Science, Long Night of Science, Science Festival, University Open Day, Children's University, Day of Open Teaching, Female in Science Day*[4] – "I am active in social events at the university, such as Children's University and Day of Open Teaching. If I had enough time, I would like to do more and participate more in similar activities." (0203VS_AC, Germany, Medical Sciences), "I participate in various events, such as Female in Science Day

---

[4] Of all the listed activities and events, only few respondents from Croatia pointed out their personal participation at the Science Festival. In other events of this type and featured here, academics, i.e. respondents from Germany engage dominantly.

and Open Day." (0208JF_AC, Germany, Natural and Technical Sciences), "I participated in activities outside the university, such as Night of Science or Open Day. These activities are part of my discipline. I represent the institution in such activities." (0523KS, Germany, Social Sciences and Humanities), "I participate in the activities outside the university if my time allows it, for example, Girls Day." (0524GP, Germany, Natural and Technical Sciences).

The second segment of *outreach* activities, which seems more common among academics, presents activities primarily aimed at promoting the university in local, regional and national settings. These types of activities are usually aimed at promoting the university among secondary school students (prospective university students) and potential funders, the media, but also the public as a whole. For example, an Irish interviewee explains:

> With regards to service to community/society, I contribute to liaising science and biology with the public by hosting science days in the university, by giving careers talks to schools and by addressing scientific needs in the media. In a functional democracy academics should have the license to criticise without the fear of being punished. (IE_19-ACA, Ireland, Natural and Technical Sciences)

Some respondents think that the 'race for the students', and, of course, financial resources, are the main initiators of these types of activities at universities, so an Irish interviewee explains:

> Community service for me means going to schools, bringing a school into a university institution, running races and Engineering Week. These activities are important because of the competition between the studies in higher education institutions in our region and you come to conclusion that you have to promote yourself ... you must be seen helping the community. (IE_35-ACA, Ireland, Natural and Technical Sciences)

The trend of participating in activities that are more targeted towards the promotion of university and science is very clear in Germany, somewhat less in Croatia. Irish respondents, however, are more turned toward creating deeper connections with the community in which they operate, in particular with previous levels of education system, so one respondent explains:

> The institution has an outreach initiative; it provides consultation to schools and performs certain tasks in the community. Such activities are recognized because the patterns of promotion contain teaching, research and community engagement, so service is one of the three academic activities that are evaluated. (IE_51-ACA, Ireland, Medical Sciences)

Respondents thus point out that in the creation of projects and (predominantly volunteer) activities they mainly work in accordance with the needs of their collaborators, with the intention of providing professional support:

> Service to community is encouraged by the Institution firstly in very self-serving way where academics visit a lot of schools to talk about the programmes they can offer to the institution/school. But there is also the encouragement to get involved with other organizations; for example, we have designed a number of training programs for the Simon Community for both their volunteers and their middle management people. (IE_41-ACA, Ireland, Social Sciences and Humanities)

(IV) Academics' Volunteering and *Pro Bono* Work

Volunteering engagement and various forms of *pro bono* engagements which academics donate to various organizations and institutions in their local community, are common for respondents from all three countries – "I'm involved in some volunteer organizations in my local community (. . .) I act as an advisor in several volunteer organizations, which includes occasional assessment of patients when it is appropriate." (IE_27-ACA, Ireland, Medical Sciences); "I personally go to schools and speak to students voluntarily about the Institution and what it can offer them" (IE_43-ACA, Ireland, Engineering). "I act as a promoter of my University in schools. I do these activities voluntarily." (0120CR_AC, Germany, Social Sciences and Humanities), "The activities which do not fall under traditional areas, such as research and teaching, for example, University anniversary or similar public events, were up till now all done by the institution. However, I personally engage myself, also. These activities are done voluntarily." (0131MP_AC, Germany, Social Sciences and Humanities). An Irish respondent thereby indicates the importance of institutional support, but certainly gives an advantage to academics' personal initiative and their willingness to engage in volunteering:

> The Institution has civic engagement and volunteering initiatives for the students to participate in and academics are also encouraged to participate in community events. The Institution facilitates us to a certain extent in doing that, but again most of it would be our own initiatives and volunteering. (IE_47-ACA, Ireland, Life Sciences)

One of the respondents from Croatia closely explains his/her attitude saying that children are a specific target group which should be addressed through such organized volunteering activities:

> In my opinion, it is most important to work with children because they are still pure enough and uncorrupted so they can be proven that society, science, education and everything else can function differently than it does. By engaging as volunteers in various activites, from blood donating, debates, popular lectures, Science Festival or any other way of volunteer work. Simply to be present, to volunteer and use your potential and the fact that we spent 15, 20 or more years on education in order to give something back to society. (HR_23, Croatia, Natural and Technical Sciences)

Irish academics/respondents more frequently emphasize this aspect of engagement compared to their counterparts from Germany and Croatia, so they appear to be more prone to personal involvement and engagement in community, volunteering in various healthcare and social welfare institutions and (local) civil society organizations, and taking care of the development of their students, regardless of the level of support from their parent institutions.

(V) Service Organized by an Institution

To respond to the growing demands of their stakeholders in the external environment, institutions of higher education turn to designing, organizing and establishing short-term and long-term activities, projects, programmes, centres, offices, coordination groups and even enterprises, with which they try to meet different needs of the environment in which they operate. In the context of organized services at the university level, or the parent institutions from which they come, the respondents emphasize lifelong learning programs through which the university offers a variety of training programs, designed adequately to meet the needs of relevant stakeholders/collaborators in the community.

Such forms of activity, as well as their personal engagement, have been identified with the respondents in all three countries included in the research –

Through various workshops and seminars intended for wider community. There are also programmes for lifelong learning, which should adapt to the needs of the community. (HR_25, Croatia, Natural and Technical Sciences),

I conduct offer-related workshops in collaboration with various stakeholders from the community and I work on Open Days. I am involved in non-academic events of social character sometimes voluntarily and sometimes on a call. (0905IH, Germany, Social Sciences and Humanities),

I personally did a lot of school visits organized by the Institution in order to attract students to our studies. (IE_49-ACA, Ireland, Natural and Technical Sciences)

(VI) Political Engagement

In his description of the academic profession, Macfarlane (2007) highlights political literacy as a significant segment of an 'ideal' academic in the function of an academic citizen. His opinion is that academic, regardless of affiliation to academic discipline, need to understand the processes of management and decision-making, not only at the university level, but also outside of it. They should be familiar with democratic processes and mechanisms which allow citizens to actively participate, to follow new policies and participate in discussions regarding the important issues for the community and society, whenever possible. He accentuate their duty, as they are most educated citizens in the community, to appropriately participate in the performance of (governing and managerial) functions at the university, but also wider, in the (local) community. Previous comparative researches on political activities of academics, in the context of their community engagement (Shin 2010; Ćulum et al. 2013), state that this is engagement activity that attracts their attention the least. The results of this part of the research also rely on previous studies – we can conclude that political engagement is the least recognized and present in the engagement of respondents. It can be seen that it is somewhat more present among the respondents in Ireland and Croatia than among their colleagues in Germany.

7.2.1 Academics and the Ways of Their Community Engagement

In the process of planning and implementation of the model of academic service-learning, while organizing student internships, conducting community-based research, as well as volunteering, research respondents, especially academics from Ireland, tend to act proactively, (individually or in a team) to identify and create interest communities as potential collaborators and partners. On the other hand, it seems that a variety of outreach activities, particularly those associated with the promotion of universities and science, are highly centralized, to which particular attention is drawn by the academics from Germany.

In this context, it could certainly mean that the governing and/or managerial levels expect this kind of engagement of academics, at least to a certain extent. The respondents thus report about their own involvement in this kind of activities usually on request, order and/or appointment from a higher managerial level: their voluntary engagement and contribution is expected. This view is captured in following comments:

> I participated in activities related to contributions to society at the university level, for example, Long Night of Science and Open Day. Such activities are carried out at the request of the university administration or superiors. (0127BK_AC, Germany, Natural and Technical Sciences),
>
> I participate in various events, for example, Female in Science Day and Open Day. I participate in such activities at the invitation of my superior because the University is in competition with other universities. (0208JF_AC, Germany, Natural and Technical Sciences),
>
> I participated in activities outside the university, such as "Night of Science" or "open day". I am asked to participate in such activities, but I do it voluntarily. (0523KS, Germany, Social Sciences and Humanities),
>
> I actively participate in socially relevant University events, like Children University for example. Such activities come as a request, but are done voluntarily. (0616AB, Germany, Social Sciences and Humanities),
>
> I participate in activities outside the university, if time allows me, for example, Girls Day. I was invited to participate in these activities, but I do it voluntarily. (0524GP, Germany, Natural and Technical Sciences)
>
> These are the activities that go beyond the usual academic work, presentations of the university and events for the students. Such activities are carried out at the request of the university administration. (0113KG _HEP, Germany),
>
> I participate in Girls Day and other events. There are no business and industry events. The activities are mandatory and are also described as those that need to be done and are rewarded. (0207SB_AC, Germany, Natural and Technical Sciences)

In this context, Irish academics talk about the university/institution as a type of a facilitator that promotes, encourages, and sometimes directs their community engagement, but they point out that their decisions, initiative and personal engagement are the main drivers:

> The institution has a civic engagement and volunteering initiatives for the students, but academics are also encouraged to participate in community events. The institution facilitates it for us, to a certain extent, but again, a lot of it is actually our own initiative. (IE_47-ACA, Ireland, Natural and Technical Sciences)

The analysis of the often important variable of gender and scientific discipline, in this part of the research, reflects some differences only in Croatia, where female respondents in the field of Social Sciences and Humanities more often than their male colleagues emphasize personal participation in various activities for the benefit of the community. Interestingly, this finding correlates with previous researches in Croatia, according to which women in academic community tend to engage in community more (Ćulum and Ledić 2012). However, it should be noted that this finding does not apply to Ireland and Germany.

7.2.2 Status of Community Engagement: Institutional Strategies and the Evaluation of Academics' Engagement

Many authors suggest that the decision on academics' community engagement to a large extent depends on their perception of the importance that is given to this activity in terms of their academic progress (Bloomgarden and O'Meara 2007; Ledić 2007). Literature and previous studies indicate that the lack of institutional support for the academics who decide to engage in community (Stanton 1994; Ward 1996; Abes et al. 2002; McKay and Rozee 2004; Harwood et al. 2005), and particularly inadequate evaluation of such engagement of academics (Abes et al. 2002), is a challenge, but also a serious obstacle in encouraging academics to a (more frequent) involvement and their engagement in the community.

Almost predictably, this research points to three basic categories in the context of institutional strategies toward promoting and evaluating community engagement: (I) a formal evaluation (typical to a certain extent for Irish higher education system), (II) informal evaluation (present in German higher education environment) and (III) the lack of evaluation (seen in Croatian higher education environment).

In Ireland, there are universities/institutions that formally recognize community engagement as one of the basic academic activities, and they include it in their formal reward system–

> (...) Community engagement is recognized in the patterns of promotion, where teaching activities, research and community engagement/service are clearly emphasized; so community engagement is one of the three activities that are evaluated. (IE_51_ACA, Ireland, Medical Sciences)

Although at some institutions community engagement is included in formal evaluation system, Irish respondents indicate that there is still a hierarchical relationship between activities that are measured: although community engagement is recognized and clearly accepted as the 'third academic activity', respondents warn that it is an activity that will not play a crucial role in ones academic career – "(...) it would not necessarily help for promotion, but it would be acknowledged" (IE_55-ACA, Ireland, Social and Behavioural Sciences),

> These types of activities are taken into account for promotions because they are the third category. It will not be crucial in improvement, but it will have a certain role. (IE_53-ACA, Ireland, Natural and Technical Sciences)

In addition to the examples of formal recognition in Irish higher education system, some interviewees point out that academics are usually not adequately rewarded for their community engagement. Activities are usually recognized "in the form of gratitude, but not in the form of reducing the workload in other areas – you do it as additional work." (IE_53-ACA, Ireland, Natural and Technical Sciences). However, some respondents believe that the issue of community engagement should not be put in (exclusive) relationship with evaluation and promotion–

> Academics should engage in community and involve in such activities because it is a good thing to do, and not because they could possibly be promoted or it could lead them further in their academic career. (IE_2-ACA, Ireland, Social Sciences and Humanities)

In Germany, the activities of community engagement are usually identified, recognized and rewarded, but for now only at an informal level. In this context, the respondents from Germany point out that these are the activities which will be recognized by the colleagues from the discipline, the institution, collaborators and the administration itself – "Activities related to serving the community/society are largely voluntary, but are recognized and respected by managers and colleagues" (0210BP_AC, Germany, Natural and Technical Sciences).

In Croatia, on the other hand, interviewees point to several dangerous tendencies. They report about a low level of recognizing the importance of community engagement and of such activities, not only at institutional level (institutions and universities), but also among colleagues. In addition, they highlight the marginalization of such activities, mocking the academics who engage in the community, and even possible threats for further development of academic careers – "If doing activities for the benefit of society and the community is in fact evaluated, then it is evaluated negatively." (HR_34, Croatia, Social Sciences and Humanities). The respondents further explain their opinions:

> Instead, there is only envy if someone succeeds. If someone goes out of the university framework, others will say, "Look how he has presented his work, like there is no better and more important thing to do." (HR_39, Croatia, Medical Sciences)
>
> These activities are not rewarded and can only cause professional damage to an individual and his/her academic career. For example, a person can 'get in the way' of some older colleagues who could decide on his/her future. Bearing this in mind, a person thinks in terms of what is wise and what is not. (HR_46, Croatia, Social Sciences and Humanities)

In a university environment where academics' community engagement is not institutionally positioned, promoted and evaluated, as is the case with Croatian universities (Ćulum and Ledić 2010, 2012), the attitudes of academics on the commitment and understanding of personal and civic responsibility for students and (local) community in which they live and work become crucial. Although in this research Croatian academics show us their positive attitudes about their role in contributing to the development of community and society, it is hard to believe and expect, as pointed out by a number of authors (Boyer 1990, 1996; Bloomgarden and O'Meara 2007; Ledić 2007; Ćulum and Ledić 2010), that academics will involve in various activities of community engagement if there are no mechanisms for their appropriate evaluation.

Conclusion

Previous comparative analysis was directed towards questioning community engagement among respondents from three European countries (Croatia, Germany and Ireland) in order to answer the research question focused on discovering activities, ways to engage respondents in such activities and the status of such engagement in the context of institutional evaluation strategies.

The results show that there are six different forms of public engagement of academics in the community, some of which are associated with the basic academic activities (teaching and research), and some occur as an additional, third activity. Identified models are mainly directed towards (field) activities in schools with the mission of promoting science and universities, and attracting new (potential) students. Academics associate with different stakeholders in the community, mainly schools and community organizations. Furthermore, they integrate teaching and research with the activities in community, they volunteer in various community projects designed by local community, civil society organizations and institutions, they offer pro bono services, and rarely are politically active. Activities related to teaching and research, such as academic service-learning and community-based research are predominantly practiced by Irish academics, while in Croatia these activities are not recognized at all.

Although it is possible to talk about a range of ways in which academics engage in community, there are certain specificities in individual countries. So, in Germany this type of activity is usually performed voluntarily, but at the request or invitation of university administration or superiors. In Ireland, academics involve in such activities pro-actively and more frequently than in Germany and Croatia, which can partly be explained through the existence of formal recognition of such activities in some institutions of higher education in Ireland. While in Germany this kind of academics' action is usually informal and publicly acknowledged, in Croatia some academics see it as a potential threat for their further academic career. Therefore, it is no wonder that Croatian respondents engage much less in such activities as compared to their counterparts from Ireland and Germany.

Following the findings on the evaluation system of the activities of community engagement, as has already been pointed out, there are obvious differences between the three countries – Ireland, where there is a formal evaluation of these activities, Germany, where evaluation is present, but on an informal basis, and Croatia, where evaluation is entirely absent, and sometimes such activities are perceived as an impediment of progress.

Finally, it should be noted that community engagement often requires academics to establish and manage partner (research) projects in the community, to design and prepare unconventional teaching programs that also promote learning connected with discipline, needs related to it, as well as

(continued)

the problems in the community. Seen in this context, their openness and willingness to change are essential in meeting the needs of the environment in which they are active. Of course, all the activities and efforts that are done for better connectedness with wider community and society seem less promising if there is no establishment of a clear and transparent system of evaluation and institutional support for such activities.

References

Abes, E. S., Jackson, G., & Jones, S. R. (2002). Factors that motivate and deter faculty use of service-learning. *Michigan Journal of Community Service Learning, 9*, 5–17.

Arbo, P., & Benneworth, P. S. (2006). *Understanding the regional contribution of higher education institutions: A literature review.* IMHE 'The Regional Contribution of Higher Education' project report. Paris: OECD.

Association of Commonwealth Universities (ACU). (2001). *Engagement as a core value for the university: A consultation document* (online version). London: Association of Commonwealth Universities. http://www.acu.ac.uk/. Accessed 11 May 2010.

Astin, H. S., Antonio, A. L., & Cress, C. M. (2000). Community service in higher education: A look at the nation's faculty. *The Review of Higher Education, 23*(4), 373–397.

Benneworth, P. S., & Hospers, G. (2007). Urban competitiveness in the knowledge economy: Universities as new planning animateurs. *Progress in Planning, 67*, 105–197.

Benson, L., Harkavy, I., & Puckett, J. (2000). An implementation revolution as a strategy for fulfilling the democratic promise of university-community partnerships: Penn-west Philadelphia as an experiment in progress. *Nonprofit and Voluntary Sector Quarterly, 29*(1), 24–45.

Bloomgarden, A. H., & O'Meara, K. A. (2007). Faculty role integration and community engagement: Harmony or cacophony? *Michigan Journal of Community Service Learning, 13*(2), 5–18.

Boyer, E. L. (1990). *Scholarship reconsider: Priorities of the professoriate.* Stanford: The Carnegie Foundation for the Advancement of Teaching.

Boyer, E. L. (1996). The scholarship of engagement. *Journal of Public Service and Outreach, 1*(1), 11–20.

Brennan, J. (2006). The changing academic profession: The driving forces. In RIHE (Ed.), *Reports of changing academic profession project workshop on quality, relevance and governance in the changing academia: International perspectives* (COE publication series, Vol. 20, pp. 37–44). Hiroshima: Hiroshima University.

Bringle, R. G., & Hatcher, J. A. (1996). Implementing service learning in higher education. *The Journal of Higher Education, 67*(2), 221–240.

Butcher, J., Howard, P., Labone, E., & Bailey, M. (2003). Teacher education, community service learning, and student efficacy for CE. *Asia Pacific Journal for Teacher Education, 31*(2), 110–124.

Cooper, C. (2005). Accounting for the public interest: Public ineffectuals or public intellectuals. *Accounting, Auditing and Accountability Journal, 18*(5), 592–607.

Correa Bernardo, M. A., Butcher, J., & Howard, P. (2012). An international comparison of community engagement in higher education. *International Journal of Educational Development, 32*(2012), 187–192.

Ćulum, B., & Ledić, J. (2010). *Civilna misija sveučilišta – element u tragovima?* Rijeka: Filozofski fakultet u Rijeci.

Ćulum, B., & Ledić, J. (2012). *Sveučilišni nastavnici i civilna misija sveučilišta.* Rijeka: Filozofski fakultet u Rijeci.

Ćulum, B., Rončević, N., & Ledić, J. (2013). The academic profession and the role of the service function. In U. Teichler & E. A. Höhle (Eds.), *The work situation of the academic professions: Findings of a survey in twelve European countries* (pp. 137–158). Dordrecht: Springer.

European Commission (EC). (2003). *The role of the universities in the Europe of knowledge. Communication from the Commission.* Brussels, 5 Feb 2003. COM (2003), 58 final.

European Commission (EC). (2005). *Communication from the Commission to the Council and the European Parliament. Mobilizing the brainpower of Europe: Enabling universities to make their full contribution to the Lisbon Strategy.* [COM (2005), 152 of 20 April 2005 and Council Resolution of 15 November 2005].

European Commission (EC). (2006). *Communication from the Commission to the Council and the European Parliament delivering on the modernisation agenda for universities: Education, research and innovation.* [COM (2006), 208 final].

European Commission (EC). (2009). *Communication form the Commission to the European Parliament, the Council, the European Economic and Social Committee and the Committee of the Regions. A new partnership for the modernisation of universities: The EU Forum for University Business Dialogue.* [COM (2009), 158 final].

Eyler, J. S. (2000). What do we most need to know about the impact of service learning on student learning? *Michigan Journal of Community Service Learning, 7,* 11–17.

Eyler, J. S., & Giles, D. E. (1999). *Where's the learning in service learning?* San Francisco: Jossey Bass Publisher.

Goddard, J. B., & Chatterton, P. (2003). The response of universities to regional needs'. In F. Boekema, E. Kuypers, & R. Rutten (Eds.), *Economic geography of higher education: Knowledge, infrastructure and learning regions.* London: Routledge.

Göransson, B., Maharajh, R., & Schmoch, U. (2009). New activities of universities in transfer and extension: Multiple requirements and manifold solutions. *Science and Public Policy, 36*(2), 157–164.

Hall, P. (2010). Community engagement in South African higher education. *Kogisano, 6,* 3–53.

Harwood, A. M., Ochs, L., Currier, D., Duke, S., Hammond, J., Moulds, L., Stout, K., & Werder, C. (2005). Communities for growth: Cultivating and sustaining service-learning teaching and scholarship in a faculty fellows program. *Michigan Journal of Community Service Learning, 12*(1), 41–51.

Howard-Hamilton, M. F. (2000). Creating a culturally responsive learning environment for African American students. *New Directions for Teaching and Learning, 82,* 45–53.

Hudson, P. B., Craig, R. F., & Hudson, S. M. (2007). Benchmarking leadership in university-community engagement: First steps and future directions for a new regional university campus. In *Proceedings Australian Universities Community Engagement Alliance* (AUCEA), Alice Springs, Northern Territory.

Jongbloed, B., Enders, J., & Salerno, C. (2008). Higher education and its communities: Interconnections, interdependencies and a research agenda. *Higher Education, 56*(3), 303–324.

Kezar, A., & Rhoads, R. A. (2001). The dynamic tension of service learning in higher education – A philosophical perspective. *The Journal of Higher Education, 72*(2), 148–171.

Krücken, G., Meier, F., & Müller, A. (2009). Linkages to the society as "leisure time activities"? Experiences at German universities. *Science and Public Policy, 36*(2), 139–144.

Ledić, J. (2007). U potrazi za civilnom misijom hrvatskih sveučilišta. In V. Previšić, N. N. Šoljan, & N. Hrvatić (Eds.), *Pedagogija – prema cjeloživotnom obrazovanju i društvu znanja* (Vol. 1, pp. 123–134). Zagreb: Hrvatsko pedagogijsko društvo.

Linton, C. J. (1995). An indirect model of service-learning: Integrating research, teaching and community service. *Michigan Journal of Community Service Learning, 2,* 105–111.

Macfarlane, B. (2007). *The academic citizen: The virtue of service in university life.* London/New York: Routledge.

McKay, V. C., & Rozee, P. D. (2004). Characteristics of faculty who adopt community service-learning pedagogy. *Michigan Journal of Community Service Learning, 10*(2), 21–33.

Myers-Lipton, S. (1996). Effect of service – Learning on college students' attitudes toward international understanding. *Journal of College Student Development, 37*(6), 659–668.

O'Meara, K. A. (2002). Uncovering the values in faculty evaluation of service as scholarship. *Review of Higher Education, 26*(1), 57–80.

Organisation for Economic Co-operation and Development OECD. (2007). *Higher education and regions: Globally competitive, locally engaged.* Paris: OECD – Institutional Management in Higher Education Programme.

Osborne, R. E., Hammerich, S., & Hensley, C. (1998). Student effects of service-learning: Tracking change across a semester. *Michigan Journal of Community Service Learning, 5,* 5–13.

Persell, C., & Wenglinsky, H. (2004). For – Profit post-secondary education and civic engagement. *Higher Education 47*(3), 337–359. Springer stable. http://www.jstor.org/stable/4151548. Accessed 9 Oct 2012.

Peters, S. J. (2000). The formative politics of outreach scholarship. *Journal of Higher Education Outreach and Engagement, 6*(1), 23–30.

Reardon, K. M. (1998). Participatory action research as service learning. *New Directions for Teaching and Learning, 73,* 57–64.

Root, S., Eyler, J., & Giles, D. (2003). The Bonner scholars program: A study of the impact of stipends on indicators of a community service ethic. *Metropolitan Universities: An International Forum, 14*(3), 97–110.

Russell Group of Universities. (2004). *Higher education community engagement model: Final report and analysis.* London: The Corporate Citizenship Company.

Schleicher, A. (2006). Europe's University challenge, *OECD Observer, 2006*(1), No. 254, 7–8

Shin, J. C. (2010). Scholarship of service: Faculty perceptions, workloads and reward systems. *RIHE International Seminar Reports, 15,* 173–188.

Singh, M., & Little, B. (2011). Learning and engagement dimensions of higher education in knowledge society discourses. In J. Brennan & T. Shah (Eds.), *Higher education and society in changing times: Looking back and looking forward* (pp. 36–44). London: The Center for Higher Education Research and Information (CHERI).

Stanton, T. K. (1994). The experience of faculty participants in an instructional development seminar on service-learning. *Michigan Journal of Community Service Learning, 1*(1), 7–20.

Stoecker, R. (2003). Community-based research: From practice to theory and back again. *Michigan Journal of Community Service Learning, 9*(Spring), 35–46.

Strand, J. K. (2000). Community-based research as pedagogy. *Michigan Journal of Community Service Learning, 7*(Fall), 85–96.

Strand, J. K., Marullo, S., Cutforth, N., Stoecker, N., & Donohue, P. (2003). Principles of best practice for community-based research. *Michigan Journal of Community Service Learning, 9* (Fall), 5–15.

Vickers, M., Harris, C., & Mc Carthy, F. (2004). University community engagement exploring service learning options within practicum. *Asia Pacific Journal of Teacher Education, 32*(2), 129–139.

Ward, K. (1996). Service-learning and student volunteerism: Reflections on institutional commitment. *Michigan Journal of Community Service Learning, 3,* 55–65.

Winter, A., Wiseman, J., & Muirhead, B. (2008). University-community engagement in Australia: Practice, policy and public good. *Education Citizenship and Social Justice, 1,* 211–230.

Wynsberghe, R. V., & Andruske, C. L. (2007). Research in the service of co-learning: Sustainability and community engagement. *Canadian Journal of Education, 30*(1), 349–376.

Chapter 8
Implementation of Quality Assurance Systems in Academic Staff Perspective – An Overview

Luminita Moraru, Mirela Praisler, Simona Marin, and Corina Bentea

8.1 Introduction

Cheng and Tam (1997, p. 23) suggest that "education quality is a rather vague and controversial concept" and Pounder (1999, p. 156) argues that quality is a "notoriously ambiguous term". The present study identifies and examines numerous challenges posed by standardisation and global approaches of quality assurance and their implications for educational restructuring, a special attention being paid to new forms of Quality Assurance Systems (QAS) covering the relation between teaching and research, students' feedback/students' implication or cross-institutional assessments. The main themes are direct statements extracted from the interviewees' responses that were considered to be the most meaningful to the central areas of inquiry. They are: quality assurance system significance; satisfaction with QAS; QAS implementation issues; QAS organizational benefits; quality vs. quantity; research vs. teaching in terms of QA; students' feedback/students' implication; standardisation/general model vs. flexible approach; structural changes; and cross-institutional assessment tools.

For a better understanding of the results presented in this chapter we should mention that each main theme presented here was covered by different members of the project team, i.e. the project team has been divided into three smaller, separate teams, each with its own tasks, in order to maximize the efficiency of the work. As a result, not all countries involved in the project managed to answer to all the research themes. Switzerland focused on the academic recruitment process, and it has not

L. Moraru (✉) • M. Praisler
Faculty of Sciences and Environment, University Dunarea de Jos Galati, 47 Domneasca St., Galati 800 008, Romania
e-mail: Luminita.Moraru@ugal.ro

S. Marin • C. Bentea
Department of Teacher Training, University Dunarea de Jos Galati, Galati, Romania

© Springer International Publishing Switzerland 2015
T. Fumasoli et al. (eds.), *Academic Work and Careers in Europe: Trends, Challenges, Perspectives*, The Changing Academy – The Changing Academic Profession in International Comparative Perspective 12, DOI 10.1007/978-3-319-10720-2_8

covered other QAS aspects, such as significance, satisfaction, student feedback and cross-institutional assessment. Croatia, for instance, failed to deal with the last two objectives. The answers from the Polish interviewees have not been included in the analysis of the cross-institutional assessment and standardisation/general model vs. the flexible approach. We would also like to add that in this study, we have only taken into account the opinions of the academic staff, without considering the opinions of the managers and the higher education professionals (HEPROs). Consequently, the respondents' opinions do not have a uniform distribution in all eight countries involved.

In addition, during this first exhaustive analysis, we analyzed the answers coming from the individual and institutional level. So, we may expect that this initial analysis will suffer significant modifications at some later point, when we will deal with all the identified aspects in a more comprehensive way.

8.2   QAS Significance

Finnish interviewees express the opinion that QAS was typed out and made clear what quality is, how quality can be assured, and the benefits of information sharing. However, sometimes the decisions related to QA are presented a little too late to the staff, so that there is very little time to react to them. From their point of view, the strength of the QAS is that it covers all levels from students and employees to external stakeholders. They all have the possibility to give feedback, and it is dealt with systematically. The weakness is that the feedback systems are partially overlapping; feedback is collected about different issues but these are not connected to each other, which makes the system a bit fragmented.

The Romanian interviewees express divergent opinions related to the importance and utility of QAS. The seniors perceive the QAS as having a strategic role in the higher education system, as affecting the level of success of the educational process or as a continuous and preventative action through an innovative vision. The juniors, on the other hand, have a more pragmatic vision. They perceive the quality system as a connection tool between the business environment and higher education, a connection that is intended to link the most required competences and capabilities and to improve the employability of graduates and employees. Juniors believe that the QAS must contribute to the development of an institutional culture focused on the concept of quality. In the seniors' view, it is necessary to clearly define the quality policy at university level, to set up short and long term objectives and goals, to strengthen the cooperation with other universities, faculties and departments. On the contrary, many juniors believe that the quality of teaching and research processes would increase if the collective decision-making bodies would give up QAS. They often perceive this system as nothing else but a bureaucratic tool and as a source of nervous and emotional consumption.

The Croatian interviewees' emphasize that the society as a whole has the same expectations to academic staff: quality education and to help the students to develop and acquire competences and qualifications they will need in performing their future jobs. These objectives are more effectively reached through QAS and its specific activities.

The Polish junior interviewees express a confused and some kind of a disappointed attitude related to QAS. They claim that despite the growing expectations of the university management in all academic fields (teaching, research and administrative duty) academics do not have any support from the university administration to fulfil these expectations. They must learn how to budget projects, learn procedures of compulsory tendering and also prepare reports for the ministry (PL16_AC, PL36_AC). In their opinion, this should be done by the administration or by HEPROs. Other juniors think that the expectations of the university management are not clearly explained in general, including quality assurance in particular.

8.3   Satisfaction with QAS

The opinions expressed by Finnish junior interviewees indicated that the current QAS is "pretty good". Here, the marketing idea applied to higher education was stated. Higher education is a service and it is necessary to refer to student behaviour as primary client and to stakeholders. They agree that the students' expectations and students' choices are characteristic to the consumer behaviour and their satisfaction depends on the relationship between their expectations and their perceptions of the actual performance. Quality of higher education institutions' services is important for 'customer' satisfaction.

Some Austrian junior interviewees express their feeling of dissatisfaction related to the increasing number of administrative tasks at the expense of the time spent on research. From their point of view, the problem is not related to the structural conditions, but to the growing personal pressure which leads to discouragement: "Pressure without anything in return." (AT32_AC) They claim support instead of control (AT41_AC, AT53_AC). They acutely perceive that the pressure comes from constant performance measurement and control. They feel that the evaluations are not used for personal feedback but rather as a leverage or form of pressure against academics. They also express their concern and dissatisfaction related to the struggle for power (senate vs. rectorat). This structural dilemma also entails the danger that the university diverges from its most important task, i.e. the education of students and the quality of the provided educational services (AT25_AC).

Generally, the satisfaction of Romanian academic staff interviewees with QAS is good. However, their opinion is that QA demands high workloads, so its implementation faces resistance from academics. A critical opinion is expressed related to the quality of the on-line education or of the distance-education programmes (RO9_AC). The opinion that the face-to-face interaction between teacher and students yields a higher quality education is often expressed.

The Croatian interviewees express a very critical point of view on the way QAS is implemented. They also disagree with the operational methods of quality assurance. In this context, they denounce the extreme lack of transparency of operations,

the absence of performance evaluations, the absence of operations' quality evaluations, the dramatic decrease of formal requests. They feel that there is no real
feedback relationship between management and employees.

Despite the fact that German interviewees are awarded on QAS, the evaluation
of research and teaching is perceived as a pointless effort. In their opinion, the
evaluation takes place for supervisory reasons. Questionnaires for evaluation are
often large-scaled and not filled in completely. This might be a reason for distorted
results. Also, they claim that the consequences of evaluations are unknown. An
interesting point of view comes from junior interviewees. In their opinion, the
evaluation is unilateral, as it does not show the real situation of teaching
(DE0601_AC, DE0607_AC). The seniors acknowledge the existence of many
teaching evaluation reports, but consider that these do not yield any conclusions
about the quality of teaching. They point out that negative evaluations remain
without consequences. Some seniors feel that many things in quality assurance
are evaluated only at "surface". The measurability of educational services is viewed
critically and many believe that the questionnaires do not reflect the teaching
adequacy.

Irish interviewees perceive the system of quality control as a positive issue.
However, both, seniors and juniors complain that more administration is required
due to the extra paperwork linked to quality assurance and other related procedures
(modular descriptors, and modular content). They believe that there "is no doubt
that these processes need to be done". However, they point out that the academics
become overloaded (IE34_AC, IE35_AC, IE42_AC). Also, the Irish interviewees
feel the external pressure to do research, to attract funding, to update the research
profile and to do the student surveys for quality assurance purposes. Still, they
underline that the internal pressure of self-motivation is even greater.

The Polish interviewees express a moderate satisfaction on QAS and a critical
view on the system. They declare that the university management is putting
growing pressure on academics to complete their academics grades and to deliver
publications in high quality peer-review academic journals (PL3_AC, PL23_AC).
Also, the interviewees feel that they are expected to do teaching mainly because it
provides funding for the university and departments. Despite these criticisms, the
juniors perceive that the university gives academics more autonomy and flexibility.
Although this autonomy covers mostly teaching, the university management leaves
some freedom to the departments regarding the way to make academic courses
more attractive for students. Opinions were expressed that even if teaching is more
time consuming and less prestigious, it is highly required keeping the university
books in balance. The management does not pay too much attention to evaluate the
quality of the service provided by academics (PL23_AC). Teaching must be done,
but nothing more than that. On the other hand, the management expects research
performance and pays huge attention to evaluate research performance. There are
respondents dissatisfied with the performance of the university administration.
They blame chaos in the organisation and management of the administrative
work, and consider it as the main factor that contributes to a negative image of
the university administration (PL24_AC, PL28_AC).

8.4 QAS Implementation Issues

Many respondents (both, seniors and juniors) see the Finnish quality assurance system organised in a complicated manner. It can be recognized but not defined. Thus, for some of them, the QA and enhancement processes going on at the university are not visible in their work or they have remained unclear. Juniors know less about QAS and quality assurance in teaching and research than seniors. The seniors are more involved in the development of QAS inside their organisations. The Finnish respondents identified themselves as being end-users and they perceive QAS as suitable for this purpose: both, transparency of each individual work and information sharing are considered very important issues, and this should be noticed in the quality of the work. The seniors believe that the QAS should be better organised. Other respondents see QAS as "conformance to specification" or "guideline documents". However, they point out that although all the documents concerning quality are available, there is so much other work to do that there is no time to have a look at them. QA should be a natural part of the academic work, and there should be clear structures and information about them. In their opinion, this goal can be reached through a more detailed discussion about quality and its structures. Other respondents express the opinion that the QAS is too formal and bureaucratic. In consequence, the academic personnel "forget the content in quality management handbooks, because they are only for bureaucratic use" (FI65_AC).

Generally, the Austrian senior interviewees correctly perceive the functions and actions of QAS. In their opinion, the typical quality assurance practices deal with the department evaluation, revision processes, reports, expert reviews and impose quality standards regarding the quality and qualification of academic staff. Still, all of them are perceived as being "time-consuming processes". In teaching, QAS deals with a permanent demand to introduce new study programmes, their coordination and a detailed description of the educational targets. Also, QAS deals with cyclical research evaluations of departments and is perceived as having "an immaterial side" through honours and awards for academia. Other seniors claim that the task of QAS is to analyse the core processes and to establish reliable criteria in human resources policy, and also to give support to young academics in their career pathway. QA is perceived as a marketing instrument and some claim that the university leadership is not interested in QA. A Good quality assurance system should promote communication and transparency. Austrian junior academic staff does not express any opinion on the QAS and their role or practices.

Romanian interviewees express a clear opinion on QAS implementation and on the strong and weak points of the system. Unfortunately, the junior academic staff paid little attention to this issue. Some seniors provide examples of decision making influence in building strategic plans, funds allocation, risk management (internal control). At individual level, they underline the influence of the QA on their professional roles, in classroom management, mentoring activities (assistance in career advancement/promotion, improved job performance, enhanced creativity), and in anti-plagiarism actions. The weakness of the system is the requirement to align the educational objectives with the accreditation requirements, with little regard for the methods or quality of the teaching/learning processes or the necessity to organize courses/trainings dealing with quality assessment problems. Other seniors believe that the main concern of the higher education management must be the continuous improvement through preventative action (RO17_AC). Regulatory self-evaluation of academic staff and evaluation made by the head of department must be an important source of information in order to establish the best management practices. Unfortunately, although these assessment activities are carried out annually, the corrective measures are missing. A junior expresses the opinion that the main problem of the QAS is the difficulty to organize effectively a dialogue between the students and the teachers or tutors. The increased participation and cooperation across departments are mentioned as strengths of the quality assurance model. In addition, funding seems to represent a key issue for the Romanian higher education system. Currently, the funding received by state universities each year depends on the number of students enrolled in each year of study, a policy that often influences the decision of universities and academics to expel poorly performing students. The latter are often kept into the higher education system due to financial reasons. Many interviewees express a clear opinion that universities should receive the state grant per student for all the academic years of the given study program, regardless of the number of years that the state funded student is actually enrolled. High quality standards in teaching and research cannot be reached without adequate financial support.

The Swiss interviewees are aware that new "Controlling and Quality Assurance" departments have been created. However, depending on the competence of the staff in charge, they consider these units as useful (clear structures) or as a disadvantage (if these positions are filled with "unqualified staff who mistake steering for control"). Some interviewees have seen QA as a form of control system although in their opinion QA does not mean control.

Croatian interviewees view the demand to improve the quality of teaching as very important. The QAS structures operate at the university level. The university defines the role of the Quality Board and determines action plans which then are distributed to its constituents. Besides didactics and knowledge on the educational process, one has to know how to treat students, how to teach and transfer knowledge, how close to get to students, what level of autonomy is acceptable, what things one can decide upon and what tasks to refer to certain professional services. Apart from teaching, they stress the fact that they are acquiring new competences in both, research and professional project management.

Surprisingly, the German junior academic staff interviewees expressed their opinion on implementation of QAS in a large number, while seniors did not really make their voices heard. Some juniors notice that teaching is evaluated and research is controlled, and consider it useful (DE0127_AC). Other juniors believe that the university is increasingly "managed" and not led. The evaluation of teaching is perceived to be neither positive nor negative. At institutional level, there has been an increase in the evaluation of the teaching activities, while the real focus on teaching was left behind. In the same context, one senior claims that although the evaluation of teaching has a long tradition and gives motivation for the new contents, the evaluation process has no consequences: "Even if I would get bad marks, it won't affect my status in the university" (DE0607_AC). The juniors are also aware of the lack of administrative consequences in case of bad results in teaching evaluation.

The main issue that Irish interviewees perceived as important is the newly created HEPRO posts. One junior interviewee makes the distinction between HEPRO posts (which are closer to quality assurance) and institutional HEPRO posts (dealing with strategic planning). The second type of HEPRO follows a pure business model. This type is more managerial, meaning that there are administration people who have started:

> intruding on academic life which I regard as detrimental and who don't understand academic life and have become quite powerful in institutions, they do not see themselves as a support service to facilitate things, they are obsessed about control and they are not facilitators (IE41_AC).

In one junior's opinion, the new legislation specific to the higher education system has created more paper work and this aspect is increased by HEPROs nowadays employed in quality assurance and human resources. The problems mentioned above may also be due to a poor communication between academics and HEPROs: one interviewee believes that the academics do not:

> fully understand my role (director of quality), even if I try to explain, but I think that's reflective of a wider misunderstanding of universities and the academic profession (IE31_AC).

Due to the last changes in the Polish higher education system, the academic staff is mainly concerned with evaluating the individual performance in research, the junior academic staff being focused on how to complete academic degrees as soon as possible. Another general interviewees' perception indicates that these changes leave academics in confusion and disbelief. In addition, respondents perceive contradictions between declarations made by the university management and their initiatives. A senior gives a relevant example: While there is a "verbal concern" about the quality of teaching, the recent increase of the minimum number of students in classes is threatening the quality of teaching (PL_9_AC). Other seniors appreciate that the university management on different levels take some measures to monitor and to improve the academic performance in both, research and teaching. Deans, in particular, try to motivate academics to improve the quality of their work. Students' satisfaction surveys are taken seriously into account. The dean, in collaboration with academic managers of smaller units, tries to identify the soft spots of teaching at the department. The same thing happens in research. The department measures and evaluates individual research outcomes and try to motivate academics who clearly underperform. Moreover, interviewees agree that teaching is important because it is the main source of funding. Academics are required to deliver solid lectures and tutorials. The Polish junior interviewees feel more acutely the discomfort, confusion and somehow the repression of personal initiatives. The situation is sharpened by growing institutional pressure to complete academic degrees as soon as possible and deliver solid publications in highly valued academic journals. Moreover, junior interviewees correctly perceive the importance of the quality of teaching as it is primarily focused on students' satisfaction as main proxy of quality of teaching (PL45_AC, PL46_AC). Academics receive feedback about their performance and they are also informed about the expectations on the three aspects of academic profession mentioned before.

8.5   QAS Organisational Benefits

Most of the Finnish respondents said that the university put in place a well organised system for an enduring culture of quality within the institution. As a result, academics really understand what quality actually stands for. The strength of QAS is that it raises awareness on "what we are doing and what we should do, but unfortunately this takes time". They believe that "you shouldn't start re-inventing the wheel again": QAS worked well before changing the structures – today it needs to be correlated to the new bigger structures (FI78_AC). Another benefit of QAS is the existence of a committee for quality issues and the fact that each department is represented in it. This committee analyses the quality indicators in research and teaching. The Bologna system is viewed as beneficial:

> Among all these recent reforms, I find the Bologna reform the most successful. The time-limits for an active study for the students at Finnish universities are a good thing in my opinion. They generate positive pressure on the students. (FI64_AC)

At institutional level, the QAS is a common "soft" instrument for organizing and implementing policies related to organisational performance in terms of quality. But many respondents claim that it is not "a transparent and open process". Another interesting idea that emerges from the views expressed by Finnish respondents is that "the higher in the hierarchy of our HEI you go, the more aware people are of these quality management issues" (FI63_AC). A junior respondent pointed out that the advantage of Finnish QAS is that the formal certification is a brand that can be used in marketing. There are also benefits perceived for the teaching activity:

> An optimal quality system for teaching would be to do the most of teaching as joint teaching projects. It would be good to be responsible of your teaching not only for your students but also your colleagues. (FI78_AC).

However, the respondents highlight a weakness of the QAS, which is manifested in the international evaluations when the cultural differences are not taken into account. In this case, the necessity to generalize the information in order to facilitate a correct perception involves a large consumption of resources (time, emotions and nerves).

The Romanian seniors belonging to all disciplines highlight that the main benefit is that the quality assurance is a tool used to bring together state and local governmental institutions representatives, academics and entrepreneurs, from Romania and abroad. The system aims to facilitate and foster networking for all these groups that promote quality assurance issues in higher education. Quality assurance possesses the capacity for the implementation and country-wide monitoring of the missions and objectives of the universities. An example mentioned regarding the quality assurance practices is benchmarking with other institutions in order to make right decisions on the internal organisation. Autonomy is seen an asset, as it stimulates all teaching and research activities.

The Croatian interviewees consider that few benefits are coming from the quality assurance system. Despite of his former position of Chancellor's Assistant for 4 years at the Centre for Quality, one senior believes that quality assurance has little impact on the academic community. The latter never considered it part of the university administration system. The quality assurance responsible communicates and establishes certain standards and criteria that may not be acceptable to all (HR53_AC).

The German interviewees, both juniors and seniors, are interested in the consequences of the evaluation process, which is seen as a part of QAS. They doubt about its benefits. Even if the teaching evaluation is considered to be positive, the "direction" is unclear to the interviewees. They claim a lack of communication between management and academia. The junior interviewees believe that evaluation is for supervisory reasons and it is a unilateral tool because it does not show the real situation of teaching. Admonitions are possible if there are incomplete data, but the consequences of the evaluation are not known. However, the self-evaluation is beneficial for their work. In this respect, the accountability to the professor or to the students is not perceived as a problem, but as an incentive and a feedback. The content of the student feedback is perceived as enrichment. The seniors perceive the evaluation as normal and unproblematic. However, one of them perceived the strong initial evaluation of the courses as being limited. The analysis was not timely made and distortional due to the students' dissatisfaction. They see the moment of evaluation as being critical, because it takes place before the semester ends. However, "more evaluation means more loss of time" (DE0124_AC). Controversial, but positive discussions exist in various teams whether the curriculum should be more compact: some members want to teach certain contents, while others want a tightening and a redistribution of the teaching program due to the Bologna reform.

The Irish interviewees view the importance and benefits of QA, but disagree with the huge amount of paperwork related to QA, which is a very time-consuming activity. They believe that QA could be done more efficiently and that QA has not had a great deal of impact on academics. The junior interviewees believe that the approach to monitoring the quality of academic work has impacted on their workload. QA includes managing student feedback through one of the internal quality assurance processes, facilitating and improving the quality through provision of continuous professional development courses.

The Polish respondents believe that QA would be more efficient if the university management clearly expressed its expectation toward the academic staff. One respondent declares that "the University is the best place to work because nothing is expected from him apart of some teaching which is even not evaluated" (PL17_AC). Another senior advocates for transparent procedures in research and teaching, in relation with students and other academics. From the Polish junior interviewees' point of view, measuring the students' satisfaction and the individual research performance are quite recent and positive phenomena at the university. These expectations have become more explicit in the last 4 years. Another important factor is associated with the increased use of the information technology.

8.6 Quality vs. Quantity

The Finnish respondents have revealed the pressure coming from management to increase 'throughput'. For example, "70 % of the students should pass" even though very few students meet the standard (FI35_AC). As a result, quantity may be in conflict with quality. Some interviewees think that the criteria set for quality assurance are based too much on quantity and too little on quality. However, international referred publications are a sign of good quality in research. Thus, in research work there is an inbuilt system of quality assurance expressed by peer review in publishing scholarly work. Increasing co-operation with international partners is also a sign of a better quality in research. Many respondents claim that administrative tasks have increased in professors' work. There is also too much teaching. There should be more time for research and less pressure to make profit, to have degrees, publications etc. (FI13_AC).

From this point of view, the Austrian interviewees express almost unanimously the same opinion: Quality assurance is all about growth and quantity and "only what can be counted and measured is highly rated" (AT08_AC). The juniors complain about the continuously increasing number of evaluation procedures. Juniors feel "over-evaluated" and disapprove of "formalized evaluation procedures" (AT53_AC, AT49_AC). Academics have to publish more. They believe that personal performance reviews and interviews are more useful. In their opinion, evaluations do not take into account the context. They believe that qualitative research is not measurable. Oftentimes the formal data entry sheets are filled out under time pressure and unwillingly. They are concerned that even if the raw data are wrong they are used as a basis for analysis. So, they express the opinion that the new quality criteria are "extremely stupid" because the quality criteria cannot be measured in numbers and the evaluators do not take time to control the content. Social science teachers claim that there is a certain closure towards society (AT52_AC). They are dissatisfied that the inter-institutional mobility and time-consuming communication are less highly valued. Current developments do not lead to "social knowledge": "local impact and social involvement is not valued and publications in practice-oriented journals are ranked less highly"(AT08_AC). In social sciences it is hard to count and to standardise.

The Romanian junior interviewees acutely feel this nexus between the quality and the quantity of their teaching and research. They claim that there are discrepancies between the quality approach, which measures the result of learning, and the quality approach, which measures the way knowledge is delivered. Most of them believe that the current form of QA implementation is not favourable and it does not encourage the development of an academic career. They did not like the fact that emphasis was placed only on articles published in ISI quoted journals listed in the Web of Knowledge database. Only the papers published in journals with high impact factor and/or significant relative influence score are taken into account for career advancement (RO15_AC).

The Swiss interviewees (seniors and juniors) feel that meritocracy and quality are the most important criteria for career advancement. While visibility and funds are the most important criteria in research, the current activity in teaching is assessed by students. However, the later results are taken into account only marginally. Some interviewees raise the question how the outputs of academic work can be measured. An academic career is based on scientific production (meritocracy), visibility (be in the right sector, i.e. life sciences now) and capability to integrate oneself in a managerial structure within university: teach, communicate, foster relations with your management:

> Publications seem to be more meritocratic, but it is a jungle there, too. How can you measure? Publications, impact factors... quality is only linked to peer review. (CH12-AC)

The Croatian senior respondents claim and criticize that the career progress in most research fields is typically based on the number of publications; they see the quantity and not their quality, as the dominant criterion for advancement to a higher position. Interviewees find these advancement criteria inadequate and they believe that these criteria need to be changed. An important number of seniors perceive as a main problem the disproportion between the number of teachers and the student population. Either the number of teachers should increase, or, which is more realistic and socially adequate, enrolment quotas should decrease. As a result, the general quality at colleges and universities will increase.

The German respondents expressed divergent opinions about accountability and peer reviewed publications. Some of the senior and junior respondents claim that there is no accountability or there are some problems with the accountability reporting requirements. Other respondents perceive the mandatory accountability reporting as positive and that the accountability requirements of the Department are manageable. The German juniors notice a change of expectations regarding publications in international peer reviewed journals. An opinion is that "at the same time thematic contents got less and it's accepted to focus on one topic, I don't like this development. I'd call it 'Americanization'". However, generally the respondents seem to deal in a relaxed way with the accountability reporting requirements (DE0215_AC).

In the same way, the Irish interviewees underline the students' quantitative issues. They make reference to the number of students, their retention rate, number of graduates and their average grades, as well as to the quantitative attitude related to performance in research. In this respect, juniors want more emphasis on quality versus quantity of publications. Some of them feel a significant pressure to increase intake, retention and graduation of students "at all costs" (IE2_AC). In the interviewee's opinion, there are restrictions placed on academics in terms of class sizes and reduction of hours. The senior respondents seem to have the same opinions. Seniors believe that students expect to be hand held. They are less inclined to think for themselves and even though "we are dealing with a lower level of student", their ability to self-direct their own learning is diminishing to a frightening level (IE34-AC). At individual level, the main issue is the lack of resources, which means there is a limited amount of money for attending conferences, presenting papers and publishing. So, "you have to earn more money in your research time to bring in the money to allow you to actually disseminate"(IE40-AC). There is a drive in the direction of trying to encourage research and apply for funding. The pressure is coming from "the senior level rather than being a department focus". Time management is a challenge, as is the quality of the student cohort and their expectations. High student numbers are needed for the financial viability of the institution, but "getting bums on seats, at what cost is that being done?" (IE34-AC).

The Polish junior interviewees also express most of their opinions on the same subjects, because they feel these pressures acutely. The quantitative approach is proeminent in the university management strategy. The main expectation of the university management is to publish papers in highly respected academic peer-review journals. These explicitly communicated expectations are a quite new phenomenon that did not exist in the past. Academics protest against such policy, but it seems that there is no alternative. Some of the interviewees say that in social sciences there is a strong theoretical orientation that overlooks their work as academics whose research produce applicable knowledge, but they do not count when it comes to academic degrees. Other juniors express the opinion that university governance is changing and the expectations addressed by the university management are contradictive (PL58_AC, PL30_AC). The respondents refer to raising a minimum number of students in classes to 25 persons. The contradiction is emphasized, on the one hand, by the desire to increase the quality of teaching and, on the other hand, by the increasing number of students in tutorial groups. Another example refers to teaching and research. In the past, expectations were dominated by teaching. Solid teaching was required by the university, with great focus on quality. Today, the university management wants academics to complete academic degrees as soon as possible, but at the same time overloads them with an increasing number of teaching hours. Only the number of students seems to count for the state universities, as they are financed by the state per student. Academics must find their way between such contradictory expectations in many aspects of their work. The same opinion is expressed by senior interviewees. The respondents complain about the admission of too many students. This is a huge problem because the staff spends most of their time on teaching.

8.7   Research vs. Teaching in Terms of QA

All Finnish interviewees agree that the scientific research and research-based teaching are the main functions of the university. It is therefore clear that assessing the quality of research is a crucially important concern in the management of universities. The respondents largely agreed that the quality indicators in research are the quality of the journals where articles are published and the citation per publication rate. The same importance presents the co-operation in international research projects. According to some juniors, in the Finnish higher education system more attention is paid to the amount of research rather than on the quality of research. Quality of teaching has been paid attention to but it is still hard to define. Quality assurance in teaching is done mostly by student feedback. The quality of teaching is more problematic because student feedback and learning outcomes should be mirrored into students' own input. From this point of view, the quality assurance systems seem artificial. QAS has certain weaknesses, as clear instructions or quality assurance procedures concerning single courses is missing; individual teachers are responsible of courses and their contents, and individuality in teaching is very much emphasised. Also, shared assessment criteria are missing. Teaching does not have a similar peer quality control as research has. A senior professor stated:

> When it comes to quality matters I would separate research from teaching. The quality assurance of research works fine through publishing in international peer reviewed journals. Also for teaching we have nominal systems of quality assurance but I am not sure that everybody follows them (FI75_AC).

The Austrian interviewees perceive themselves both as teachers and researchers. However, the seniors feel that in the last 2 or 3 years they have been viewed more and more as a teacher by their professional environment; thus, good quality of teaching is expected. Society also views academics mostly as teachers. In the same time, the growing number of students has led to emphasis on teaching. Austrian juniors express a slightly different opinion. They believe that the scientific environment expects continuously more international publications, good seminars in continuing education, linking science and consulting, initiating useful learning processes for students and seminar participants, developing expertise in project management and leadership, and initiating critical reflexion processes in communities. Also, juniors notice an overloading of managers and academics by the "industrial evaluation". They consider this an additional effort that does not contribute to quality. Evaluation is important in the analysis of learning processes, while criteria that are represented only in numbers are problematic. Through quantifying the QA measures, the social realities are not taken into account.

The Romanian interviewees perceive both the practical side and the immaterial side of quality in teaching and research. The majority of them believe that an academic career is based on research excellence and a high level of quality in teaching activity. They believe that an academic career is based first of all on research excellence and on hard individual work, patience and perseverance.

Unfortunately, high performance in teaching and research activities is expected without providing any financial support though. Regarding the teaching activity, there were many changes in the university curriculum contents and methodology. Research is the one that prevails and this affects the quality of teaching duties. Due to a continuous decrease in the student population and associated enrolments during the last decade, promotions have not been available for junior position (assistant and lecturer) during the last years. This affects the quality of practical activities because laboratory and seminar classes are taught nowadays by PhD students. If there is a solid background in research, the teaching profession offers the opportunity to share knowledge and build or form human resources. This is the way to gain visibility or notoriety in national and/or international environment. The junior interviewees quickly lined up to these new requirements: today the unique way in which academics' careers may develop is through research. The quality of the teaching activity is neglected (RO21_AC). The interviewees express the necessity to participate in international projects, work in national and international scientific teams and publish in International Data Base journals. In terms of publishing activity, they think that things are reversed: they are more researcher than teacher.

According to the Swiss respondents, the University structures are shifting towards the academic type, but their roles and positions are organized according to research funds: "the only thing you can quantify here is project funding, the more money, the more research, how bigger your team is" (CH15_AC). However, the respondents have the freedom to organize their own teaching and research activities. There are many possibilities to orient the topics of the research activity. In teaching there are some limitations, although it is possible to implement changes in curricula. The department executive management can influence the course of action, e.g. by taking responsibility in teaching modules. The interviewees notice the need to quantify the quality of research. The "ranking atmosphere" is present and even if people say "we don't believe in rankings, they are not important", everybody is interested in them (CH58_AC).

The Croatian junior interviewees view the publications as a measure of academic quality and prestige. This forced the academia to change their focus from teaching to research in order to succeed in academic environment. However, the juniors pay attention to the quality of teaching. The first requirement is to produce scientific articles of high quality and to engage in high quality teaching work. However, nobody reviews the quality of teaching work and the institution does nothing to measure the quality/success, nor does it reward teaching accomplishments. Another interviewee said that the good quality research outcomes should pass on to the students through the education process. Otherwise, there is no difference between the higher education system and the secondary education system. A senior has stressed out that advancing to higher teaching positions is highly related to advancing to a higher research position. He perceives this as being a problem because such system obstructs the advancement of university teachers who may prefer teaching work to research work and who are really great at teaching. Another senior professor noticed an increase in the quantity of workload: it is increasing in teaching, in the context of research production, in requirements to attend additional trainings and in expectations to work for magazines etc. (HR28_AC). All these activities result in newly established strict criteria for promotion and in high expectations the institution has of the academic staff. Another interesting point of view is expressed by a senior who believes that teachers expect the Quality Board only to confirm evaluations of teaching processes (for they need it to advance). Interviewees would like the teaching process to be discussed more frequently.

The German junior respondents express opinions mainly on the issue of teaching vs. research. The teaching is perceived as a more and more school-like system as there is less freedom for the juniors in research, as they depend on the project situation (DE0113_AC). Moreover, the teaching evaluation is described as ambivalent. On the one hand, it promotes the doctrine of an overall improvement. On the other hand the employees who want to improve teaching are under pressure.

For Irish interviewees both teaching and research quality are important. Thus, there is a greater emphasis on quality assurance with regard to courses and to student interactions. A growing emphasis is placed on the students' viewpoint on the actual programme. There is a desire by the institution that academics are research active and "from a personal perspective I can't imagine not doing any research" (IE39_AC). Another opinion coming from a senior is related to career pathway. The application form for promotions has a separate component on research in terms of quantity and quality of projects, funding and publications. So, research is seen by the university as a very important aspect of an academic job and "your research profile is very dependent on your outputs" (IE40_AC).

The Polish interviewees believe that the lack of research outcome will no longer be acceptable. Today, research requires more involvement and time than teaching; however it is unimaginable that teaching and research could be separated at certain universities. Some junior respondents admit that university management wants academics to conduct their teaching duties but it is nothing special. This is what academics are paid for. Although teaching is important for the university because it provides funding, the quality of teaching is not important at all. For the university, the funding of quantity (i.e. number of students) not the quality of education is an essential factor. In contrast, research performance is not explicitly required and paid, but the management pays special attention to research outcome and development of academic professional careers. In other words, academics are paid for teaching but they are expected to deliver research outcomes. The message from the university central management is clear: "publish or perish" (PL8_AC, PL18_AC). As a result of this management approach, the level of professionalism in performing administrative tasks and quality of teaching strongly depends on individual consciousness of each teacher. Many academics take an 'easy ride' and minimize resources invested in teaching. What really counts for the university management, on both, central and departmental level, is the number of publications in respected academic journals, in particular those indexed in JCR or ERIH, and external research funding.

8.8 Students' Feedback/Students' Implication

All Finnish interviewees are aware and agree that the students' feedback is an important tool in quality assurance of teaching but it is hard to get relevant information only through this mechanism. According to some juniors, the challenge for QAS is the fact that students' feedback is the only quality tool to assess the teaching activities, and so little attention is paid to the quality of teaching. Many respondents (both juniors and seniors) believe that this mechanism should not be overemphasised, because some students are satisfied if they only pass the course. This process should be clearly defined and better systematised, as many basic processes are still not described. Despite these critics, the Finnish interviewees recognize the visibility and utility of students' active implication in developing the quality of teaching and the teachers need to react to it. Moreover, the students' voice could be heard even better if every student had access to good quality teaching regardless of the campus he or she is attending.

The Austrian interviewees' perception is that, in the past, there was immediate feedback by students in teaching and an open relationship. Now, there are formalized evaluation procedures and little feedback information. Deterioration began in the 1990s and continued with the new Austrian University Law 2002/04, when an increasing privatisation and economisation of universities took place.

In the Romanian higher education environment, the students have no influence at any level of decision. The weight of their influence is very low, even in evaluating teaching. Although the importance and practical value of student feedback is correctly perceived, the evaluation results are distorted due to the dissatisfied students. From the seniors' point of view, it is necessary to strengthen the internal infrastructure of communication in the university. It is mandatory to involve students in this internal infrastructure of communication and to encourage students to share ideas and suggestions.

The German junior interviewees perceive the teaching evaluation by students as helpful and important. The respondents think that the consequences are beneficial to the contents and that they contribute to the improvement of teaching. In the same time, there are no consequences for the labour condition. Teaching evaluation is accepted by seniors. However, students are not very interested in evaluating teaching (less than 20 % of the students participate), practically passing up their influence. Teaching evaluations have little impact, although bad teaching performance and a high failure rate among students are provoking critical comments of the department's leader. Also, the seniors have questioned the practical value of the students' feedback (DE0124_AC). The results of the evaluations are disturbed by the dissatisfied students.

The Irish respondents see the students' evaluation as positive. The students "are very vocal" because each programme committee includes a student member and they can voice their opinions (IE17-AC). The approach to monitoring the quality of academic work has an important impact on the academic staff workload, as the quality assurance includes managing student feedback through one of the internal quality assurance processes.

A consensual point of view is expressed by Polish interviewees when it comes to students' expectations: the students want nothing more than just a quick and easy assignment. The Polish juniors who are closer to the student cohort have sadly realized that students' expectations are getting lower. They do not show any interest in exploring fields of study. In a vast majority they just want to pass exams, get assignments and go home. The only students' demand that have risen in recent years is to provide "fancy teaching" with the use of modern technology (PL12_AC). Traditional lectures are no longer attractive because everyone wants presentations. But at the same time, they radically increase their demands in terms of form of lectures. Dates and timetables are expected to be adjusted to their obligations outside the university. The respondents think that massification of higher education brought a new type of students at the university. "They expect an easy and nice go through higher education" and these attitudes are fundamentally different than 10 years ago. Only master students who are just about to graduate reveal some interest in the practical applications of knowledge they absorb during their studies (PL25_AC). One junior interviewee reveals some "fundamental contradictions". Students want from academics practical knowledge and skills that help them to find attractive and well-paid employment. As a result, the academics teach students but they do not have any feedback if their work is useful and have any added value on the labour market. The former students are not interested to close the "learning circle".

8.9 Standardisation/General Model vs. Flexible Approach

This theme has received a wide range of responses from Finnish interviewees. The expressed opinions are inconsistent regarding the degree of generalisation or individuality of the model quality. They have stated that there are quality handbooks which guide their actions and share best practices. However, this issue of standardisation seems to be more accessible to managers than to the academic staff. Some seniors believe that there are too many different evaluations going on at the moment and these parallel and time-consuming activities make them feel frustrated. Others perceive the quality assurance systems as varying a lot from faculty to faculty in their large university. The proposed solution is to build a uniform quality assurance system. In their opinion, the QAS must follow the bottom-up model. The junior staff did not express their opinion on this topic.

The Austrian seniors and juniors express different opinions regarding the utility of standards and standardisation in QA. Juniors doubt the usefulness of ongoing standardisation practices: "Universities appear like large, inflexible organisations in an ever-changing environment" (AT57_AC). In contrast, the seniors disagree with the fact that there is no central regulation for study programmes and this is decided by universities themselves. They consider this practice "counterproductive and cost-intensive." (AT50_AC)

The Romanian interviewees are aware that quality system is implemented and based on standards and procedures. The weakness of this standardized approach is that some of this quality standards and procedures must be improved and others must be strictly applied. The seniors agree with QAS, but they pointed out that the system progress depends on the quality of human resources. The juniors stand on other positions. Generally, they do not approve of the imposed degree of uniformity/standardization in all Romanian university organisational structures. They view as a weakness of this model the lack of any comparisons of performance indicators along the time. So, until now it cannot verify the efficiency of the imposed standards and methodology at the national level. Other juniors agree with the effort of the university management to re-configure the system of quality assurance and align the system to international standards.

The Swiss respondents are aware that networks among academics are very important. The university management has to cope with these social and human relations. Standardized methods and procedures are used for efficient and prompt handling of the quality assurance system but it takes time and energy to bring about change in order to standardize the evaluation criteria for the academic work.

Croatian interviewees claim that the changes in the higher education system are constant, but "their direction is constant as well" (HR7_AC). They believe that there is no deterioration in the quality assurance system, but some prescribed standards are not feasible.

The German senior respondents complain about the important variability of the level and the focus of the examination. They criticize that every university conceptualizes its own examination regulations, and as a result these are changing too often. They describe the change of the examination regulations as a learning-by-doing process. In their opinion, to overcome this drawback it is necessary to develop a trans-national coordination of this process as a part of QAS.

The Irish respondents think that QAS ensures that standards and institutional practices are aligned with the European standards and guidelines for quality assurance. In this context, the Irish university system is converging to the European organisational model and thereby it becomes more standardized than before. This process involves reviewing schools and research institutes, a process that is undertaken every 6–7 years to yield innovation and ensure that best practices are applied.

8.10 Structural Changes and Their Effects

The perception on the important structural changes at structural level is quite different in the case of Finnish respondents. Some of the interviewees would like to have stability in the structures because implementing changes is very time-consuming for the institution, as well as for individuals. The juniors claim that the changes at the national level have increased uncertainty, but they consider that these changes did not affect their actual work as teachers. From the point of view of quality assurance, the respondents highlight that every campus has a quality work team, which consists of employees and students. However, despite the idea that a polytechnic network is good, it seems to cause challenges for achieving quality. Campuses function very individually, and it is questionable how similar the degree programmes are in different campuses and how equal the positions of the students are (FI30_AC). More cooperation between campuses is imposed. As a result of the changes that occurred during the last 3 years in the Finnish higher education system, the quality work has decreased since the departments were merged. Another consequence of these structural changes is the necessity to reconsider the quality of the handbooks and to update them.

The Austrian interviewees experienced a lot of changes during the last years and the impact is not perceived as entirely beneficial. Among the changes in recent years they list: the teaching load has grown due to changes in university policy (large number of students, many exams); also the project-management activities (project leadership) are increasing; the project management duties take up a substantial amount of time and effort. Other changes in teaching in the recent years are the following: the salary has decreased, the qualification requirements for teachers have decreased (formerly the doctorate was a requirement) and administrative tasks have increased at the expense of research.

During the last 2 years, Romanian respondents have experimented a comprehensive academic reform consisting in political, structural and financial changes, such as: changes in administration and management from bottom-up to top-down; reduced basic financial provision for academic staff and universities; extension of research activities in the detriment of teaching; a rising of alienation in the academic staff; reinforcement of the external evaluation. Serious financial strains in higher education began with the deep budget cuts that started with the 2010–2011 academic year, which generated vacant positions and harsh salary reductions. It is difficult to predict the long-term consequences of these austerity measures, especially if some universities will have to alter fundamentally their instructional production functions. The juniors consider that both the Bologna Process and the implementation of the system for quality assurance in higher education represent changes that are intended to encourage the development of higher education. They claim that the changes in the organisational structure can relatively influence the academic roles, tasks, activities and responsibilities.

The Swiss universities have changed and became complex structures. A senior who was involved in several academic bodies and functions over time appreciated the efforts to ameliorate internal governance but he/she is still unsure whether the outcome of such reforms will be sufficiently positive. "The university is undergoing a transformation, too many resources are used and changes are not satisfactory." (CH25-AC) Juniors express the opinion that in this new environment, funding is a more important issue.

The Croatian interviewees perceive that most of the changes in the national higher education system are connected to services and administration. They say new services are being established at their college, such as services for international cooperation or for ECTS coordination. They are satisfied with them for now. However, they believe there are two distinct generations in the university administration. They have had mostly negative experiences with the older university administration. A new generation is emerging in these new services, for example in the Centre for Postgraduate Studies, International Cooperation, and Office for Quality Management etc. Here one can find young people who really work hard and well, "a person can really rely on them." (HR11_AC)

The German respondents expressed different opinions on the structures and on structural changes at all institutional levels. The structures are perceived as flexible, varied, democratic or catastrophic. Generally, the juniors have a positive perception on the organisational structures. They consider that the structures are oriented towards the optimisation of the research. On the contrary, the seniors criticize the organisational structures for various reasons. Thus, they view the structures as becoming more and more differentiated because the university's challenges to become bigger and bigger (e.g. internationality; support of work-life-balance; gender-development, career service). They find a gap between the demands of planning and the implementation of the higher education management. Another senior describes the structures as being catastrophic despite the desire to be better controlled. There are more and more students, although the universities are not growing to accommodate this situation. The Bologna process has created many problems. In addition, significant disharmony is seen in the collaboration between teaching/research and administration: "These two levels are not meshed well. This is why something like a 'corporate identity' can't take place."(DE0901_AC) At the same time, these structures are called ridiculous, because they induce a growing bureaucracy and, as a consequence, the teachers respond with more bureaucracy. Another senior describes the existing structures as democratic, although there is still a lack of transparency of the university's administration about expectations and guidelines.

Following the same tendency, the Irish national higher education system has experienced various changes. The interviewees say that every year there has been "massive change and it is growing and growing" (IE17-AC). Semesterisation has been recently adopted, which meant a huge intake of students and a considerable staff effort. The higher education institutions have been restructured, which has led to more bureaucracy and a quite intense quality assurance system that involves feedback from students, lecturers and tutors.

Polish junior interviewees acutely perceive the changes at management level. The university management does not have long term and coherent expectations from the academic community. Another change appears on the level of importance of the research activity and capacity for research. The university did not bother very much about it in the past, but this changed since 2005/2006. The respondents admit that the management takes academic research performance very seriously and outcomes are controlled on annual basis. Another junior perceives the dramatic change in the way the university treats students. Nowadays, students are much more important than academics and they know it. This approach has changed the university and makes it a students' center organisation (PL15_AC).

8.11 Cross-Institutional Assessment Tools

Related to the QA system, the Finnish respondents highlighted the opinion that this system must be fitted to a network of higher education institutions and it should be confirmed that the quality of teaching and research is at the same level in all campuses.

The Romanian academics view the lack of the cross-institutional assessment tools as a weakness of the quality system. These tools are useful to identify those proper actions for developing institutional policies. The Romanian academia experiment a "cultural change" (RO5_AC). Advanced performance measurement requires changing from a culture of reporting to a culture of evidenced-based decision-making and action. Often, these efforts are initiated by members of institutional boards and/or QAS members. In this context, the cross-sector analysis is a tool to better connect the "learning outcomes" to graduates' competencies provided within the curriculum.

German interviewees believe that cooperation within university is welcome (e.g. research-clusters or advancements of the university's profile) because there is a growing demand for a faster progress. The teaching performance of professors should be compared through more identical forms of graduation, so that students' quality can be compared. It is then easier to define requirements grades. Otherwise, it remains in an unjust initial situation with the acceptance of grades and performance if they want to change the university. A senior interviewee criticizes that every university conceptualizes its own examination regulations and they change again and again. A trans-national coordination of this process would be beneficial.

Discussion and Conclusions

Research findings showed that the QAS has so far been implemented in all analyzed higher education systems. This study was based on the academic staff perceptions on the QAS implementation. The research was performed in eight countries and was focused on a number of QA activities, taking into account the QAS implementation stage and characteristics.

A general impression that emerges from this study is that in order to make higher education system more competitive, universities have been under tremendous pressure from governments, internal and external stakeholders to restructure/reinvent the education systems. According to Carnoy (2000, p. 50), education reforms within the context of globalisation can be characterised as finance driven reforms emphasising decentralisation, privatisation and better performance. Regarding the impact of the standardisation demands and the new holistic assessment criteria of the academic staff's activity on the university management vision and strategy, most of the academics believe that government and university management have to respond to external pressures generated by globalisation.

Because there is great emphasis on 'efficiency and quality' in higher education, universities now encounter far more challenges, and are being

(continued)

subjected to an unprecedented level of external scrutiny. The 'public account-ability' leads all HEIs to accommodate increasing financial constraints and to change their governance by adopting the model based on the scientific performance judged according to international classification criteria and standards. But it is essential that these classifications do not become for a university an objective in itself, but rather to become a consequence of its mode of organisation. In the opinion of many respondents a dangerous tendency is that universities lose sight of something essential in the evalua-tion of teachers, namely the teaching performance; the evaluation criteria currently rely more on research, reflected in publications in recognized international research journals, i.e. the so-called ISI publications.

Without any significant exceptions, all respondents consider QAS being important for the university, but the way in which it is used and the require-ments on which it focuses are different from one educational system to another. Those requirements are either accepted or they become the cause of a great disappointment. Overall, the interviewees perceive the bureaucracy introduced by the QAS in the educational system as a major weakness. As a result, most of the tasks assigned to the academic staff are either confusing or outright denied, as some of the interviewees stated that QAS is just a pointless waste of time and money. The lack of QA effects is especially perceived in the case of the teaching process. Young teachers understand that teaching quality is an important factor which is mainly manifesting itself as student's satisfaction.

Depending on the existence/absence of employee training systems on quality assurance and on the personal involvement of the academic staff in quality assurance activities, there is a significant variance at the level of personal perception as regards the impact of QAS in the academic activities.

Satisfaction with the implementation of QAS and quality assurance pro-cesses covered a wide range of comments. We concluded that "quality assurance system is a complex and multifaceted concept" that can be described from different perspectives. The analysis of the QAS implementa-tion problems indicates the main factors that influence the academic staff perception: competence and organisational resources (staff training, proce-dure development, development of work instructions, lack of information and of financial resources), policy (quality policy definition and quality goal setting), and staff resistance to the QA implementation (bureaucracy, time-consuming processes, overloaded work).

The analysis of the respondents' perception on QAS at institutional level benefits show that there are three main factors: improved work quality (both in teaching and research), improved responsibility (transparency of the work and decisions and communication), and improved organisational

(continued)

performance (improved structural organisation, financial situation, reputation and visibility).

The analysis of the answers provided by the respondents indicates that even if QAS is very time and money consuming, it is an important instrument for a university, because it can be used to build the university's reputation. The exception is the German respondents, who consider QAS as nothing more than a unilateral instrument, used only to track their career progress. Junior respondents reveal a much more pragmatic way of dealing with the QAS because they perceive the formal certification as a marketing instrument used to advertise the quality and prestige of the university and according to what they say, the cooperation between the academic and business environments is welcome.

Martin and Stella (2007, p. 45) refer to two pillars of quality in education, namely "the golden standards" and "the fitness for purpose". The first approach states that it is possible to identify certain key aspects of higher education quality. The second approach assumes that a wide variety in types and objectives of HEIs makes it almost impossible to establish quantifiable criteria or standards. However, during the last years the necessity to handle with quantitative data in order to compare the performance among individuals, departments and institutions has lead to the introduction of a quality rating mechanism related to performance in research (peer review as qualitative judgement and the number of publications in highly ranking journals as quantitative judgement). Regarding the students' issue, the qualitative judgement refers to trace studies as a method for knowing the pathway of their graduates and the relationship between their study and their professional reward, while the quantitative approach refers to the number of students, their retention rate, number of graduates and their average grades. The academic staffs are forced to make them visible to their co-operators outside the university and they need to focus on quantified research outcomes such as publications in prestigious journals. The general respondents' opinion is that quality assurance is based too much on quantity rather than on quality; quality cannot be measured in numbers.

A "significant reconfiguration of the academic work" has taken place and brought a shift in the balance between teaching and research (Altbach 2005, p. 147). As publications have become a measure of academic quality and prestige, the academic work changed their focus from teaching to research in order to succeed in the academic environment. The promotion decisions in universities are based on the requirement of "pressures for scholarly productivity and increased research activity". However, the emphasis on scholarship has led to a decline in teaching quality. There are strong arguments in terms of teaching and learning support (Boyer 1990; Court 1999; Braxton 2006; Altbach 2005; Tierney 2004). In the past, solid teaching was required by

(continued)

the university, the focus being on quality. Today, the respondents claim that the focus has moved on research and on the outputs of the research activity. At the same time, the number of teaching hours remained high. The respondents perceived the lack of the QA effects especially at teaching level.

At European level, many institutions contribute to ensure a consistent quality system and to provide feedback not only from the individuals (e.g. students), but also from departments, faculties or from the universities. Among the many possible sources providing feedback (e.g. course documentation, progression rates, curriculum design processes, teaching committees, etc.), the students are the most important source of input for teaching evaluation. The key issues in using the students' feedback for teaching evaluation is: how competent and objective students are to make judgements on teaching and course quality; how effective the collaboration between teachers and students is. Although it is important that students assess the teachers, oftentimes the students pass their influence by doing this evaluation in a formal way. All of the respondents consider that a key aspect in using student feedback during the evaluation of the teaching process is the objectivity of the way in which students rate the quality of their classes/workshops, the selected teaching technique and the collaboration between students and teachers. Although it is of vital importance that students evaluate their teachers and their ways of teaching, it seems that in many cases students consider this evaluation a formal task. Only Irish students are considered an active part of this process.

Looking at the organisational structures of the European universities, we can conclude that they are relatively similar in terms of institutional missions and strategic plans, faculties, educational processes, methods of evaluation and ranking the research outcomes. Significantly different approaches can be found only in human resources policies. The quality assurance system, by nature of its intrinsic goals and through its standards and quality indicators, leads to the homogenization of higher education. In time, this may lead to the rigidification of the higher education institutions.

Most of the respondents stated that the existence of a national agency which deals with teaching quality is a positive initiative, but they point out that a necessary condition is that the same evaluation criteria should be applied for all the universities. Finnish respondents are against this uniformity, as the differences between different types of higher education structures are too important to be uniformly evaluated.

A "general model" of quality assurance does not universally apply. However, some basic elements are present in all national system. If there is a "general model", then this provides the guidelines. The general model is sustained by: the purpose of making international comparisons; the increase of programmes run by institutions in other countries (including foreign campuses); the students' mobility between countries as part of their

(continued)

programmes. A big challenge for QAS is to have the flexibility to avoid both the homogenization and rigidification tendencies in internal and external quality assurance mechanisms. Diversity enriches the educational experience. However, the benefits of standardisation cannot be denied. The quality standards provide minimum requirements in the quality assurance process and it is the task of QAS to adapt these standards to the uniqueness and individuality aspiration of the university. The opinions are diverse and this nexus needs further analysis.

Most of the changes in national higher education systems are connected to the financial restrictions imposed on universities. All these challenges impose improving the national competitiveness, quality in higher education system, productivity and strengthen social cohesion (Kyvik 2004; Liefner et al. 2004; Musselin 2007; Teichler 2006). As Bleiklie and Kogan (2007) highlight, "the notion of the university as a republic of scholars" is shifting "towards the idea of the university as a stakeholder organization". Mohrman and colleagues (2008) call for "an emerging global model of the research university". The respondents believe that it is difficult to predict the long term consequences of the financial austerity that affected the state universities during the last years, especially if some of them will have to alter their instructional function fundamentally. All the analysed educational systems have gone through or are still going through reorganisation processes at all institutional levels, and the opinions of the respondents are very different from one another. The Finnish respondents acutely feel the structural changes of their educational system. The merging process has posed some difficulties to QAS. In this context, the Finnish respondents believe that the QA activities have had a little relevance: after the merging process, new good practices need to be implemented. The new demand to increase the number of students in study groups and the low quality of the new employees are criticized by all respondents from all countries.

Many institutions have implemented various procedures to measure and analyze performance and value. The cross-institutional assessment concept highlights that without a measure for the outcomes of educational and research processes there is no possibility for the HEIs to evaluate their position on the worldwide market of education. Cross-institutional assessment tools identify sources of support and resistance for valuable initiatives, which helps derive effective educational policies, objectives, and programs. The benefits of cross-institutional assessments include: identifying and benchmarking leaders and best practices; finding common goals, experiences, and methods. This assessment may become a tool to measure progress toward excellence in teaching and research and also in accomplishing the third mission of the university. As a feature of the recent years, higher education institutions have placed a greater degree of importance on reputation (prestige) than on improvements in academic performance.

References

Altbach, P. (2005). Academic challenges: The American professoriate in comparative perspective. In A. Welch (Ed.), *The professoriate: Profile of a profession* (pp. 147–165). Dordrecht: Springer.

Bleiklie, I., & Kogan, M. (2007). Organization and governance of universities. *Higher Education Policy, 20*, 477–493.

Boyer, E. L. (1990). *Scholarship reconsidered: Priorities of the professoriate*. Princeton/ San Francisco: Jossey-Bass.

Braxton, J. M. (Ed.). (2006). *Analyzing faculty work and rewards. Using Boyer's four domains of scholarship* (Special issue. New directions for institutional research, 129). San Francisco: Jossey-Bass.

Carnoy, M. (2000). *Sustaining the new economy in the information age: Reflections on our changing world*. University Park: The Pennsylvania State University Press.

Cheng, Y. C., & Tam, W. M. (1997). Multi-models of quality in education. *Quality Assurance in Education, 5*(1), 22–31.

Court, S. (1999). Negotiating the research imperative: The views of UK academics on their career opportunities. *Higher Education Quarterly, 53*(1), 65–87.

Kyvik, S. (2004). Structural changes in higher education systems in Western Europe. *Higher Education in Europe, 29*(3), 393–409.

Liefner, I., Schätzl, L., & Schröder, T. (2004). Reforms in German higher education: Implementing and adapting Anglo-American organizational and management structures at German universities. *Higher Education Policy, 17*, 23–38.

Martin, M., & Stella, A. (2007). *External quality assurance in higher education: Making choices* (Fundamentals of Educational Planning, No. 85). Paris: IIEP-UNESCO. http://unesdoc.unesco. org/images/0015/001520/152045e.pdf

Mohrman, K., Ma, W., & Baker, D. (2008). The research university in transition: The emerging global model. *Higher Education Policy, 21*, 5–27.

Musselin, C. (2007). The transformation of academic work: Facts and analysis. In M. Kogan & U. Teichler (Eds.), *Key challenges to the academic profession* (Werkstattberichte; 65, pp. 175–189). Paris/Kassel: UNESCO Forum on Higher Education Research and Knowledge & INCHER-Kassel.

Pounder, J. (1999). Institutional performance in higher education: Is quality a relevant concept? *Quality Assurance in Education, 7*(1/3), 156–163.

Teichler, U. (2006). Changing structures of the higher education systems: The increasing complexity of underlying forces. *Higher Education Policy, 19*, 447–461.

Tierney, W. G. (2004). Turning the lights out: Tenure in the 21st century. *The Journal of Higher Education, 75*(2), 228–233.

Chapter 9
Academics and New Higher Education Professionals: Tensions, Reciprocal Influences and Forms of Professionalization

Barbara M. Kehm

9.1 Introduction

The academic profession is being perceived in public discourse and in higher education research as an ambivalent profession shaped by changing conditions and contradictory expectations. With the emergence of the knowledge society since the 1990s, the pace of change affecting the academic profession has accelerated. Concurrently and related to this, substantial changes have occurred in the organisational fabric of higher education institutions. Both developments are in turn related to an increasing diversity in higher education that also affects the academic profession. New settings for the tasks and functions of the academic role have emerged, new forms of division of work and cooperation between the academic profession and other professionals within higher education institutions are being developed. This is often described as a combination of the increasing socio-economic importance of universities and a growth in external control as well as internal diversification (cf. Altbach 2000; Enders 2001; Farnham 1999; Locke and Teichler 2007).

However, it also should be pointed out that the growth in external control is a different one than before. External control of higher education institutions in most continental European countries was predominantly state control. Since the early 1990s – in some countries later, in others somewhat earlier (cf. Kehm and Lanzendorf 2006) – governments have been withdrawing from close control of their higher education institutions, thus granting them more institutional autonomy with the expectation that this will enable them to react faster and more flexibly to external demands and challenges. In exchange for this institutional autonomy

B.M. Kehm (✉)
Robert Owen Centre for Educational Change, University of Glasgow, St. Andrew's Building,
11 Eldon Street, Glasgow G3 6 NH, UK
e-mail: Barbara.Kehm@glasgow.ac.uk

© Springer International Publishing Switzerland 2015
T. Fumasoli et al. (eds.), *Academic Work and Careers in Europe: Trends, Challenges, Perspectives*, The Changing Academy – The Changing Academic Profession in International Comparative Perspective 12, DOI 10.1007/978-3-319-10720-2_9

higher education institutions were subjected to a higher degree of public account-ability and external control through stakeholder representation in boards of gover-nors which reflected the increased socio-economic importance of higher education in the emerging knowledge societies. The growing organisational autonomy with its increasing capacity for strategic decision-making also required a strengthened and professionalised leadership and management. University presidents and their teams are nowadays more often appointed rather than elected from among the professo-riate in a given institution. Even deans tend to be appointed in a number of European countries. For both groups important appointment criteria are leadership and management competences.

In addition, there is another phenomenon which has been accompanying these changes. This is the growth in numbers of new groups of mostly highly qualified professionals which have been recruited to support organisational change and decision-making. They are not primarily active in teaching and research, although they might be involved in some teaching and some research, but entrusted mainly to prepare and support decisions of the management, establish new services or professionalise existing ones, and actively shape the core activities of the organi-sation. They can be found at the central level, in departments or faculties, and in central units outside the departmental or faculty structure. We have called this group the new "higher education professionals", HEPROs for short (cf. Kehm 2014).

It becomes evident that the academic profession is confronted not only with societal changes but also with changed institutional settings both impacting on their values, attitudes, and professional practices. However, academic norms will in turn mediate and influence these changes and new institutional settings. In this contri-bution we will analyse in a cross-national comparative approach involving eight European countries the tensions, reciprocal influences, and forms of professional-ization resulting from the interaction between institutional management, new higher education professionals and members of the academic profession. Around 60 interviews were carried out in each of the eight countries involved with repre-sentatives of all three groups coming from various universities and universities of applied sciences, the academics also from different disciplines.

In the following a brief overview of the existing definitions of HEPROs will be provided together with a brief discussion of the state of research. Furthermore, our starting hypotheses will be presented. This is followed by country studies on the HEPRO phenomenon and the interaction between HEPROs, management and the academic profession of all eight countries involved in this study. A synthesis from the country studies is then followed by conclusions trying to reflect on the hypotheses.

9.2   Definitions, Theoretical and Methodological Approaches, Hypotheses

In the first volume presenting the results of the EuroAC Project (cf. Kehm and Teichler 2012), Schneijderberg and Merkator (2012) provided an extensive overview of the state of international research on the new higher education professionals (HEPROs). This particular group of people has been analysed in a number of studies, mainly by British, Norwegian, Australian and US researchers, but was referred to by using a variety of categories. Whitchurch (2008) calls them "third space professionals" because they operate in a largely independent space which is neither strictly academic nor strictly administrative. Macfarlane (2011) calls them "para-academics" because their concrete job tasks often are the result of an up-skilling of formerly administrative and professional support staff or of a de-skilling of formerly academic staff. Rhoades (1998, 2001) refers to them as "managerial professionals" or "support professionals", and Deem (1998) as "manager-academics" meaning a particular sub-category of mid-level managers best illustrated by the role of Deans who, after serving their term of office as managers, are returning to the ranks of the academic profession. For the purposes of our HEPRO definition, however, Deem's "manager-academics" would not be part of the group of HEPROs but of the group of managers instead.

All studies demonstrate an important issue, namely that it is time to overcome "the prevailing simple dichotomy of administrative versus academic staff" (Rhoades 1998, p. 116). The growing demands for organisational development and professionalization of university governance at central and departmental levels have been identified as causes for the evolution and differentiation of functions and tasks in the area between administration, management and academic work in teaching and research. Teichler (2006) has identified four basic areas of HEPRO activities:

–   Preparation and support of management decisions (e.g. assistants to the rector or president or dean, heads of central administration units, institutional researchers);
–   Professionalised services (e.g. librarians, career consultants);
–   A new hybrid sphere between management and services (e.g. quality managers, heads of international offices, coordinators of study programmes, doctoral programmes or graduate schools);
–   Differentiation of teaching and research functions (e.g. student counsellors, curriculum designers, coordinators of research clusters or large scale distributed research groups).

The two phenomena of a (growing) culture of management and a more traditional academic culture within universities open the realm for a discussion of the interface between management and academics which is exactly inhabited by higher education professionals (i.e. Whitchurch's "third space"). Nevertheless, it needs to be pointed out that recent studies (Schneijderberg et al. 2013) were able to show that the emergence and increase in numbers of higher education professionals is closely related to the degree of managerial governance in higher education institutions. Thus, higher education professionals are as yet hardly regarded as a distinguishable phenomenon in Central and Eastern European countries (for example, Poland, Croatia and Romania) while they have become an important part of university governance in forerunner countries of managerial governance approaches like the UK and the Netherlands (cf. Kehm and Lanzendorf 2006; Kehm 2013).

Methodologically the phenomenon of HEPROs has been approached from a quantitative and from a qualitative angle (cf. Schneijderberg and Merkator 2012). Early quantitative studies were carried out in the USA (e.g. Leslie and Rhoades 1995 or Gumport and Pusser 1995) and in Nordic countries (e.g. Visakorpi 1996 for Finland and Gornitzka et al. 1998 for Norway). These studies focused mainly on changes in the composition and quantity of administrative staff in universities reporting an increase in the number of professional and higher level administrators and a decrease in the number of clerical positions. More recent quantitative studies can be found on Germany trying to determine changes in the composition of administrative staff in universities (Blümel et al. 2010) and describing in more detail the phenomenon of the emergence of HEPROs (Kehm et al. 2010; Schneijderberg and Merkator 2011).

Qualitative approaches in the analysis of HEPROs also emerged in larger numbers in the first half of the 1990s mainly being single country analyses (USA, Australia, United Kingdom, Norway), many attempting to determine the relationships between academics and administrative staff in the context of institutional cultures (e.g. Becher and Kogan 1992 as well as Barnett and Middlehurst 1993 for the UK; Lockwood 1996 for Australia; Boyer et al. 1994 for the USA, Gornitzka et al. 1998 for Norway). Among the newer qualitative studies (e.g. Naschold and Bogumil 2000 as well as Schneijderberg and Merkator 2012 for Germany; Gordon and Whitchurch 2010 for the UK) we increasingly find a focus on issues of governance and power relationships as well as professionalization and the impact of managerial approaches in university governance on academic work and academic cultures.

Generally speaking, the impacts of new forms of (managerial) governance in higher education and the forms of professionalization as well as the shifts in power relationships among administration, management and academics resulting from this nowadays have become the main focus of studies analysing the phenomenon of HEPROs. Thus, the question what factors trigger professionalization in higher education and what forms of professionalization can be observed was one of the main foci in the study the results of which are presented in this volume.

Accordingly our starting hypotheses were threefold:

– The factors triggering professionalization processes within higher education institutions were identified as (a) the emergence of knowledge societies; (b) the diversification of institutional roles within higher education systems, and (c) internationalisation.

- Furthermore, we assumed two main forms of professionalization: (a) a professionalization of academic staff through job enrichment, i.e. the taking over of
  tasks going beyond the core business of teaching and research; (b) a professionalization through a growing division of labour and resulting specialisation
  among academic staff and among institutional management.
- In trying to determine the effects of such processes of professionalization we
  assumed that the academic profession would either (a) experience a thinning out
  of their own professional role or (b) engage in processes of their own professionalization by acquiring new skills and taking over new tasks or (c) experience a
  loss in function or career opportunities through division of labour and increasing
  segmentation.

9.3 Results of Country Studies

In this section the results of eight country studies (Austria, Croatia, Finland,
Germany, Ireland, Poland, Romania, and Switzerland) will be presented derived
from interviews with three groups of persons: members of the academic profession,
HEPROs, and representatives of institutional management (central as well as
departmental or faculty level). The focus of this particular part of the interviews
(for a full account see the Introduction in this volume) carried out in the framework
of the EuroAC Project was on the interaction between these three groups, possible
tensions, reciprocal influences on each other's work and possible forms of professionalization resulting from the interaction.

Two issues should be mentioned at this point. First, at the beginning of the
Project HEPROs seemed to be an unknown species in universities in the three
Central and Eastern European countries involved (Croatia, Poland, Romania). The
assumption was that this might be related to the fact that managerial approaches to
university governance in these countries are either not yet implemented or if at all,
only in their early beginnings. However, the interviews showed that HEPROs are
being recruited in these countries as well, although they are regarded as part of the
institutional administration (at central and at faculty level). Thus, HEPROs do exist
in Croatia and Poland, less so in Romania, but the general perception of academic
staff with regard to specific HEPRO roles is not yet very pronounced. The image
that emerges from the interviews is one of lowly paid and overworked academic
staff fighting with the bureaucracy of the central university administration which
prefers to do things as they have always been done and refuses to learn new things.
However, there are also exceptions and the story will be told. Second, and closely
related to the first point, is a certain blurring of boundaries between what our
interview partners called "administration" and what we define as HEPROs. This
is not surprising given that HEPRO roles are a relatively recent phenomenon in
most countries and the perception of academic staff of HEPRO roles versus
administrative roles is not yet clearly differentiated. Basically, all job roles that

are not academic are then either managerial or administrative. Thus, in the mind of many academic staff HEPRO roles and administrative roles are synonymous.

The country studies will be presented in alphabetical order, the variety in length is related to the fact that the focus of the interviews differed to some extent in the eight countries involved due to the matrix structure chosen for the interviews. Thus, the Austrian, Finnish and Romanian team concentrated their interview focus on the theme of governance, the Polish and Swiss team on the theme of academic careers, and the Croatian, German and Irish team on the theme of professionalization which then included an inquiry into HEPRO roles and their relationship to academic staff and management.

9.3.1 Austria

Despite the Higher Education Law from 2002 which made universities completely independent, the necessary reorganisation of institutional management in most cases did not result in a pure managerial approach to university governance. Co-determination by academic staff is still in place, although a loss of power has been observed. HEPRO work is frequently taken over by junior and middle rank academic staff. Thus, HEPROs at Austrian universities consider themselves mostly as academics working in the middle management of the universities. In addition, academic positions at Austrian universities are very difficult to attain, competition for the few opportunities is high and tenure is granted only at a relatively late stage of the academic career. Often women are switching from academic assistant positions (doctoral and post-doc positions) into part-time administrative positions due to a better compatibility of work and family life. This switch does have career consequences: on the one hand academic qualification work tends to be neglected due to the administrative burden, and on the other hand – HEPRO roles being a very recent career path – there is a lack of stable career models in this work. But also job descriptions of other academic staff in permanent positions include up to one third of the regular working time to be spent on administrative tasks.

Typically HEPRO tasks comprise documentation and collection of data, reporting, service and support, much of which is related to the increased public accountability burden of Austrian universities. One interviewee being part of the institutional management saw a clear relationship between appeasement of the academic profession for their loss of power and increased HEPRO work: "If I can offer university administration that covers all aspects of teaching etc., it becomes easier for a professor to accept a loss of power" (AT26_MAN). In contrast to this, professors consider the number of HEPROs as being too many and would prefer the university to provide a higher number of academic positions. As it is, the increase in administration and accountability (data collection, reporting) is taken over by permanent middle level academic staff or female part-timers with the danger of losing research capacity.

9.3.2   Croatia

Croatia was one of the three countries of which we anticipated that HEPROs and their tasks were a rather unfamiliar phenomenon in universities. However, the picture is somewhat split. Junior academic staff tends to see neither a professionalization of the university administration nor is there a perception of HEPRO roles and their potential difference to administrative roles. However, junior academic staff notes an increase in the amount of administrative tasks that have to be carried out by junior and senior academic staff alike. Those academics – mostly senior ones – that have at least some experiences with HEPRO roles were positive about them and contrasted HEPROs clearly to the administrative staff with the former being younger, better educated and more efficient in their work and the latter being unprofessional and bureaucratic. But due to the fact that HEPRO roles are still very new and also small in number, HEPROs have not managed to develop the capacity to provide the sort of systematic support that is expected from them.

HEPROs in Croatian universities are mostly recruited in the fields of international cooperation, quality management and to support the implementation of the Bologna reforms (e.g. ECTS coordination). But they can also be found in technology transfer offices and research support offices. HEPROs mark the beginnings of a new type of administration and there is a relatively clear split between a younger generation of HEPROs and an older generation of traditional administrators. Institutional management tries to modernise the administration by offering additional training for existing administrative staff and recruiting younger persons with higher levels of education for open or new positions. But there is also another split: while the traditional administrative staff is lowly paid but having permanent contracts, the younger staff being newly recruited as HEPROs or into the general administration might be somewhat better paid but often having fixed-term contracts. Still, HEPRO salaries are considered as being too low to retain the high performers while the older generation of administrators remains on their permanent contracts. One interviewee, a senior academic and current Vice-Chancellor at his university, stated that "university administration is the biggest problem at Croatian universities" (HR42_MAN) and deplored the lack of managerial spirit in university administration. He claimed that "new competences are absolutely necessary, especially in the management segment my position is based on" (HR42_MAN). Interestingly this interviewee did not exclude himself and his own work from the need for professionalization. A junior member of academic staff who had worked in the university administration for 2 years voiced scepticism with regard to the potential for professionalization in the university administration. He was noting an increased number of newly hired employees in the administration of his institution but did not see much progress in terms of efficiency: "(...) when you see how many people work in administration, you expect some major progress will occur regarding the support it provides to academics. And then when you start working at the university and seek their support you either don't get it or you don't get it in the form you expected. (...) They do exist, but I often wonder what those people actually do" (HR41_AC).

The HEPROs themselves report positive experiences with academics and more mixed ones with institutional management. Especially HEPROs working in departments and faculties are assigned tasks by the dean or head of department and sometimes tend to see that as a restriction of their autonomy. HEPROs working in the area of quality management and quality assurance state that there are good experiences with younger academic staff but also some resistance, especially from the older generation of academic staff, against the new quality assurance instruments in teaching and learning.

9.3.3 Finland

Finnish academics report that there are many new professionals in the faculty administration leading to a new administrative layer which is perceived by some as a higher degree of control over academic work by the administration. On the other hand the traditional support staff (e.g. secretaries) has been decreased and centralised which in turn leads to a higher administrative workload for the academic staff. "I think that the organisation of administrative work at universities has changed a lot. The administrative and technical staff that used to work close to us at our departments has been moved to service centres. (...) Administration frustrates many nowadays and therefore this work is not as attractive anymore" (FI77_AC). By centralising administrative (and clerical) and technical staff and moving it away from the academics the latter are being forced to do a higher amount of administrative work themselves. Or as one senior academic bitterly formulated: "There's professionalization going on in management and administration and there is a lot of highly competent personnel in those positions. But the trend in expert work nowadays is that one has to do secretarial work oneself" (FI68_AC).

Both the new competence requirements for academic staff (e.g. supervision, project management) and the higher administrative work load are seen by some members of the academic profession as having a negative impact on creativity. Generally, academic staff has to acquire "more knowledge about more things" (FI16_AC) as one junior academic stated, while a senior academic specified that academics have to acquire "more expertise in governance" (FI17_AC). Among the academic profession views tend to be divided whether these additional requirements impact negatively on time for teaching and research and thus is a form of professionalization outside traditional academic tasks or whether these developments should be regarded as a positive trend because they require academics to reflect more on their own activities, make them more visible and more structured and help in setting goals and working on them (FI18_AC, FI19_AC/MAN).

A number of Finnish academics who were interviewed in the course of our research stated that the actual academic work in terms of teaching and research has not changed very much but that higher education institutions are currently professionalising their management and administration. In the course of these changes also new support structures are being created for research and study administration. This in turn leads to a higher amount of reporting, e.g. when new databases are established, which has to be done by the academic staff.

However, one Vice-Rector pointed out that "research is getting more professional as one has to create new ideas all the time. Professionalization can be seen in management as well; roles are clearer than before (...). Traditionally departments have had responsibilities but now responsibilities are getting more personalised and therefore attitudes towards own tasks have become more professional as well" (FI20_MAN). The statement demonstrates at least four changes:

– All main status groups working within the university are professionalizing;
– There is a more pronounced division of labour;
– Responsibilities are allocated to people rather than to organisational units and
– People are being made accountable for their work.

Interestingly Finnish polytechnics seem to lag behind somewhat in terms of these developments and the resulting changes. A HEPRO from a Finnish polytechnic stated in the interview: "Management is getting more professional. Strategies have a bigger role nowadays and they guide everyday life. This has caused a lack of competences in the management of polytechnics because traditionally expertise in one's own subject has been respected, but now there is a need for expertise in management. There is a need to train management staff to develop these competences or to recruit professional managers" (FI29_HEPRO).

9.3.4 Germany

German academics' perspective of HEPROs alternates between HEPROs producing more work for academics and HEPROs being really helpful because they unburden academics from administrative work or provide useful services. By far not all junior researchers are familiar with or knowledgeable about HEPROs and their work. Those academics that are familiar with HEPRO roles generally expect that the work of HEPROs will become more important in the future. Academics report that they have no outright negative experiences but there is a certain tension with the classical committee structure for institutional and departmental (or faculty) decision-making. Especially senior professors characterised HEPRO activities as intransparent and resulting decisions as opaque here and there: "HEPROs lead a life of their own" (DE0308_MAN).

HEPROs themselves see their work as important for a specific clientele (e.g. students or academic staff) but foremost for the university as an organisation which has to be competitive in many respects and areas. Their work is influenced by requests from university management or deans. Most HEPROs consider themselves as service oriented but perceive in their activities a certain tension between meaningful service projects and administration, the latter being linked to negative connotations. The experiences of HEPROs regarding their cooperation with representatives of the central management and of the academic profession vary to a considerable extent. Apart from their service orientation they also perceive themselves as working at a variety of interfaces. Most HEPROs, though highly qualified and often having a doctoral degree, have had no particular training for their job. Often they are recruited to help solve a particular problem, cater to a specific need, or support the university in dealing with new challenges and requirements. HEPRO work often starts as project work on fixed-term contracts. If they succeed in making themselves and their work indispensable or if the university believes that the tasks will have to be carried out on a continuous basis then HEPRO contracts become permanent.

HEPRO work in universities of applied sciences is somewhat different because it is more student and teaching oriented. However, universities of applied sciences are currently also under pressure to develop an applied research portfolio. Therefore we can safely assume that new HEPRO roles will be created at universities of applied sciences in the future.

HEPROs are perceived differently by the academic profession and by management. The academic profession see HEPROs as well qualified people taking an administrative or organisational burden off them which is related to teaching and research but an unloved element. Academics tend to emphasise the service function of HEPROs. Representatives of central and departmental (or faculty) management seek HEPRO support to deal with new challenges and requirements and provide information and data for decision-making. They tend to see HEPROs as a means to professionalise their own work.

9.3.5 *Ireland*

The interviews carried out in Ireland with HEPROs, academic staff and representatives of management show a picture that is riddled with tension in the interaction between these three groups. Academics complain about the "bean counting" aspects of HEPRO activities and feel that "they no longer have any power or any control over their subjects" (IE23_AC). Managers require academic staff "to see the bigger picture and be part of the team" (IE28_MAN), and HEPROs point out that academics "are difficult customers to please" (IE58_HEPRO) who "prefer the status quo and don't want to do any extra work" (IE10_HEPRO).

Many HEPROs in Irish universities seem to have moved from previously academic positions into HEPRO positions and academics tend to think that not all HEPROs are suited for middle management tasks. However, there are also voices that make a more detailed distinction among HEPROs by dividing them into "enablers" or "facilitators" and "bean counters obsessed with control and performance indicators" (IE5_AC; IE12_AC/MAN; IE41_AC). HEPROs in supporting and facilitating roles (e.g. in the field of quality assurance) have a better relationship with members of the academic profession than HEPROs in more managerial positions supporting institutional management (e.g. in the field of strategic planning).

Both HEPROs and members of the academic profession feel that too much routine administrative work has to be done by them. Thus, an academic stated: "Institutional managers have influenced the role of the academic by reducing the budgets which has resulted in academics doing more administration work than before" (IE20_AC). And a HEPRO pointed out that there were many menial things she was expected to do ("I almost feel I should be checking the toilet roles in the toilet", IE6_HEPRO) which did not allow time for conceptual or strategic thinking. And both HEPROs and members of the academic profession voiced harsh words about each other. The tension seems to arise from different expectations what the respective other group should do. HEPROs feel that academics expect from them to do work that is academics' work (IE58_HEPRO) and academics feel that HEPROs are increasing their workload and tend to create bureaucratic structures, superimposing complicated procedures and requesting information that is not necessary (IE46_AC).

It seems that one main group of HEPROs at Irish universities constitutes an additional layer of hierarchy related to accountability and competitive requirements while a second main group of HEPROs is involved in quality assurance issues. The activities of the first group are seen by academics as a "power shift away" from them "to more of the accounting and finance and HR people" (IE15_AC/MAN) which creates most of the tension. The second group is widely accepted by the academics as being helpful and facilitating.

9.3.6 Poland

Polish academics see the university as a bureaucratic institution with an administration that does routine work and refuses to professionalise. And while many junior academics have no concept of HEPRO roles and accordingly do not observe any changes in university administration, there is indeed a slow emergence of HEPRO roles at Polish universities. This is due to the fact that new administrative units are being created for which younger and better educated staff are recruited. The new administrative units are often closely related to the new challenges and demands with which Polish universities are confronted, e.g. participating in larger EU-funded research for which new administrative procedures and financial regulations have to be applied, competing for international students who require new forms of support and advice. "There is observable change in raising the quality of the university administration. (. . .) The reason for such a change is that new people had to be employed who are better educated and have a different approach to problems that need to be addressed" (PL13_AC). In particular, English language skills have become much more important for administrative staff than before.

What seems to be particular about the Polish way of dealing with new issues is that nobody expects much of the traditional administration any longer and parallel structures are created with more professionalised staff rather than tackling the issue of professionalising and modernising the existing administration. Another interviewee from the group of academics provides an explanation for this situation: "Administration is in many places badly organised and produce tons of useless papers for internal purposes. The problem of the administration is that there are conflicts between different units which struggle for power, bigger budgets and influence. As a result one unit of the administration can easily block the initiative of another unit. Tribal wars and lack of strong leadership undermine the authority of the university administration" (PL14_AC). The university is described as being dominated by a "help yourself system" (PL16_AC) in which academics do not have any support from the university administration, and a senior member of the University Senate sees his university as "a perfect example of the lack of professionalism in any possible dimension. (. . .) A sad thing is that the university management does not care if there is professional performance or not" (PL17_AC).

However, some academics are more optimistic because they believe that the recruitment of younger, better educated and more professional staff for new tasks in the administration will positively influence the others or they hope that there might be a spill-over from more professionalised areas of the administration (e.g. student services) to other areas (cf. PL20_AC/MAN). It seems that the most visible HEPRO roles can be found in student services and in the support of attracting and managing third party funded research projects. In these areas HEPROs are offered better salaries. Concerning the central university administration the problem is their low salaries so that it is not possible to recruit and retain young and well educated staff. "The same administrative staff has been already working here for 30 years and it is difficult to teach an old dog new tricks" (PL23_AC).

The overall trend emerging from the interviews is that junior academics tend to see the university administration as useless, inefficient and reluctant to change. In contrast, the more senior academics more often see some progress in terms of professionalization of the university administration. But it remains somewhat unclear whether these signs of progress are related to the hiring of younger, more flexible and better educated staff or whether the traditional university administration has started to change.

9.3.7   Romania

The one notion that can be found in the Romanian interviews again and again is "outside professionalization" or "imposed professionalization" or – taken together – "professionalization imposed from outside". What this notion implies is that Romanian higher education is importing models from other European countries to deal with the ongoing social and economic changes. With "professionalization imposed from outside" Romanian universities are reacting to demands of their external social and cultural environment and to challenges resulting from Romania's EU membership and the implementation of the Bologna reforms, for example in terms of modernising curricula, implementing quality assurance mechanisms or establishing transfer activities. These are typical HEPRO tasks in most of the Western European higher education systems. In Romania these tasks are mostly carried out by academic staff "unpaid, at home and in their free time" (RO4_AC). This is seen by the academic profession as taking time away from their teaching and research duties. Academics also complain about the fact that changes are implemented in a highly bureaucratic manner while university management is not professionalising at all.

Overall, academics' views are split whether the additional tasks required from them actually constitute a reconfiguration of job roles and tasks or whether they are just an additional burden beyond the core business of teaching and research. The sometimes bitter undertone in the interviews is related to the fact that academics receive very low salaries – there was a 25 % reduction of salaries in 2010/11 – and that there are few resources for research. The "professionalization imposed from outside" is seen as a form of excessive and additional bureaucracy coming from an incoherent and unprofessional institutional management and influenced by managerial attempts to align Romanian higher education with European standards (especially in quality assurance). Together with the lack of resources for research and low salaries this does not only lead to academics' feeling that they have a high overload of work but also to a high level of job dissatisfaction among academics.

The perspective of manager-academics (e.g. deans and heads of departments) is somewhat different from that of the academics. The former see the new requirements as a normal evolution related to the modernisation agenda of Romanian higher education. But even representatives of the management believe that there is too much administration and not enough professionalization: "We are still de-professionalised because we have to do too much administration at the expense of important professional issues. (...) Unfortunately there is an overload for the few who actually get involved and there is still an amorphous mass that mimics commitment" (RO64_MAN). And a vice-rector stated: "Today very little attention has been paid to how teachers prefer to engage in their own professional development, in particular the development of teaching practice. All attention is focused on the imposition of external control ..." (RO67_MAN).

Thus it seems that not much progress has been made in Romanian higher education in terms of professionalization and further differentiation of job roles. Instead, academics are given an additional workload with the task of implementing a "modernisation agenda" borrowed from EU 'higher education speak' which only few academics and representatives of management tend to support and which is seen as an imposition from outside. No emergence of HEPRO roles can be observed so far.

9.3.8   Switzerland

Swiss academics report about an increase in administrative tasks they have to do which is mostly related to reporting and accountability requirements. As in most of the other European countries involved in our study academics tend to see all work that is not directly related to teaching and/or research as "administration" and they feel that they are required to do more of that without additional means or resources. "Administrative work takes a lot of energy. Even though there have been reorganisations in order to improve efficiency, academics waste too much time" (CH25_AC). Switzerland also was the only country among those involved in our study in which academics observed a progressing differentiation between teaching and research roles.

In particular younger academics still in their qualification phase as post-docs tend to take over HEPRO roles in addition to their research work and possible teaching duties. They often have to divide their time between the two job tasks but find it difficult to manage: "It is difficult to be an assistant and a CEO of the department at the same time. I do this because of my financial situation" (CH27_AC/HEPRO).

The few HEPROs who were interviewed by the Swiss team represented a notable divide: those doing HEPRO work at the departmental or faculty level were part-time HEPROs and part-time academics having to reconcile the demands and challenges of both job roles. Those doing HEPRO work at the level of the central administration (e.g. in the international office) are mostly on full-time contracts and involved in implementing strategies designed at the central level. However, one HEPRO stated "that the strategy of the institution is too far from the departmental strategy" (CH55_HEPRO) which makes implementation difficult.

Overall, the Swiss interviews convey a somewhat fragmented picture with more administrative work for the academics, an increasing differentiation of academic work, and strategies of the institution not being properly aligned with strategies of departments or faculties.

9.4   Synthesis

The case studies of the eight countries involved in the EuroAC project presented in this chapter provide information about four main issues which can be synthesized by the following key points: professionalization, changes in job roles and tasks, the role of administration, and tensions between the three groups of academics, HEPROs and representatives of management.

9.4.1 Professionalisation

Professionalisation is understood in different ways in the higher education cultures of the countries involved in this study. Among the younger academics the perception of professionalization is most often related to the acquisition of additional skills and competences related to new forms of the organisation and practice of teaching and research. For example, there is more emphasis nowadays on the systematic and certified acquisition of teaching skills and pedagogical tools; for research competences have to be developed concerning successful applications, calculating a budget, exercising project management and cooperating in international and interdisciplinary teams. Among the more senior academics the perception is widespread that new forms of governance and HEPRO activities have not really influenced their work in teaching and research. However, the burden of having to take on additional administrative work which is a complaint voiced by academics in most countries is not at all perceived as a form of professionalization. Instead it is regarded as threatening creativity and taking time away from the core activities of teaching and research. HEPROs are regarded in two ways by academics: they are either part of the "bean counters" trying to control academic work by unreasonable requests for data and reports, or they are the "facilitators" providing helpful and useful services to increase quality and effectiveness of teaching and research.

In most of our eight countries involved in the study the academic profession sees a need for further professionalization of the (central) administration and in some countries also of the institutional management. In turn, HEPROs often reported the impression that it is the academic profession which is resisting change and can't be bothered with the tasks resulting from institutional accountability duties. In two of the three Central and Eastern European countries participating in this study HEPRO roles are only just emerging (Poland and Croatia) while in Romania, typical HEPRO tasks are taken over by members of the academic profession. In Poland and Croatia HEPROs constitute a younger, better educated, more flexible and more professional administrative group in contrast to the old style bureaucratic administration. HEPROs themselves report that they have received hardly any systematic training for their jobs and 'learning by doing' and 'learning on the job' is the most common form of professionalization. Frequently younger, often female academics tend to take over HEPRO roles or are part-time employed as academics and part-time as HEPROs.

In those countries in which HEPRO roles in higher education institutions are relatively established we see a further form of professionalization, namely that of the management professionalizing itself through the deployment of HEPROs. The increased expectations with regard to a more professional management of higher education institutions are in part dealt with by recruiting HEPROs to deal with accountability issues and collect data for informed and evidence-based decision-making by the institutional management. Therefore the group of HEPROs seen by academics as the "bean counters" tend to work in the central administration for the institutional management and the group of HEPROs seen by academics as the "facilitators" tend to either work in central service units or at the level of departments and faculties.

9.4.2 Changes in Job Roles and Tasks

In particular, the younger members of the academic profession, in the Central and Eastern European countries also the more senior ones note considerable changes in their job roles and tasks. Though we had anticipated a more progressed differentiation into teaching only and research only positions, this seemed to be the case in Switzerland only. The changes are basically threefold: First, and as mentioned in the previous section, more and more professional competences are required for teaching and research, such as intercultural competences and teaching in the English language in the face of growing internationalisation as well as improved pedagogical and didactic skills or skills to write successful grant applications and being able to manage larger, often international and interdisciplinary project teams. Second, additional professional competences are required such as becoming more involved in university third mission activities or participating in committees for internationalisation or for developing departmental strategies. Third, and for younger academics perhaps most importantly, there is an increased attention to one's own career management. Managing to stay in academia and getting tenure has become increasingly more difficult and is highly competitive. The building up of competences, qualifications and experiences that might contribute to career progress is approached much more strategically than before. The other side of this coin is the fact that some young academics, often women, are either switching from academic jobs into HEPRO jobs or become part-time academics and part-time HEPROs.

Senior academics mostly report that they do not observe any great changes in their job tasks as far as teaching and research are concerned but that they are increasingly required to take on additional tasks as "manager-academics" or in supervision of PhD candidates. There were only few cases in which a senior academic reported that his or her task was almost exclusively confined to writing grant applications and managing the research team. However, there are higher expectations in terms of leadership and managerial skills when it comes to taking over fixed-term functions as dean, head of department or director of a research institute.

Finally, HEPRO roles are becoming increasingly differentiated, although mostly without preceding systematic training and with unstable career progression. Many HEPROs are moving into their roles from being an academic, many tend to work in structures similar to fixed-term project work with fixed-term, often part-time contracts. Only when they manage to provide helpful services that are needed continuously they have the opportunity to receive a permanent contract. Typically HEPROs are better educated and have higher level qualifications, often a doctorate, than the average staff in the university administration. But HEPRO roles are in most cases not linked to any model of career progress. On the other side of the coin HEPROs get involved in the professionalization of other groups within the university: of the academic profession by offering services in the field of staff development, for example; and of representatives of the institutional and departmental management by providing data and information for more effective and evidence-based decision-making.

9.4.3 The Role of Administration

The phenomenon of academics having to carry out more administrative and even secretarial tasks was surprisingly widespread in our case studies and an issue of equally widespread complaints. It seems that in many countries and many universities secretarial support staff has been reduced and the remaining staff centralised so that access to such support is increasingly restricted. This indirectly confirms the findings of earlier studies that university administrations have been restructured by reducing clerical staff positions and increasing the number of higher level administrators. Among these higher level administrators we can find many HEPROs who are involved in implementing the new forms of managerial governance. Academics greatly resent having to do more administrative work and tensions arise when they try to shift these tasks to HEPROs.

The situation in the three Central and Eastern European countries involved in this study is somewhat different. In Poland and Croatia HEPRO roles are just emerging and seen by academics as a better, more helpful and more effective group of administrators compared to the traditional (central) university administration which tends to be old-style bureaucracy. However, this new group of HEPROs seems to form parallel structure or layer which is not integrated into the existing administration. This enables academics to avoid the traditional university administration, although these HEPRO jobs tend to be instable, dependent on external funding and riddled with a high level of fluctuation because the "high performers" are hard to retain in the face of typically low salaries in regular administration and no constant flow of external funding. It remains yet to be seen whether the new HEPRO roles will have an impact on the traditional university administration or whether an instable parallel structure becomes the norm.

Romania is an exceptional case as here the phenomenon of HEPROs seems to be the least known and common compared to our other countries of comparison. Instead, HEPRO tasks are being given as additional, mostly unpaid tasks to academics who feel overburdened by them because they reduce the time for teaching and research as well as private time.

9.4.4   Tensions and Reciprocal Influences

In trying to summarize and synthesize possible tensions and reciprocal influences resulting from the interaction between the academic profession, HEPROs and institutional management, six major issues can be observed:

–   Tensions arise when institutional management is using HEPROs for its own professionalization in areas such as institutional accountability, introduction of new public management instruments and evidence-based decision-making. Academics see the resulting requests for generation of data and production of reports as bureaucratic approaches that increase their workload.
–   In many areas related to the core business of teaching and research members of the academic profession tend to professionalize themselves, however support from HEPROs is welcomed when it comes to new forms of organising and administering teaching and research.
–   HEPROs in central service units or located in faculties and departments (rather than in the central administration) are mostly seen as helpful and useful by the academic profession, but HEPROs sometimes suffer from expectations to also carry out menial tasks which might have been done by clerks and secretaries before.
–   The shift towards recruitment of higher level administrators and decrease of clerical positions in institutional administration has led to a higher administrative workload for academics which they feel is keeping them from their core business of teaching and research.
–   HEPROs see themselves as dominantly service oriented but often meet with resistance from academic staff not willing to change.
–   In the Central and Eastern European countries a traditional and rather bureaucratic administration tends to be confronted with new challenges resulting from a Europeanisation and modernisation agenda. Their unwillingness to professionalize results in the recruitment of younger and better educated HEPROs which are not integrated into the institutional administration but constitute an unstable and fluctuating additional layer. Academics prefer to cooperate with these new HEPROs in order to circumvent having to deal with traditional administrators.

Conclusions
Overall we can say that HEPROs are a visible phenomenon in those countries in which a high degree of institutional autonomy coupled with a professional institutional management can be observed. Both elements have to be present as the examples of Austria and Poland have shown in different ways where we have a very high level of autonomy for higher education institutions on the one hand, but a lack of professionalized institutional management on the other hand. According to Musselin (2013), the evolution of universities from

(continued)

being institutions to becoming organisations is leading to new structures characterised by a stronger division of work, a differentiation of job roles and a new construction of the relationships between the academic profession and the higher education institution at which they are employed. The earlier these changes have started, the more established and differentiated are HEPRO roles.

HEPROs are mostly working at the interface between institutional management and academia as the new forms of higher education governance strive to achieve a tighter organisational coupling of the various units a higher education institution consists of. Among other things this tighter coupling is linked to a variety of attempts to convert the prevailing "unclear technologies" in teaching and research into objective knowledge (e.g. by developing standards, defining criteria, and evaluating in terms of efficiency and effectiveness) which can then be managed. HEPROs play an important role in this process acting as pioneers and as change agents at the same time because their job tasks consist mostly in the development of structures and processes to deal with new challenges and demands the institution has to face.

Looking at the emergence of HEPRO roles in universities of different European countries we can observe a variety of roles and heterogeneous forms of organisational integration. In addition we find national and institutional path dependency related to the history of national higher education systems and forms of institutional cultures. This of course, impacts on the employment situation of HEPROs but also on their interaction with academics.

The emergence of HEPRO roles is currently related to hybrid forms of professionalization either by academics taking over HEPRO tasks or by administrative staff through upskilling. This was most visible in Austria, Croatia, Poland and Romania. In the other countries included in this study we observe a more professionalized management of higher education institutions leading to the gradual development of established occupational roles for HEPROs. Still, as Kottmann and Enders (2013) have pointed out in a comparative analysis of six European countries, HEPRO tasks first emerge ad hoc and incrementally in reaction to new (internal as well as external) demands and challenges higher education institutions are confronted with. But while countries with more professional and managerial approaches to higher education governance react with strategic and planned processes of differentiation of tasks, other countries in which traditional collegial models of governance dominate are reacting more ad-hoc and incrementalist. Although the six European countries which were analyzed by Kottmann and Enders are not identical with the countries included in this study (the only overlap is Austria), the results seem to be similar for our eight countries of comparison: Finnish and Irish higher education institutions have a more

(continued)

strategic approach, Austrian, Croatian and Polish institutions show an ad hoc approach, German and Swiss institutions present a mixed picture, and at Romanian higher education institutions no HEPROs have emerged as yet. Instead, their work is taken over by academics on an ad hoc basis.

But let us have a final look at our starting hypotheses. The first one was that there are three main factors triggering processes of professionalization, namely the emergence of knowledge societies, the diversification of tasks and functions of higher education institutions, and internationalisation. It is possible to establish links to all three factors. The emergence of knowledge societies has led to an increased importance of higher education institutions in and for societies because higher education institutions are producing, disseminating and conveying knowledge. In order to react more flexibly to the new demands and challenges they were given more institutional autonomy in exchange for more public accountability. Increased autonomy requires a more professional institutional management and public accountability requires more data gathering, more reporting, and proof of efficiency and effectiveness in terms of services, outputs and outcomes. This is achieved with the help of HEPROs who support institutional management in designing appropriate strategies and establishing evidence based decision-making processes.

But the increased importance of higher education institutions in and for knowledge societies has also led to a growing diversification of tasks and functions, sometimes referred to as "mission overload": fund raising, marketing and branding, technology transfer, recruitment and retention of students, providing advice and counselling to a more international and more heterogeneous student body are just a few examples of new or more professionalised tasks and services that higher education institutions today have to master. Because many of these tasks clearly go beyond the core business of teaching and research, new higher education professionals have been recruited to take them over or improve them. In part this has led to shifts of some tasks which were part of the typical portfolio of academics to HEPRO activities; in part these were new tasks for which neither the traditional administration nor the academics felt appropriately qualified.

Internationalisation in higher education is a very multi-faceted and ongoing process, no longer restricted to the organisation of student and staff mobility. There is much competition for best talent going on, active recruitment abroad, offshore provision of transnational education and establishment of branch campuses in other countries. There is also a broad spectrum of activities related to internationalisation at home, starting from the internationalisation of curricula and reaching to the necessity of English language knowledge in the administration, in support services, the provision of teaching and cooperating in international research teams. However,

(continued)

internationalisation has also led to the spreading of good practice models, to imitation of standards and procedures, even to isomorphism where it comes to competition. In this area as well a variety of HEPRO roles have developed to support the higher education institutions in their endeavours. This has not remained without any impact on academic work.

Our second hypothesis was that there are two forms of professionalization going on in higher education institutions: First, a professionalization through job enrichment, and second, a professionalization through a division of labour. Although we can observe both forms in most of our countries included in the comparison, job enrichment especially in the form of upgrading and upskilling traditional administrative work and division of labour through taking particular tasks out of the portfolio of academic work and making them part of the new occupational roles of HEPROs, the more prominent phenomenon right now seems to be a hybridisation of professional roles (cf. Noordegraf 2007). For the most part HEPRO work is not (yet) established as a stable occupation with permanent contracts and opportunities for career progress. Instead, there are many academics on part-time contracts working as HEPROs on part-time contracts as well. There are former academics working as HEPROs but still doing some teaching or some research. And finally, there are academics having HEPRO work as part of their contractual duties (e.g. in Austria) or as additional, unpaid duties (e.g. in Romania). However, there are some European countries in which a more systematic training and qualification has been established for HEPRO roles (Germany, for example) so that it can be expected that the hybridisation of HEPRO roles is only a transitional phenomenon. But a more general picture emerges as well. In the framework of the interaction between management, the academic profession and HEPROs each of the three groups is professionalising in a relatively distinct form: Institutional management professionalises through HEPROs, HEPROs professionalise through job enrichment, and academics professionalise through being confronted with new demands which are coming at least partially from HEPROs.

Our third and final hypothesis was that the effects of such professionalization might either lead to a thinning out of academic roles or to an acquisition of new skills, or to losses in function through division of labour and segmentation. The verification of this hypothesis is not quite as straightforward as originally assumed. This is probably also the area in which most of the tensions between the academic profession and HEPROs arise. Academics typically do not see a thinning out of their role through HEPRO activities. Instead they either find HEPRO activities useful because they unburden them from unloved "administrative" tasks or they find that HEPROs add to their workload because they make unreasonable requests for data supply and reporting. Also an acquisition of new skills can be observed on both sides.

(continued)

With regard to members of the academic profession this becomes most visible among the younger generation of early career researchers who have to go about their career management and career progression in a much more systematic way than before and sometimes even are required to produce certified course work in terms of teaching skills and a variety of other general competences and key skills. Among the more senior generation of academics we can note that there is an increased emphasis on project management, successful grant application and requirements to improve their skills in doctoral supervision. However, the senior members of the academic profession do not see many changes in teaching and research as such. Among HEPROs the acquisition of new skills is a widespread phenomenon because they are confronted every day with tasks for which they have not received any systematic training. In this situation 'learning by doing' and 'learning on the job' are common. Finally, we could hardly note the perception among the academic profession that HEPRO work leads to losses in function through division of labour and segmentation.

Concerning the relationship between the academic profession and HEPROs we find a number of ambiguities. Members of the academic profession appreciate the work of HEPROs as long as it is service and support oriented and unburdens them from what they consider 'administrative' work which is not directly related to teaching and research. However, additional demands coming from HEPROs in terms of reporting, evaluating or data generating is not at all appreciated by academics. In turn, HEPROs miss appropriate recognition of their work from the side of the academics and often feel saddled with menial tasks. Actual interaction between HEPROs and academics happens mostly when HEPROs are integrated into the functioning of department, faculties or research units, less so when HEPROs are integrated into the work of the central administration. In departments and faculties HEPROs often take over tasks such as coordinating committee meetings, administration of teaching and study programmes, provision of information and advice, and coordination of research support. In addition, the office of the dean typically has at least one HEPRO acting as an office manager. Conflicts between HEPROs and the academic profession arise most often when HEPROs take over controlling and monitoring tasks or have the power to sanction.

It remains to be seen whether in the future the professionalization of HEPROs advances to such an extent that we can speak of the emergence of a new occupation located between administration, management and the academic profession or whether we are currently observing the beginning of a blurring of boundaries between academic and non-academic areas and activities within higher education institutions.

References

Altbach, P. G. (Ed.). (2000). *The changing academic workplace: Comparative perspectives.* Boston: Boston College, Center for International Higher Education.

Barnett, R., & Middlehurst, R. (1993). The lost profession. *Higher Education in Europe, 18*(2), 110–128.

Becher, T., & Kogan, M. (1992). *Process and structure in higher education* (2nd ed.). London: Routledge.

Blümel, A., Kloke, K., Kruecken, G., & Netz, N. (2010). Restrukturierung statt Expansion. Entwicklung im Bereich des nichtwissenchaftlichen Personals an deutschen Hochschulen. *Die Hochschule, 20*(2), 154–172.

Boyer, E., Altbach, P., & Whitelaw, M.-J. (1994). *The academic profession. An international perspective.* Princeton: Carnegie Foundation.

Deem, R. (1998). 'New managerialism' and higher education: The management of performance and cultures in universities in the United Kingdom. *International Studies in Sociology of Education, 60*(3), 203–228.

Enders, J. (Ed.). (2001). *Academic staff in Europe: Changing contexts and conditions.* Westport: Greenwood.

Farnham, D. (Ed.). (1999). *Managing academic staff in changing university systems. International trends and comparisons.* Buckingham: SRHE/Open University Press.

Gordon, G., & Whitchurch, C. (Eds.). (2010). *Academic and professional identities in higher education. The challenge of a diversifying workforce.* New York: Routledge.

Gornitzka, A., Kyvik, S., & Larsen, I. (1998). The bureaucratisation of universities. *Minerva, 36* (1), 21–47.

Gumport, P. J., & Pusser, B. (1995). A case of bureaucratic accretion: Context and consequences. *The Journal of Higher Education, 66*(5), 493–520.

Kehm, B. M. (2013). Die neuen Hochschulprofessionen als europäisches Phänomen. Deutschland im Vergleich mit ausgewählten europäischen Ländern. In C. Schneijderberg, N. Merkator, U. Teichler, & B. M. Kehm (Eds.), *Verwaltung war gestern? Neue Hochschulprofessionen und die Gestaltung von Studium und Lehre* (pp. 369–387). Frankfurt/M: Campus.

Kehm, B. M. (2014, forthcoming). The influence of new higher education professionals on academic work. In U. Teichler & W. Cummings (Eds.), *Forming, recruiting and managing the academic profession.* Dordrecht: Springer.

Kehm, B. M., & Lanzendorf, U. (Eds.). (2006). *Reforming university governance. Changing conditions for research in four European countries.* Bonn: Lemmens.

Kehm, B. M., & Teichler, U. (Eds.). (2012). *The academic profession in Europe: New tasks and new challenges.* Dordrecht: Springer.

Kehm, B. M., Merkator, N., & Schneijderberg, C. (2010). Hochschulprofessionelle?! Die unbekannten Wesen. *Zeitschrift fuer Hochschulentwicklung, 5*(4), 23–39.

Kottmann, A., & Enders, J. (2013). Die neuen Hochschulprofessionellen in Europe: Ausdifferenzierung und Aufgaben im internationalen Vergleich. In C. Schneijderberg, N. Merkator, U. Teichler, & B. M. Kehm (Eds.), *Verwaltung war gestern? Neue Hochschulprofessionen und die Gestaltung von Studium und Lehre* (pp. 305–333). Frankfurt/M: Campus.

Leslie, L. L., & Rhoades, G. (1995). Rising administrative costs. Seeking explanations. *The Journal of Higher Education, 66*(2), 187–212.

Locke, W., & Teichler, U. (Eds.). (2007). *The changing conditions for academic work and careers in select countries.* Kassel: University of Kassel, INCHER (Werkstattberichte 66).

Lockwood, G. (1996). Continuity and transition in university management: The role of the professional administrative service. *Higher Education Management and Policy, 8*(2), 41–52.

Macfarlane, B. (2011). The morphing of academic practice: Unbundling and the rise of the para-academic. *Higher Education Quarterly, 65*(1), 59–73.

Musselin, C. (2013). Redefinition of the relationships between academics and their university. *Higher Education, 65*(1), 25–37.

Naschold, F., & Bogumil, J. (2000). *Modernisierung des Staates: New Public Management in deutscher und internationaler Perspektive* (2nd ed.). Opladen: Leske & Budrich.

Noordegraf, M. (2007). From "Pure" to "Hybrid" professionalism. *Administration & Society, 39* (6), 761–785.

Rhoades, G. (1998). *Managed professionals: Unionized faculty and restructuring academic labor.* Albany: New York State University Press.

Rhoades, G. (2001). Managing productivity in an academic institution: Rethinking the whom, which what, and whose of productivity. *Research in Higher Education, 45*(5), 619–632.

Schneijderberg, C., & Merkator, N. (2011). Hochschulprofessionen und Professionalisierung im Bereich der Qualitaetsentwicklung. *Qualität der Wissenschaft, 5*(1), 15–20.

Schneijderberg, C., & Merkator, N. (2012). The new higher education professionals. In B. M. Kehm & U. Teichler (Eds.), *The academic profession in Europe: New tasks and new challenges* (pp. 53–92). Dordrecht: Springer.

Schneijderberg, C., Merkator, N., Teichler, U., & Kehm, B. M. (Eds.). (2013). *Verwaltung war gestern? Neue Hochschulprofessionen und die Gestaltung von Studium und Lehre.* Frankfurt/ M: Campus.

Teichler, U. (2006). Introductory thoughts about qualifications for a professional higher education management: New study programmes in Germany (in German). In Stifterverband für die Deutsche Wissenschaft (Ed.), *Qualifizierung für Hochschulprofessionen. Neue Studiengänge in Deutschland. Positionen 8.* Essen: Stifterverband für die Deutsche.

Visakorpi, J. K. (1996). Academic and administrative interface: Application to national circumstances. *Higher Education Management and Policy, 8*(2), 37–41.

Whitchurch, C. (2008). Shifting identities and blurring boundaries: The emergence of third space professionals in UK higher education. *Higher Education Quarterly, 62*(4), 377–396.

Chapter 10
Academic Careers and Work in Europe: Trends, Challenges, Perspectives

Tatiana Fumasoli, Gaële Goastellec, and Barbara M. Kehm

10.1   Introduction

This is the third and last volume of a series presenting the results of a European comparative research project analysing changes of the academic profession in Europe (EuroAC). The project involved higher education researchers from eight countries (Austria, Croatia, Finland, Germany, Ireland, Poland, Romania and Switzerland), who were funded by their national research councils while the overall project was supported by the European Science Foundation as part of their EuroHESC Programme (Higher Education and Social Change).

While the first volume of the EuroAC series (Kehm and Teichler 2012) presented the results of an extensive study of existing research on the academic profession, academic careers and forms of professionalisation, the second volume (Teichler and Höhle 2013) portrayed the results of a comparative survey of the academic profession in 12 European countries focusing on their career paths, their job satisfaction, their workload and changes in their work situation over time. This third volume complements the two previous ones by offering insights derived from

T. Fumasoli (✉)
ARENA Centre for European Studies, University of Oslo, Blindern, P.O Box 1143, Oslo 0318, Norway
e-mail: Tatiana.Fumasoli@arena.uio.no

G. Goastellec
Observatory Science, Politics and Society, University of Lausanne, Quartier UNIL-Mouline, Bâtiment Géopolis, Lausanne 1015, Switzerland
e-mail: Gaele.Goastellec@unil.ch

B.M. Kehm
Robert Owen Centre for Educational Change, University of Glasgow, St. Andrew's Building, 11 Eldon Street, Glasgow G3 6 NH, UK
e-mail: Barbara.Kehm@glasgow.ac.uk

© Springer International Publishing Switzerland 2015
T. Fumasoli et al. (eds.), *Academic Work and Careers in Europe: Trends, Challenges, Perspectives*, The Changing Academy – The Changing Academic Profession in International Comparative Perspective 12, DOI 10.1007/978-3-319-10720-2_10

more than 500 interviews (around 60 in each of the eight countries involved) with institutional leadership, junior and senior academics as well as with new higher education professionals (HEPROs). As detailed in the introductory Chap. 1 of this book the interviews were carried out by using a matrix structure with a common core of questions followed by three thematic focuses, on governance, on academic careers and on forms of professionalisation in higher education. The researcher teams from Finland and Romania focused on the effects of new forms of institutional governance on the work situation of academics; the researcher teams from Austria, Poland and Switzerland on changes in academic careers; and the researcher teams from Croatia, Germany and Ireland on professionalisation processes among various groups within higher education institutions. In addition to the particular thematic focus each researcher team also carried out a smaller number of interviews on the other two focuses so that all three focuses could include a comparative perspective of all eight countries involved in the study.

In the following sections of this final chapter a synthesis will be provided for each of the three thematic focuses and some conclusions will be offered about the overall results and insights that can be derived from the interviews.

10.2 Governance

Structural and formal changes in higher education have affected the academic profession: mass education, globalisation in terms of interdependencies and increased competition, diminishing support from the state particularly with respect to funding, etc. Policy-wise these developments have led to reforms granting more institutional autonomy to higher education institutions across Europe with the assumption that a more autonomous university would enhance its efficiency, effectiveness and strategic profiling. At the same time, the control over university functioning has been organized around accountability and quality assurance.

These changes have been perceived differently by the members of the European academic profession for several reasons. National contexts and path dependencies – systems based on internal or external careers, more or less tenured positions –, institutional types – universities, colleges, polytechnics – and disciplinary affiliations – social sciences, humanities and natural and technical sciences, basic or applied – have framed distinctively how academics make sense of on-going changes. Moreover, academics' perceptions are also illustrations of changing configurations of actors: thus, the rise of the administrative and executive domains is noticed by respondents, even if with different shades of (dis-)agreement.

When it comes to quality systems, the increasingly significant role played by European policies becomes an additional layer to the complexity of the picture. The EuroAC interviews reflect shared expectations of standardization of practices of quality enhancement within universities, as a signal towards more accountability, transparency and fairness in appraising academic performance. Interestingly, opinions on quality assurance are quite positive in this regard, what is criticized is the partially missing feedback between evaluation and improvement policy. This seems to be related both to an administration not able to fully implement quality systems and to senior academics' reluctance to take the necessary steps and modify structures and processes.

The diffusion of practices of quality assurance is striking: all countries, all institutional types and all disciplines have internalised a "discourse" on quality and its underlying rationales. Differences emerge with regards to missions and activities within higher education institutions: hence students are the main (and practically only) evaluators of teaching, quantity is the primary criterion for research output, services remain rather undefined and hardly measurable. Different implications can be derived when it comes to how university core activities are affected by quality systems: there is no reputation gain with students rating classes high, as there is no particular incentive in relation to personnel policies (e.g. promotion). Measurement of research excellence through indicators triggers competition not only among higher education institutions, but also within the same university, as academics are now able to rank themselves and negotiate better working conditions, e.g. less teaching, more PhD students and postdocs, and/or laboratories and other facilities.

Interestingly, one area that according to Moraru and colleagues (Chap. 8) is not perceived as significantly impacted by quality assurance is human resources. Incentives are not clearly linked to evaluations, particularly in teaching and services. In parallel, in traditional universities recruitment procedures seem to be still tightly in the hands of professors, who are able to influence such processes according to their own (normative) ideas of scientific excellence as well as according to their negotiating power. More generally, it can be observed that a tension exists between academic cultures (and relevant quality criteria) and institutional affiliations, whereas institutional leadership and administrative realm try to build common practices. Finally, research continues to remain the most autonomous academic activity, for it is largely driven by academics who are able to determine strategic priorities at the level of their research group and then affecting institutional strategies.

Broadening the perspective to academics' perceptions on governance, control and coordination of their activities, the picture presented by Aarrevaara and colleagues (Chap. 5) illustrates a sense of increasing complexity: different and conflicting logics as well as multiple actors have come into play. Academics feel that societal expectations are increasingly shaping how they work and, more specifically, the rationale underpinning teaching, research and services.

Hence students have become customers able to choose from among different options often following reasons that are alien to higher education traditional values. Research excellence is redefined through categories and indicators that are, at least partly, provided by administrative sources. University third mission constitutes a significant part of the academic work, articulating differently according to institutional type and disciplinary field (e.g. technology transfer or media appearances).

Different logics are at play when it comes to define and legitimize the academic work. The traditional academic logic based on peer review in the framework of publications in scientific journals and of research projects is pulled together with an administrative or bureaucratic logic supported by indicators measuring mainly quantity. A corollary to this is the overlapping and conflicting understanding of excellence by academics as professionals and by universities as organizations. A meaningful insight into this tension is provided by the observation that academics are required to comply *internally* with organizational processes and structures, while at the same time they are able to find the necessary financial resources for conducting research *externally* through national research councils and European programmes. The decoupling between institutional affiliation and significant resources appears to be increasing.

The third logic at play is a "socioeconomic" one, endorsed by policy makers at national and European level. According to this logic higher education has to contribute explicitly and concretely to society's progress. This is visible in teaching, where an instrumental rationale (preparation for the labour market) has replaced higher learning as a goal *per se*. It can be detected also in the discourse on applied research, even though in this case academics seem to be more able to insulate themselves and their research activities from external influences.

The recent reforms introducing binary systems in Switzerland and Finland are claimed to have strengthened the New Public Management ideology. Universities of applied sciences are more permeated by ideas supporting a reinforced management, enhancing efficiency and effectiveness, measures of quality and their links to incentives. The difference between universities of applied sciences and traditional universities can be observed in recruitment processes: in the universities of applied sciences different criteria (e.g. leadership and project management) are taken into account and an increasing number of actors participate (e.g. management and administration). It still remains to be seen whether these practices will also diffuse into traditional universities.

Finally, what emerges from the interviews of the EuroAC project is the transforming nature of the academic profession. The above mentioned external changes, be they globalisation or policy reforms, are connected to an on-going stratification and division of labour within universities and in the academic profession. The university as a collegial system run by professors is turning more and more into an organization where different actors are involved, both internally and externally. Institutional leadership, faculty leadership and departmental leadership coordinate strategies and affect more and more the allocation of resources. While a professorship appears to become increasingly difficult to achieve in the course of an academic career, differentiated roles and positions are created and new paths are experimented with in order to manage the variety of human resources (e.g. assistant and junior professorships, non-tenured professorships). Forces of competition are visible at different levels, e.g. between universities, between researchers, between national systems, thus creating more complex dynamics and expected as well as unexpected outcomes. The redefinition of institutional autonomy taking place in the last two to three decades is putting under pressure academic freedom, which also being reframed. One possible consequence might be that academic freedom will be experienced – and indeed institutionalised – differently according not only to junior and senior positions, but also according to institutional affiliations, disciplinary fields and financial endowments.

10.3   Academic Careers

The changes in institutional governance observed during the last decades have not only transformed the nature of the academic profession but also led to in-depth transformations of academic careers through increased structuring, formalisation and competition.

Structuring concerns the different stages of academic careers, their expected lengths, but also some differentiation processes. As underlined by the interviewees, an academic career can be divided into four main stages: doctoral studies, post-doc and junior positions, lower-level senior and higher-level senior positions that are being defined increasingly precisely. For example, doctoral studies are reduced in their duration and their content is formalised with the development of doctoral schools and the contractualisation of the relationship between the doctoral student and his/her supervisor and institution. As for post-doctoral positions, previously a feature of the hard sciences, they are becoming a general characteristic in most disciplines.

The comparison shows that the doctorate affirms itself as an entry requirement to academic careers in most countries and higher education sub-sectors. Differences between countries concern the level of competition for PhD positions, already high in some places, nearly non-existent in others. More broadly, interviewees suggest that an academic career has now the form of a funnel, with the number of available positions going down as one goes up the career ladder. Indeed, while access to permanent positions appeared relatively easy when higher education systems were growing in size, stagnation is now observed in most European countries generating an imbalance between the number of newcomers and the number of available advanced positions.

At the same time, changes in funding nurture the development of externally funded positions that introduce a variety of professional situations at different stages of an academic career, from PhD student to professor. Fixed-term contracts are increasing also corresponding to broader flexibility demanded by human resources and to the emergence of cross employment between institutions and professional sectors. Here, national science foundations and European foundations play an important role by promoting collaborative projects that imply externally funded academic contracts but also early career professorial positions (such as the "fellow professors" in Switzerland or the "*Juniorprofessuren*" in Germany). These new positions reduce the dependency of junior academics on senior professors that used to structure the historical German Chair model. With the introduction of tenure track processes not only more precocious careers are promoted, but also academics perceive them as an instrument to clarify career trajectories and related expectations. Still, academics also underline the fact that the number of tenure tracks positions remains too low to allow a complete change of the academic career model.

Nevertheless, this differentiation facilitates the re-structuring of academic careers and in particular the slow replacement of the chair model by a department-based model. Indeed, the creation of these temporary positions allows to go against the historical hierarchical structure and to promote accelerated careers for a small number of distinguished junior scholars. Even if the number of individuals concerned remains marginal, the existence of these new career models signals the possibility of an alternative and constitutes incentives for universities and disciplines to rethink the internal structure of academic careers.

This diversity of status at the same stage of an academic career also seems to constitute a lever for the formalisation of recruitment processes and professional activities contents. As shown by Fumasoli and Goastellec Chap. 4, academic recruitment processes structure the organisation of academic markets and reveal a trend towards formalisation and advertisement of positions. These formalisation processes can be observed for all levels of academic recruitment, from professorial to doctoral positions. It also corresponds to the length of university engagement through the recruitment: in case of a long term investment, the university leadership is more often involved and the process more formalised. In case of a short term investment, the recruitment is more often organised by a single professor or at a department level. Formalisation of recruitment criteria goes along with the formalisation and specification of contractual terms and conditions regarding professional activities and relevant negotiations when it comes to top notch academics.

In spite of variations in recruitment criteria, depending on the country, the university and the discipline, university and non-university sectors are converging in terms of requirements in recruitment processes. Regulated internal academic markets emerge through the formalisation of career structures and recruitment processes.

This integration of the academic labour market comes with an increased competition among academics for positions, financial and symbolic resources (prestigious fellowships, publications in top journals of the discipline, etc.). Competition also takes place between institutions for the "best and the brightest" leading to "the winner takes it all" market as shown by Kwiek and Antonowicz (Chap. 4). This competition between institutions values international mobility as a signal of excellence. As underlined by Brechelmacher et al. (Chap. 2), international mobility is not being generalised as a necessary step of academic careers but is becoming a distinctive feature that facilitates early careers and recruitment. International mobility is perceived by the interviewees as an opportunity to network and accumulate social capital as well as to increase independence and self-assertion. Specifically, post-doctoral international mobility is a tool to increase the chances to obtain a position in the home country. The effectiveness of such a strategy depends on the organisation of the local labour market and the networks established there. Internationalisation is thus far from signaling the integration of an overall European labour market.

In the end, the comparison reveals that traditional and flatter hierarchical models coexist, however to a different extent depending on the discipline. In disciplines in which a generational change is already at play among senior professors, we find flatter relationships, new career structures, independence through international experience, competition for external funding.

What is striking is that mentoring is still perceived in all contexts as a central element, as much for seniors as for juniors. Changes in the structure of academic careers and changes in governance have not transformed the importance of mentoring for younger academics. Finding the right mentor, either in the old chair structure or in the new collaborative structures appears central. Thus, pairing of doctoral students and senior academics can enhance a PhD experience, for expertise and networks can be built and used in academic markets. Indeed, against the backdrop of increasingly competitive labour markets marginal differences between individuals have more impact on careers than before, meaning that "small differences matter". "Luck", "chance", and "opportunity" that were historically important in academic careers are becoming even more important, while networks count more. As one interviewee explains, "meeting a good academic mentor is a milestone in academic career". And universities acknowledge the centrality of the mentoring process. In Switzerland, for example, mentoring programmes specifically dedicated to female PhD students have been developed by equality offices to combat the gender disadvantages in academic careers. Indeed, interviewees have underlined that academic careers are problematic for women, for both work-life balance and family planning.

10.4   Forms of Professionalisation

The changes in governance and academic careers, which have been synthesized in the previous sections, have also impacted on various forms of professionalisation within higher education institutions. Clarke et al. (Chap. 6) have focused on the changes of professional roles perceived by academic staff in terms of their teaching, their research and their institutional embeddedness.

What is striking in this respect is the fact that academics today are much more than ever before expected to contribute to the success and performance of the institution that employs them. This does not only mean that academics' performance in teaching and research is more closely monitored and reinforced through incentives, i.e. high performance in areas deemed important by the institution is rewarded, but they are also expected to take on a higher administrative workload because secretarial and clerical roles have been centralised and reduced in numbers. In addition, as the chapter of Ćulum et al. (Chap. 7) points out, academics are also expected to become more engaged in institutions' third mission activities, e.g. pro bono services, cooperation with industry, community engagement, etc. This is strongly related to the fact that universities today have to be accountable to the public and society at large in order to legitimize their public funding. Research is no longer seen as the disinterested pursuit of truth serving the progress of a given discipline, the results of which are communicated within a given scientific community. Instead, most research funding applications today have to include a section reasoning why that particular project idea or grant application should be funded and what it contributes to society at large. There is also an increased emphasis on research being carried out in larger groups and networks, preferably also including partners from societal stakeholder groups and companies, i.e. non-academic partners.

Concerning the teaching role, academics are expected to professionalise not only in terms of the quality of their delivery but also by acquiring new pedagogical skills, working with new technologies, and engaging in curriculum development which demonstrates the role of an academic education for the employability of the graduates. Here too, the purpose is no longer exclusively to provide students with the knowledge base of a given discipline or field of studies by making them competent in the use of the relevant theories and methodologies, but also to channel towards students the potential utility of knowledge, skills and competences to fit the labour markets.

Accordingly, academic careers have changed as well. Not only do we observe a considerable increase in fixed-term and part-time contracts, but we also note a variety of new requirements in terms of competences, skills and experiences which are acquired in a more structured and systematic way by giving more shape and structure to the doctoral and postdoctoral phase. In addition, competition for tenured positions and professorships has become fierce in most countries.

But there are also new forms of professionalisation in other groups of the university population. The new responsibilities in terms of institutional leadership and management that come with a growing autonomy of universities have led to what is commonly called a "New Public Management" approach in their governance. This has contributed to steeper hierarchies within the institutions, a loss of collegial academic self-regulation, an attention to institutional efficiency and effectiveness coupled with more evidence-based decision-making. Institutional performance is increasingly benchmarked and ranked on the basis of more or less appropriate numerical indicators. In some countries the allocation of state funding is increasingly made dependent on the outcomes of evaluations of institutional performance or on the fulfillment of externally set targets. Universities are developing into organisations in order to become actors on markets and react flexibly and efficiently to the continuous and ever changing demands and expectations of their environment. This requires different forms of management and leadership than the traditional idea of the rector or president as "the first among equals".

Despite the fact that there is an increasing number of offers in terms of induction seminars and management workshops to convey the "tricks of the trade" to newly elected or appointed members of institutional leadership and management, the latter tend to professionalise themselves with the help of new higher education professionals and by recruiting highly skilled experts for the central administration. The latter are responsible for collecting data and reports on institutional performance and prepare for evidence-based strategic decision-making. These developments are clearly more pronounced in the Western European countries than in the Eastern European countries.

The third group which has been analyzed in the framework of the EuroAC project in terms of its professionalisation are the new higher education professionals (HEPROs). Their work is located at the interface between institutional management and academia and regardless whether they are part of the central administration or work in the faculties and departments, they appear to be genuine change agents in terms of turning universities into organisations. They are not administrators in the traditional sense but rather highly qualified university graduates, often having a doctoral degree, responsible for professionalising services, managing and implementing change and for collecting data and information for strategic decision-making. They often have a somewhat ambiguous role within the institutions. Academics look at them with the expectation of being unburdened from unloved administrative tasks, institutional management uses them to implement strategic decisions and changes at the "shop floor", and the HEPROs themselves see their tasks as service oriented but not administrative.

It is typical for HEPROs that the majority of them has no systematic training but is recruited first on a project base to achieve something or get something done which is either new or more traditional but requiring additional expertise. So their process of professionalisation is mostly on the job through learning by doing. Our analyses have shown that the development of HEPRO roles is uneven in the countries involved in the EuroAC study. They are less prominent in the Central and Eastern European countries, while in the Western and Northern European countries the differences tend to be more related to their previous training. On the one hand we find an up-skilling of traditional (central) administrators to take on additional and more strategic responsibilities. On the other hand we find mid-level academic staff moving into HEPRO work without giving up all of their academic activities in teaching and research. This latter trend points to a hybridisation of occupational roles (neither academic nor administrative but a little bit of both) and it remains to be seen in which direction professionalisation processes for this particular group of people will develop.

It is difficult to assess which of the three groups within academia analysed here (academic staff, management, HEPROs) has undergone the most far-reaching professionalisation process. But our results provide evidence that the academic profession has been affected most by the changes described. Senior academics are often expected to acquire the new skills on their own – although in some countries human resource development is much further advanced than in others – while young researchers often have the opportunity to acquire new skills and competences in a more systematic way as part of their training to become independent researchers and academic teachers. However, HEPROs are mostly on their own as well. The difference to academics might just be that their tasks are more specialised and in a narrower field while academics not only have to acquire new skills and competences in the traditional areas of teaching and research but are also getting more involved in administration and in fulfilling universities' third mission.

In principle we can say that the observed new forms of professionalisation are in their early stages and much in flux. They certainly are impacting on academic work already now, but only the future will show whether considerable parts of this professionalisation in all three groups will result in hybrid roles or whether it will develop into new forms of division of labour within academia.

Conclusions

An academic career is a social process that has been greatly transformed during the recent decades. Academic careers have been impacted by at least three intertwined dynamics emerging in the 1960s and accelerating from the 1990s onwards: the emergence of "knowledge societies", the institutional diversification of higher education and its internationalisation.

Indeed, after being first a tool of the reconstruction after the Second World War "knowledge is today recognized as the object of huge economic, political and cultural stakes, to the point of justifiably qualifying the societies currently emerging" (UNESCO 2005, p. 5). Higher education represents the main instrument of knowledge production, transmission and dissemination. Institutional diversification goes along with the rise of knowledge societies: the highly qualified human capital required to nurture these societies' calls for an enlargement of the higher education sector in order to train more individuals with more diverse competences. This enlargement has led to a growing number of higher education institutions that admit different types of students to be trained for different activities and professions. As for the internationalisation process, it "includes the policies and practices undertaken by academic systems and institutions — and even individuals — to cope with the global academic environment" (Altbach and Knight 2007, p. 290). Internationalisation tends to be perceived as an appropriate characteristic of higher education, especially when it comes to academic labour markets, and is associated with quality by higher education policy makers.

How does this changing institutional context impact on the academic profession?

Previous research has already shown that while increasing in size and importance, the academic profession experienced a loss of status, a growing workload and a gradual reduction of professional self-regulation (Enders 2004). But what is at play at the beginning of the twenty-first century is highly complex. These three characteristics of the transformation of the higher education context have led to an increasing number of incentives affecting the three missions of the academic profession: teaching, research and community service.

First, rankings are leading to an enhanced scrutiny of research activities and strategic management of academic staff (Fumasoli 2014). More importance is given to raising research funds, building research teams, publishing in high impact journals, participating in international research projects, etc.

(continued)

It has been shown elsewhere that internationalisation is perceived at institutional, national and European level as a desirable outcome of academic labour markets: being internationally attractive is associated with quality by policy makers (Marginson and van der Wende 2009; Musselin 2004). "Competition to attract the 'best and brightest' generates in return the internationalisation of academic careers and markets and cognitive standards of its desirability. Internationalisation thus seems to appear as two sided: it works both as a *normative standard* of quality judgment and as an *instrument of standardisation* regarding individual careers, institutional profiles and the composition of national markets, but also, more generally, of higher education organisations" (Goastellec and Crettaz Von Roten, submitted).

Second, in knowledge societies with higher education being accessible to a larger proportion of the population, the academic profession is hold always more accountable for the professional destiny of its graduates and, more broadly, of what it gives back to society. Thus, the academic profession is more and more responsible for the alignment of the type of training it provides and the needs of the labour market the graduates are heading to. Changes in the profile of the student body and the missions attributed to higher education along with the development of new technologies are profoundly modifying the ways of teaching in higher education institutions, implying a renewal of techniques and pedagogical styles with a focus on shifts from teaching to learning. Learning by doing is becoming increasingly important, in contrast to the large lectures that were previously characterising the university pedagogy.

More broadly, the enlargement of the role played by higher education systems comes with a public demand that its value to society be demonstrated, including community service, science communication, public understanding of science. The multiplication of demands has put the academic profession under great strain. What are the consequences?

The multiple processes at play can be divided into four main dimensions: a diversification of the academic profession itself, increased integration of national labour markets for higher education graduates, some disconnection between academic status and academic activities, and last but not least the multiplication of tasks to fulfill and competences to acquire.

Regarding the diversification of the academic profession itself, the main dynamics are related to the increase of fixed-term positions in academe (including externally funded positions), the development of cross-employment by different universities or by universities and firms, and finally a trend towards less secure working conditions resulting in performance pressure and increased competition. This leads to a pyramidal division of labour with academics on short terms contracts often being hired to carry out a single task (in teaching or in research) while permanent academics face a diversification of their activities. At the same time, the chair model, in which PhD students and post-docs as well as an intermediary body of academics

(continued)

were subordinated to a professor, tends to disappear. In a number of European countries, reforms have been introduced to foster earlier academic independence. Career patterns as well as employment and working conditions are changing leading to new forms of division of work and more uncertainty for academics.

While the diversification of the higher education landscape has come with a diversification of the academic profession, these developments push towards more conformity of academic profiles and career structures. For example, the doctorate is becoming a prerequisite for access into the academic profession in almost all countries. Doctoral schools are developed leading to an extended formalisation and professionalisation of doctoral studies as well as to collective socialisation process. A post doc phase becomes a normal step in the academic career and, due to an increased number of doctoral students, a filter to entering the academic profession. The post-doc phase is acknowledged by the academic profession as the most competitive phase in the academic career. Furthermore, tenure track positions exist in more and more countries although in numbers that are considered too small by academics. International mobility is perceived as important already at these first stages of the academic career. At another level, the pressure on individuals to internationalise their trajectory transforms international mobility into a resource for an academic career, a tool to increase networking, accumulating social capital, increasing independence and self-assertion. Certainly, the role played by the international dimension differs according to the higher education system and the respective career organisation. It depends on the degree of internationalisation of the national academic profession: very important in countries where a large part of the academic profession is international (such as in Switzerland), but with effects less clear in countries with very low levels of internationalisation (such as Poland). National context and societal characteristics impinge on the reforms at play, and lead to the national and local appropriation of global trends. These trends testify an increased integration of national labour markets for higher education graduates, the same career norms being diffused within the systems and these norms being made public (for example through international recruitment calls and processes).

At the same time, academics also observe an increased disconnection between academic status and academic activities supported by an intensification of the competition among individuals and by its location outside the higher education institutions. The development of research funding at the level of national agencies and at the European level is affected by this change of rules from academic status to competition. Simultaneously, the academic career structure is partly being redesigned. As a result, a generational rivalry or "generation clash" can be perceived in the discourses of the academics, with the youngest feeling first, that they have to work much more than the older ones had to, second, that their environment is more insecure.

(continued)

Finally, there is a multiplication of tasks academics are supposed to carry out in research (e.g. doing research, raising funds, hiring, training, valorising, organising conferences, publishing, mentoring), in teaching (e.g. new course development, support to students, different teaching skills), and with regard to other activities related to teaching and research (e.g. being able to build a website, to use teaching platforms, to develop MOOCS, to communicate to a wider public than the sole scientific community). Academics are now asked to develop more skills that include management and communication skills, teamwork capacity, proficiency in foreign languages, networking, information technology competencies.

The search for societal and economic relevance in teaching and research leads to an intensified monitoring of research and teaching performance. Academic discourses echo both, the perception that little attention is paid to teaching quality in the course of a career, and the perception that teaching quality is becoming more important. Flagship institutions, in which research is very relevant, can focus on teaching quality to improve their profile, while middle ranked institutions that are less visible in the academic research market might be tempted to put all their efforts into improving their research visibility, thus disregarding the teaching dimension, at least when it comes to academic incentives.

This explosion of academic activities goes along with a new division of work characterised by the growing importance of research managers who compete for external funding by building research projects that will later on be carried out by doctoral and post doctoral students. The development of quality assurance also adds bureaucratic tasks to the academic and managerial work and functions as a connection tool between the business environment and higher education. More broadly, documentation and reporting has become significantly important. New administrative tasks emerge while academics are asked for a greater involvement in research activities and academic responsibilities.

The national and increasingly international embeddedness of higher education institutions has turned them into more complex organisations than ever before. Accordingly, new forms of professionalisation among various groups within the institutions have emerged. In the previous paragraphs the new demands on the academic profession have already been described. Be it through learning by doing or through participation in more structured and systematic training, academics today are obliged to acquire a considerably broader set of skills and competencies than 10 or 15 years ago.

In addition, institutional management is becoming more professionalised not only due to the growing institutional autonomy but also due to the increasing international competition on the one hand, and due to the augmented external expectations with regard to institutional performance on the

(continued)

other. As has been pointed out members of the institutional management dominantly professionalise themselves with the help and through the support of a new group of experts, the new higher education professionals, who prepare strategic and evidence-based decision-making and act as change agents in the implementation of managerial decisions.

The picture that emerges with regard to the new higher education professionals is ambiguous though. In quite a number of countries involved in the EuroAC study we have noted a hybridisation of professional roles with academics taking over HEPRO tasks and vice versa. These processes cannot be characterised simply as a de-skilling of academics and/or an up-skilling of administrators. The mixture of tasks has more far-reaching consequences in terms of blurring boundaries between the academic sphere on the one hand and the middle management sphere on the other.

However in countries in which managerial governance of higher education is more progressed HEPRO roles seem to be more stable and more distinct from other roles – be they academic or be they managerial. However it is not yet clear whether the developments in the majority of countries will lead towards more established occupational roles and career structures for higher education professionals or whether hybrid roles will become the norm. The results of our analyses indicate that we need to think in new ways about theories of professionalisation in order to theoretically ground and explain some of the phenomena described and analysed in this study.

References

Altbach, P. G., & Knight, J. (2007). The internationalization of higher education: Motivations and realities. *Journal of Studies in International Education, 11*, 290–305.

Enders, J. (2004). Higher education, internationalisation, and the nation-state: Recent developments and challenges to governance theory. *Higher Education, 47*, 361–382.

Fumasoli, T. (2014). Strategic management of personnel policies: A comparative analysis of Flagship universities in Norway, Finland, Switzerland and Austria. In F. Ribeiro, Y. Politis, & B. Culum (Eds.), *New voices in higher education research and scholarship*. Advances in Higher Education & Professional Development, IGI Global.

Goastellec, G., & Crettaz Von Roten, F. (n.d.). The internationalisation of academic labour market: Normative standards of quality judgements and instruments of standardisation. Submitted to *IJHE,* December 2013.

Kehm, B. M., & Teichler, U. (Eds.). (2012). *The academic profession in Europe: New tasks and new challenges*. Dordrecht: Springer.

Marginson, S., & Van der Wende, M. (2009). Europeanisation, international rankings and faculty mobility. Three cases in higher education globalisation. In OECD (Ed.), *Higher education to 2030: Vol. 2. Globalisation* (pp. 109–144). Paris: OECD.

Musselin, C. (2004). Towards a European academic labour market? Some lessons drawn from empirical studies on academic mobility. *Higher Education, 48*, 55–78.

Teichler, U., & Höhle, E. A. (Eds.). (2013). *The work situation of the academic profession in Europe: Findings of a survey in twelve countries*. Dordrecht: Springer.

UNESCO. (2005). *Towards knowledge societies*. Paris: UNESCO.

Printed by Printforce, the Netherlands